RACE CAR ENGINEERING
AND MECHANICS ∘∘∘∘∘∘∘∘∘∘∘∘∘∘∘∘∘∘∘∘∘∘∘∘

RACE CAR ENGINEERING

ooooooooooooooo ILLUSTRATED WITH PHOTOGRAPHS AND DRAWINGS

AND MECHANICS°°°°°°°°°°°°°°°

Paul Van Valkenburgh

DODD, MEAD & COMPANY °°°°°°°°°°°°° NEW YORK

All photographs and drawings in this book are by the author unless otherwise credited.

Library of Congress Cataloging in Publication Data

Van Valkenburgh, Paul.
  Race car engineering and mechanics.

  Bibliography: p.
  Includes index.
  1. Automobiles, Racing—Design and construction.
I. Title.
TL236.V38   629.22'8   75-22057
ISBN 0-396-07201-1

ACKNOWLEDGMENTS °°°°°°°°°

I owe a great many thanks to all the people who have contributed to my store of knowledge. In many places I discuss their ideas and discoveries and data without giving them specific credit. But since it would be distracting to stop and identify the proper person at each point, I can use this page to recognize certain individuals.

First, there are all the anonymous racing engineers and technicians I worked with at Chevrolet Research and Development on the semi-official racing team, and whom I listed in my first book, *Chevrolet Racing*. But individually, I have to give special credit to:

Don Cox, a former associate at Chevrolet and now chief engineer for Penske Racing, who probably knows more about race car technology than any other person I know.

Mark Donohue, who shared part of his vast storehouse of practical personal experiences with me as I worked on his autobiography, *The Unfair Advantage*.

Carroll Smith, who wrote the most informative race car preparation articles ever published, in a series he did for *Sports Car Graphic* while I was technical editor there.

750506

And finally, all those other personal friends whose technical comments have added to or changed my thinking about race cars:

Don Gates and Mike Pocobello of Antares Engineering

Bill Milliken and Doug Rowland of Calspan (Cornell Aero Labs)

Jim Hall of Chaparral Cars

Karl Kainhofer, Earl MacMullin, John Woodard of Penske Racing

Jim Travers and Frank Coon of Traco

Paul Lamar of Lamar School of Race Car Design and Development

Dick Guldstrand of Guldstrand Racing

Bernie Pershing of Aerospace Corporation

Bob Liebeck of All-American Racers

Mary, my wife, who *really* changed my thinking about race cars

CONTENTS ∘∘∘∘∘∘∘∘∘∘∘∘∘∘∘∘∘∘∘∘∘∘∘∘∘∘∘∘∘∘∘

INTRODUCTION ∘∘∘∘∘∘∘∘∘∘∘∘∘∘∘∘∘∘∘∘∘∘∘

In a way, I'm using this book to say good-by to all those people I've raced with or who have read my automotive journalism. By the time this book is published, I'll be finishing my Master's Thesis on "A Systematic Integration of the Behavioral Sciences," and moving on to other *social* challenges. But as I get out of the racing game, I want to leave something to show for my efforts. I would like it to matter that I was ever involved at all. So with this book, I'm leaving most of my racing knowledge behind. I don't expect to be using it where I'm going, so I'm putting it down in print before I forget it, in the hope that other racers can put it to good use.

It is possible that many of the things I write here were previously known only by a very few professional racers. However, that doesn't mean I'm so smart that I know everything there is about racing. It merely means that I found the time and the initiative to do the job before other qualified people I know could have. Don Cox and Mark Donohue and I talked about a combined effort for years, but they were so involved with reality that they couldn't possibly spare the time. With the exception of Carroll Smith, most other people haven't been fortunate to have the engineering education, or the driving experience, or the mechanical experience, or the writing experience to do the job. I can't boast, though, because I recognize just how little is really known by anyone in this business. I did generate a lot of original knowledge about race cars while a Research Engineer for Chevrolet, but so did all the others. But the most humbling knowledge is that the more you learn about anything, the more you realize how little anyone knows for *sure*. If anyone tries to give the idea that he knows all the answers, you can be sure that he really doesn't even know the questions very well. I leave this book—and the profession—with a lot of fascinating unanswered questions and potential for improvements.

At any rate, I have tried to cover all the areas of race car engineering, theory, development, and mechanics as completely as possible and in a balanced manner. That is something that (to my knowledge) hasn't existed before. Naturally, in trying to cram the greatest amount of factual information into the least amount of space, I must expect arguments about my point of view and complaints that I was not thorough enough. But you can't please all the people all the time. For those who need more basic information, or more advanced information, or verification of some of my more unbelievable comments, I have provided frequent references and an extensive bibliography in the back.

If anyone is the least bit curious about why I'm moving away from engineering, racing, and writing about race cars, when thousands of excitement-seeking young men are anxious to get into the business, I don't mind explaining. I have been exposed to some of the greatest, wisest, and most successful people in racing. I've seen the top, and discovered that for me for one reason or another it didn't seem to be worth the effort to get there—and to stay there. I was fortunate to know the taste of winning—building and driving my own car—in my own limited sphere, and felt that these successes were hollow. It seemed all too easy for me to go through life racing my heart out, winning more than my fair share, and still ending up with nothing more than a bunch of trophies and some fading fame to show for it. I feel that I have relatively well satisfied my drive for competitive success, and I'm anxious to redirect my efforts into other areas which are more humanistic and cooperative than racing.

It is perhaps a broad statement of my philosophy to say that I don't believe anyone should ever have to compete with an unfair disadvantage—whether on the track, or in real life. Even if I were still driving, I would be willing to tell a competitor everything I know, and then let the best man win. But I suppose it is fortunate that there wasn't enough room in this book to reveal some of my more esoteric accumulated knowledge, because someday I might *have* to go back to making a living as a race car engineer or driver.

1

HOW TO WIN ○○○○○○○○○○○○○○○○○○○○○○○○○○○

PEOPLE, KNOWLEDGE, PREPARATION

This book will show you how to win any automobile race. And it's very easy to do. That is, it's very easy to *show* someone how to win a race—but it's usually an incredible challenge in time and money to actually do the job. But the better anyone understands and uses everything in this book, the more likely he is to win—assuming his car is at least equal to the others in basic design factors such as power-to-weight ratio, body size and shape, and tire size. Unfortunately, all cars are not created equal, and race sanctioning groups can't always make classifications equitable between different makes or designs. Until they can create an accurate handicapping system, any car may be at a basic disadvantage, which the driver and mechanic will have to overcome by even greater efforts. If this chapter seems to be more about the philosophy of racing than the engineering and mechanics, it's because a tremendous personal commitment is of primary importance in winning races.

No book is big enough to include everything a driver or mechanic needs to know about race cars. Therefore, it is assumed that the reader already has a basic knowledge of automobile service and mechanics. If not, it can be picked up from an ordinary auto mechanics text, preferably one written for the Junior College student. There are thousands of good potential race car mechanics who already have a lot of experience in garages and dealerships, but who don't know all the necessary specific details of racing. Qualified aircraft mechanics perhaps have even better training. Similarly, there are thousands of graduate engineers who could be a great asset to a racing team, but who don't know what all the problems are or the factors involved. So this book was written for either the experienced non-racing mechanic, or the non-racing engineer. If you know how to engineer a car, or how to rebuild one completely, this book will show how to apply your knowledge specifically to racing.

The first distinction between a race car mechanic and an ordinary repair mechanic is perfection. The average garage mechanic can make a few mistakes and get away with it. He just fixes his fixes the next time around. But a racing mechanic has to be more professional, because, like a doctor, he may not have a second chance. Sometimes he may be able to recheck his work before the race starts and correct any problems if there's time. But as the old saying goes, "When the flag drops, the bullshit stops." Racing is very unlike school, where 60 or 80 percent correct may be a passing grade. There are thousands of components in a race car, and 99.99 percent right is not close enough. If the mechanic misses *one* thing, the results are likely to be serious. Not only is the race certainly lost—and in professional racing the mechanic may be losing out on a share of the winnings—but the most serious aspect is that a man's life is at stake, and possibly the lives of innocent bystanders. Sometimes, in longer races, it may be possible to correct an error during a pitstop and still have a chance of winning. In that case, the mechanic is more like an emergency medic, in that slow, methodical, and precise work is not as important as his ability to instantaneously diagnose and cure the problem.

Good race car mechanics are hard to find or train, and they are therefore very valuable. Top men can make more money than engineers or executives, and the work is a lot more exciting—if also demanding in terms of hours worked and miles traveled. The best investment in a race team can be one or two of the best mechanics available. Otherwise, all the money spent on the most exotic equipment, not to mention the other expenses of racing, is totally wasted. Unlimited dollars won't win a race without some people with a lot of knowledge and experience. And if the best man available starts making serious mistakes—he's out. He can lose races, he can lose money, and he can lose the driver's life.

If a mechanic or engineer lacks experience in racing, a lot of book learning can make up most of the difference. There may not be enough space here to go into great detail about all the aspects of race cars, but at least there is a mention of almost every area and potential problem that should be considered, and references for further study in depth. The book also presents a systematic overall approach to the entire package, treating the race car, driver, and team as a system.

But if anyone wants to keep up with race car technology and the state of the art, it will be necessary to do a lot of reading. First, it's mandatory to have a copy of the particular sanctioning body's regulations—and to know them by heart. Even if it never becomes necessary to recite a certain rule to a technical inspector or official, everyone on the team must know exactly what they can and cannot do—to the car, or in the pits, or on the track. In addition, automotive enthusiast periodicals, whether monthly slick magazines or weekly newsletters, often have the latest technical advances or scoops on a competitor's new device. At the very least, they are always a good source of information on the availability of new products through the advertisements. Very little information is given in this book on brand names or sources of racing products. Both change so rapidly that it's impossible to keep up in a hardcover book which may take a year to publish. Any good racer should have enough initiative and imagination to find whatever he needs through the ads or by simply asking around. Another good source of information is through the manufacturers themselves. Any speed equipment or automobile manufacturer who appreciates good racing exposure will probably have a lot of up-to-date technical data available on their products. It can also be helpful to read race reports to get an idea of the causes of vehicle retirements. A person with a great deal of excess time could compile a tremendous check list of potential failures—and their frequency—by tabulating the published race DNFs (Did Not Finish) from the past few years.

For the engineers who want to keep up with the latest theoretical advances and more esoteric technological information, there are a number of valuable engineering trade journals. The Society of Automotive Engineers also puts out a few hundred technical papers each year. Most of the information will be directed toward passenger car applications, but the fanatic race car engineer will always be able to see any conceivable connection with his own needs. And finally, there are a few other hardcover books which cover limited areas of automotive—if not race car—engineering, most of which are listed in the bibliography.

As far as the information in this book goes, most of it is assembled relatively sequentially. The first half, for example, builds slowly up to a total comprehension of handling. Therefore, the chapter on Handling won't make much sense if you haven't read the previous chapters. However, a mechanic with a specific problem or area of interest can concentrate on individual chapters, or specific areas within a chapter, such as theory, hardware, development, or maintenance.

NOTE: This is an important disclaimer to keep in mind, regarding all general statements and especially mathematical equations in this book. In the interest of saving space, a lot of the theories and equations have been simplified a great deal. It is possible for a person who doesn't have a good engineering background to get into trouble by misinterpretation or extension into unrelated areas. There are innumerable pitfalls for the person who doesn't do some research behind a theory or equation, or who doesn't follow up with some sort of test verification, or who bases an entire vehicle on a single theoretical premise. It's happened to the best of us. It could save a lot of time, money, and frustration to get further advice from a qualified mechanical, aerospace, or race car engineer. Experienced race car mechanics are also good consultants, although they have a terrible tendency to say, "It won't work—because it hasn't been done before." Or, perhaps, because they didn't think of it first.

Besides specific information, here are a few basic philosophical generalizations worth mentioning. There is such an infinite number of tasks to be performed in winning races that there has to be some established series of priorities. It isn't possible to build and race a car successfully if everyone simply concentrates on what is fun, or familiar, or simply easy to do. In the basic assembly of a race car, there will be three categories of jobs to do: Must, Important, and Also. These will range from the safety items necessary to get through technical inspection, to final appearance detailing. It won't do a bit of good to have a polished and pinstriped body if the engine can't be installed in time. This assembly priority list is also a good reference for scheduling critically important components, which must be bought or built before many other assembly jobs can follow in sequence.

There is no reason to ever go to a race until the car is ready to be raced. That ought to be obvious. But so many people are so anxious to be racing that they will take their unfinished, unprepared car to the track anyhow, hoping to be able to get it ready at the last minute. They literally push themselves into total frustration and exhaustion by packing, unpacking, searching for parts and tools, correcting mistakes, making continual adjustments by intuition, and going without food or sleep. Then they wonder what's wrong with the car or the driver that kept them from winning. So the first preparation priority is to have the car *finished* before ever leaving for the track.

The oldest truism in racing is—you've got to be able to finish before you can win. In any given race it's quite likely that half of the cars which start will not even finish the race at all. Therefore, any car that is prepared well enough to stay together for the length of a race has already beaten at least half the field before the race even starts. Those priorities ought to be obvious—*first,* the car has to be safe and durable, and *second,* it can be made faster. So if there is ever any thought about what ought to be done next—and that should be a constant consideration—then the most rational sequence is: (1) have the car assembled on time, (2) make it safe and durable, and (3) try to make it faster. If the car is ready to race as it is rolled off the trailer, except for adding fuel and checking tire pressures, then it is probably already in the lead at that point.

A few things ought to be mentioned about radical innovation, and a related subject, intentional cheating. Simple observation and a lot of practical experience shows time after time that the wildly innovative car will practically never win a race—until it is also well developed. Almost invariably, it is the best developed, old reliable design that finishes first. There can be thousands of test miles on a faster, more exotic race car, and yet it hardly stands a chance of finishing its first races. If innovation and experimentation are felt to be more important than winning early races, that's fine, but, once you're behind, it will be extremely difficult if not impossible to catch up again in a particular championship series.

As for intentional cheating—don't bother. It isn't worth the time. There will *never* be enough time to do all the perfectly legal assembly and development work described in this book. It may be easy to increase engine displacement or to use exotic fuels or to increase fuel capacity, but it's even easier to recognize and uncover such blatant cheating. The more sophisticated techniques take a great deal of time and money to make them stand up under scrutiny. Racers are usually suspicious enough so that a winning car *will* be carefully scrutinized, officially or otherwise. And once a cheater is exposed, no matter how light the penalty, he will never again be able to celebrate an unquestioned victory. The only exception is under those sanctioning bodies where cheating is commonly accepted among some competitors who may have unwritten rules of their own, regardless of the official rules. At least they still remain relatively equal among themselves, but that makes it doubly difficult for a newcomer to become competitive. Sometimes you can't simply follow the book.

Auto racing seems to be moving toward better equality in cars, if not proven and *guaranteed* absolute equality between cars, so that the contest will be more between drivers. Until then, it is the intent of this book to make the situation at least *academically* more equal. There is nothing here that most professional and other consistently winning teams shouldn't know already. But this may balance the scale a little by making most of the necessary information available to everyone. If every racer were to follow everything in this book, at least more cars ought to finish more races—and hopefully more competitively.

2
TIRES AND WHEELS ०००००००००००

Racing tires seem simple enough. You buy the biggest ones you can fit on your car, or the biggest ones the rules will allow, or whatever is being used on a faster car. You put them on your car, inflate them, and race. Since you can't design your own or modify what you get, what else matters? However, to understand practically everything else about race car engineering, you have to know how a tire works. And, when you understand tires, it becomes apparent that there are a large number of factors that can be controlled to optimize their performance. The racer who knows how to get the most out of his tires has a definite advantage over anyone else whc is using the identical tire.

THEORY

There is more knowledge to tires than the "black art" technology the racing tire companies would lead us to believe. It's true that the design of internal cord bodies is based largely on experience, and the formulation of rubber compounds from hundreds of basic elements is more experimental than scientific, but a great deal of research has

7

gone into the theory and operation of tires. To get down to the very basics, it's important to know how rubber acts in contact with the ground. The most complete research and theorizing in this area is by Kummer and Meyer, although their work is probably beyond most tire engineers, much less race car mechanics. To over-simplify, they explain how rubber generates friction by a combination of mechanical gripping of irregularities, and molecular adhesion between the rubber and these microscopic contact areas. They further explain how both conditions can be optimized through modification of many other factors, most of which, unfortunately, are up to tire builders.

These theories explain how a tire is able to produce "something for nothing," or is able to produce a cornering, accelerating, or braking force greater than the weight resting on it. In other words, a tire carrying a load of 1000 pounds could have a maximum friction force of well over 1200 pounds, depending on the tire construction and road surface. The ratio of these numbers, or force/weight, is referred to as the coefficient of friction (Cf), and is one of the most important considerations in the discussion of tires. This coefficient has many important relationships to ordinary driving, but in this book, it represents the *maximum* coefficient of friction for a tire, since race cars ideally operate at that maximum at all times. The greatest Cf that can be obtained from a production passenger car tire is probably about 0.8 to 1.0 under ideal conditions. A race car tire, however, is generally capable of a Cf between 1.0 and 1.4, depending on tire construction and the vehicle. Now we will see how a number of factors affect this all-important number.

TEMPERATURE

The most significant consideration with respect to racing tires is the temperature of the rubber under operating conditions. As Fig. 1a shows, there is an optimum temperature at which the rubber operates, and there is a significant loss in traction on either side of this peak. The temperature peak is determined by the rubber compound, and generally varies between perhaps 150 degrees for a rain tire on a lightweight car, to over 250 degrees for a NASCAR stocker on high banks. A given amount of friction work being done generates a given amount of heat, which raises the temperature of the tire until it balances with the amount of heat it can dissipate in airflow. That is the temperature at which the tire compounder tries to design the tire to have its highest Cf. Various factors which affect tire temperature are: weight of the car, cornering capability, average speed, airflow to the tire, road temperature, air temperature, heat transmitted from brakes or engine, tire pressure, tire tread thickness, and, of course, tire construction. The last two are primarily the responsibility of the tire engineer, and explain some common characteristics of race tires. Tread thickness is always at a minimum, to prevent the unreinforced rubber mass from storing excess heat to the point where it degenerates and separates from the cord body. Likewise, the sidewall has only enough rubber to keep air from leaking past the cords. Heat is also generated by flex of the carcass as it contacts the ground, which is one reason for stiff cord bodies, as in belted or radial tires. The rest of the factors are a matter of matching the proper tire to the proper conditions, or modifying the conditions, and are covered in other sections.

SLIP

A second consideration is the relationship of the Cf to slippage in the rubber contact area. Whether a tire is accelerating, braking, or cornering, it has some small degree of slippage. In a longitudinal sense it is referred to in percent slippage, and in cornering it is represented in terms of slip angle, or the direction the tire is traveling compared to the direction it is pointed. Longitudinal slip (Fig. 1b.) is obvious in its extremes: in acceleration the limit is wheelspin, and in braking the limit is lockup. The extreme of cornering slip angle is 90 degrees, at which point the tire is sliding sideways. What is less obvious is that the tire has its maximum Cf at some very small degree of slip—say 5 percent of rotation or 5 to 10 degrees slip angle, and that the Cf drops slightly beyond that point, when the tire goes into a slide. (Fig. 1c.) Both of these factors have been explained in detail, by Harvey and Ressler, although tire companies seldom report them and the only meaning they have to the racer is in the feel of the tire, or the warning it gives at the limit of breakaway. A race driver automatically tries to maintain his car at these limits by steering angle and throttle control. No matter what slip angle the peak Cf is at, however, whether 5 degrees for a race tire or 15 degrees for a production tire, the peak should be rounded and not drop sharply, or the driver will be unable to get close to the limit without losing control. The reason for small slip figures in race tires is that the slip accounts for wasted forces in the form of drag, and because this wasted energy contributes to heat buildup. Passenger car tires are designed to accept these losses for softness in ride and handling. The concept of slip angle also affects oversteer/understeer in the consideration of an entire vehicle, but as long as the front and rear tires have about the same characteristics (which is why you should never mix bias-ply tires with radials) it is primarily theoretical and mathematical. Likewise, longitudinal slip figures are most valuable in the design of anti-skid brake systems and drivelines.

CAMBER

The Cf is also affected a great deal by the camber angle or inclination of a tire. Obviously, as a wide tire is tilted, one edge is raised off the pavement and traction is lost. A rubber tire may be expected to flex somewhat to keep an even pressure footprint, but this flex also allows

Figure 1. Coefficient of Friction as a Function of Tire Variables

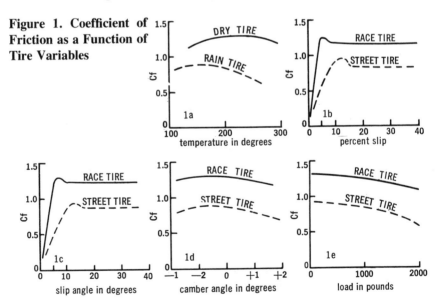

the tire carcass to roll under when subjected to extreme cornering forces. The curve in Fig. 1d indicates how camber reduces the Cf of a typical race tire and also shows that in fact, a slight inward inclination of perhaps ½ degree actually increases the Cf. It is not clear whether such test data is accurate to this degree of precision, however, because it becomes difficult to measure angles under these forces and deflections. It is quite possible for the wheel to be deflected half a degree, and the tire to be deflected over one degree with respect to the wheel. Since tire companies don't provide the information anyhow, it's necessary to determine the actual optimum camber angle for each tire on each vehicle.

PRESSURES

Tire pressure is another factor that can affect the Cf, although it is difficult to determine with respect to other factors, and practically impossible to generalize upon. The proper pressure is one at which there is an even rubber pressure in contact with the road, all across the tire patch. Pressure must also be at a minimum, to get the maximum rubber area on the ground and to provide some bump absorption, and yet it must be high enough to minimize heat-generating tire deformations. In addition, the generation of heat during a race will raise pressures by 5 to 15 psi and cause pressures to vary from one side of the car to the other depending on which tires are working hardest at any one time. Regardless of what pressures are recommended as ideal by engineers from their experiments on flat test surfaces, it always comes down to determining the actual pressures to fit a particular car and track surface. The most general statement that can be made is that in the range from 20 to 40 psi, the Cf goes up slightly with increasing pressures, except as it can be greatly decreased by track roughness. It's worth mentioning that enough pressure is also required to keep the tire bead seated on the wheel rim, as centrifugal forces try to pull it off.

LOADING

Another property of the tire Cf is that it varies with the total load on the tire, as seen in Fig. 1e. As unit pressures rise anywhere in the rubber contact patch, the rubber is less able to resist frictional shear-ing forces. In other words, a tire that has a Cf of 1.4 on a 2000-pound car, might have a Cf of 1.2 on a 3000-pound car. Where this factor gets more complicated, however, is in the lateral weight transfer under cornering, when the outside tires are more heavily loaded and the inside tires less so. At first glance, it would appear that there would be no loss in total cornering capability, because the outer tire gains as much weight as the inner one loses. In fact, how-ever, the change in Cf is not so linear, and the outer tire loses Cf more than the inner tire gains it. Typical figures are as follows:

$$\text{no weight transfer}\begin{cases} \text{outside tire } 500 \text{ lbs} \times 1.30 = 650 \\ \text{inside tire } 500 \text{ lbs} \times 1.30 = \underline{650} \\ = 1300 \text{ lbs cornering force} \end{cases}$$

$$\begin{matrix}\text{typical} \\ \text{weight transfer}\end{matrix}\begin{cases} \text{outside tire } 750 \text{ lbs} \times 1.27 = 952 \\ \text{inside tire } 250 \text{ lbs} \times 1.31 = \underline{328} \\ = 1280 \text{ lbs cornering force} \end{cases}$$

These figures don't seem to show a great deal of loss between the two conditions, but even the loss of twenty pounds' force in cornering power can affect the handling when it is at one end of the car. Also, these figures are for lightweight race cars on very large tires. As the loading increases, as with NASCAR sedans on 8-inch-wide treads, the effect increases. This factor demonstrates one reason why the race car builder tries for the lowest center of gravity, to minimize lateral weight transfer in cornering.

OTHER FACTORS

Finally, it is important to realize that the Cf varies a great deal with respect to the surface the tire is on. This is true not only in such an obvious condition as a wet or oily track, where the Cf can drop to 0.3 or less, but in the variation from a dirty to a well-used section of the same dry track. Even an invisible layer of dust or rubber particles can have a noticeable effect. Measured coefficients can vary by 10 per-cent around the same track with the same tire on the same day. The driver of a race car automatically discovers these variations and takes them into consideration, even if it's not always possible to find and drive on the areas with the highest Cf. The point is that a specific Cf can never be assigned to a tire, except under impossibly limited conditions. The numbers are always relative, but so important to the ultimate performance of a race car that they must always be considered.

There are other factors in tire construction or use that ordinarily would be of no interest, except that they could be the cause of some problems, and therefore should be mentioned. As the tire is essentially a flexible device, it has a spring rate and some internal damping. These rates are so high compared to the suspension spring rates that they are generally ignored. However, they can become harmonic with the chassis under certain conditions, and create a destructive chatter or wheel hop. A tire also has a self-aligning torque, which tries to keep it traveling in a straight line, and obviously, the wider the tire, the greater the tendency. If the steering kingpin were located in the exact center of the tire, it would be very difficult to steer it. The tire would have to be twisted in its own contact patch. Offsetting this pivot point allows the tire to tend to roll around one edge. Another property is pneumatic trail, which means that the forces on the tire move the contact patch away from the geometric center, upsetting static geometry. It should also be noted that tires can be made (intentionally or unintentionally) assymetrical in cornering capabilities. This might be an advantage on an oval track, or a definite disadvantage if it happens accidentally on a car intended to corner in both directions. Finally, most of these factors are related to steady-state conditions, whether in high-speed straightaway driving or low-speed cornering. In practice, everything is always changing, or transient, and can't be isolated. When the suspension allows the tire to oscillate vertically and/or move laterally over bumps, the Cf always loses.

The most ignored concept in tire dynamics is the friction-circle theory. This is related to the obvious fact that a tire has relatively equal traction capabilities in any direction—accelerating, braking, or cornering, as shown in Fig. 2. Actually, it's more of an ellipse, with more traction in the longitudinal plane for most tires with tread grooves, but a circle is a close enough approximation. In any transient operation of a race car, say from braking to cornering, there are two ways to get from one limit of traction to the other. The driver

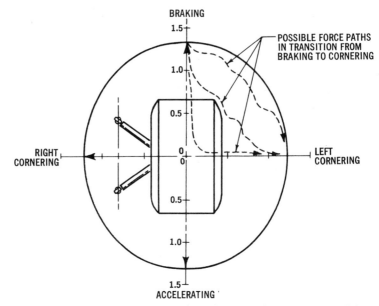

Figure 2. Ellipse Representing Peak Tire Coefficient in Any Direction

may either suddenly get off the brakes and turn the steering wheel, or he may ease off the brakes while he gradually applies more and more steer angle. As can be seen from the force paths, the first option allows the car to go through a short period where no work is being done by the tires. This is wasted time, no matter how short, because the car cannot instantaneously change its motion from straight-line braking to a curved path. It has been mathematically and experimentally proven (by Mark Donohue) that the second option—trying to keep the tire and car on the perimeter of the friction circle at all times—is a measurably faster way around a race track. Not only that, but it reduces the stresses on the car and tires which are created by sudden movements, and it is almost the definition of smoothness in driving technique.

TIRE DESIGN

The internal construction of different types of tires ought to be familiar already from any number of articles or tire company handouts.

Currently, however, the only designs available in racing tires are the fabric-cord bias-ply carcass (with a lower than normal cord angle) and the racing radial. The bias-ply carcass appears to be so well suited to racing needs, with its high stiffness both laterally and torsionally, that it's surprising the racing radial ever appeared. It would seem that the radial would inherently run at higher slip angles which would account for more wasted forces in traction. It's only advantage may be in the promotion of production tires. So there isn't much choice concerning construction.

SIZES

Tire size is the most apparent criterion in selection. It's obvious that with all other factors such as tire compound and pressures being equal, the more rubber on the ground, the greater the traction. But another advantage is that the greater contact area permits the use of softer or stickier compounds. Not only is there more rubber to wear away for the same tire mileage in a race, but there is a larger surface area to dissipate the greater heat generated. There appears to be no basic physical limit to the overall width of a tire tread. The greatest difficulty in making them wider has been in construction and the machines that are required. Any flexible, inflated structure tends to take a spherical shape, while it's necessary to keep a tire tread area flat across its surface. Because thick rubber shoulders are not rigid enough, and they store too much heat, the tire engineers have been slowed by the technology in designing flat cord bodies.

Tire sizes and size designations change so fast that any specific description would soon become obsolete. The only sure way to make a selection is with a tape measure. The first interest is in tread width, and specifically, that part of the tread in contact with the ground. Currently, the widest tires available are the rears for Can-Am cars, at about 19 inches. While that *may* be too wide for a small-displacement race car, it has never been conclusively demonstrated that there is such a thing as too much tire. The greatest current problem is in sanctioning groups which limit the rim width, forcing tire engineers to design for radical overhangs. When SCCA sedan rim widths were at 8 inches, some treads were over 10 inches wide. As long as there are no restrictions, however, select the tire first, and then follow the manufacturer's recommendations as to proper rim size. Each tire is designed to have the tread flat with the beads a certain distance apart, and if this distance varies by a few inches, evenness of the rubber contact area may suffer. Finally, it is possible that a wider tire will not always be faster, because of other over-riding effects such as compound or geometry changes. Width alone is not an adequate criterion.

A secondary consideration is tire diameter. Here it's not quite so easy to make a clean-cut decision. There are conflicting considerations. In the first place, there can be a choice of wheel diameters, which have recently ranged from 16 inches down to 10 inches on various radical race cars. The current selection for most professional formula racers is between 15 and 13 inches, and it's not uncommon to see different sizes front and rear. Then the question of section height, or overall tire diameter, is added to that.

Since the tendency seems to be to try and reduce diameter from the typical 26-inch tire on a 15-inch wheel, we should consider both the advantages and disadvantages of this reduction. The most obvious advantage is that it reduces the rotational inertia of the assembly, which is equivalent to weight in pounds when accelerating or braking. Reducing diameter also lowers the center of gravity of each tire and wheel, although this has a small effect on the car as a whole. And considering there is a required minimum ground clearance, it doesn't lower the chassis any further. Another advantage can be gained in suspension geometry, in making it possible to get the roll center closer to the ground without other negating effects. And finally, on open-wheeled cars, the smaller-diameter tire obviously has less air drag.

The disadvantages are almost as great. As diameter goes down, the contact patch grows shorter—in theory, at least—and the shorter and wider it gets, the more unstable it is for the driver to control. More important, as section height is reduced, there is less distance for the sidewalls to deflect, and the tire becomes more rigid and less able to absorb road roughness. On a very smooth track this is no problem, but it can cause severe chatter on other surfaces. On a heavy car, a

Comparison of the inner and outer tires under hard cornering shows the extreme lateral tread displacement with respect to the rims.

smaller-diameter tire will also have a tendency to run hotter. Not only does it have less working rubber in its circumference, and rotate faster, but there is less surface area to radiate heat to the air. And finally, on heavy, enclosed cars, a small-diameter wheel simply doesn't have room for an adequate brake assembly—whether disc or drum—much less enough cooling airflow for it. The most common application of 13-inch wheels is on the front of formula cars, which have little weight on the front, and frequently have chassis-mounted brakes.

It may be too obvious to mention, but it's worth keeping in mind that tire diameters also affect gear ratios. On cars with quick-change ratios, this can be corrected relatively easily. Conversely, on cars with more difficult differentials, a change in diameter can take the place of a gear change. Another point to consider with really high-performance lightweight race cars is the variation in tire roundness and diameter. Racing tires are usually more carefully built than production tires, and there is less tolerance for error. But it's still possible to get a tire that has a 0.1-inch diameter difference or out-of-

A tire inner sidewall that has been cut nearly to the point of disaster. A suspension component cut through three layers of fabric.

roundness. It's worth checking with a dial gauge and tape measure, especially if the car has a high-speed vibration, or pulls to one side under acceleration or braking.

Clearances are another very important consideration, particularly on production sedans and sports cars. It's hard to visualize the extent to which a wheel and tire normally travel, and the amount which the tire will deflect on a rim. The only real way to find whether a tire will fit in a limited wheelwell is to mount the tire on the correct wheel and try them on the car. It's usually easiest to remove the suspension springs, and manually move the suspension and steering through all extremes of travel. Then, additional clearance must be provided to allow for wheel and bearing deflection (which can amount to one degree off the axle centerline), and lateral tire deflection on the wheel. The worst examples of tire shift are probably the cantilevered sidewall tires on narrow rims, which can move as much as 1.5 inches laterally. A quicker but potentially much more expensive method is to try the tires on the track. With a good ear and good luck, a driver can hear a tire rubbing before it gets cut or worn. With bad luck he can destroy the tire and possibly the car. When there are doubts as to whether the tire is occasionally touching somewhere, the inner side-wall can be marked with chalk and then examined to see if it gets rubbed off. Clay can also be used, by building it up on suspicious metal surfaces and checking how far the rotating tire wears into it. Chassis constructors often use a template of the tire's radial cross-section mounted on the axle to check clearances.

TREADS

Once the tire size is determined, there may not be much choice in tread design, except between different manufacturers. For many years it was assumed that some sort of grooves (circumferential) and sipes (lateral) were necessary on a race tire, to allow for deflections in the contact patch and to swallow dirt from the track. Recently it has been concluded that for dry pavement it is far more important to have the maximum amount of rubber in contact with the road, and slicks seem to be the rule. Apparently, then, it would seem that whichever tread has the least cut out is the best bet, all else being equal. Even the slickest of tires, however, needs some sort of wear indicator, such as holes sparingly molded into the tread surface. All race tire treads are as thin as possible anyhow, to reduce heat and inertia, and ideally, should be no thicker than required to last one race in a really competitive class. If the tire is only half-worn at the end of a race, perhaps a softer compound would be better, or perhaps even starting the race on half-worn tires.

By the time all else is decided, there may not be much in tire compounds to choose from unless it is a very important race where competing tire companies are participating, such as Indianapolis, Daytona, or some other professional series. The only way to determine compound on a cold tire sitting in the pits is to read the manufacturer's identification number stamped in the sidewall, and then ask their tire engineer. At that, about all he can say is whether it is a gumball, or very sticky qualifying tire, an intermediate, or a very hard compound. If some testing has been done recently, he might even know about how many laps it will last, and whether it's likely to overheat and blister the tread off. For the amateur racer who buys tires at the warehouse, especially older or discontinued lines, it's im-

Various tire tread patterns; from the bottom: an older "semi-grooved" tread, two types of rain grooves, and the latest "slick" or treadless tire.

portant to remember that they aren't designed for storage or long life. Advances in rubber compounding cause race tires to be obsoleted almost monthly, and even if not, the rubber ages rapidly. A race tire that is stored for a year or two will continue to vulcanize on its own until the rubber is harder and more brittle, and not only does it have less adhesion, but it will tear more easily.

Rain tires are a special case in both tread and compound. According to the theory of tire traction, there are two considerations when moisture enters the picture. A light film of water, such as fog, dew, or mist coating the track, reduces the molecular adhesion. But it is only when the water film gets thick enough to prevent the mechanical gripping of irregularities that a different tread is required. So there are stages of wet-track requirements. As long as there is a light film—which is likely to be rapidly evaporated or thrown off anyhow—a perfectly smooth tire tread may still be best. However, the moisture will cause tire temperature to drop, and a softer compound would be advantageous. When the water reaches a point where it fills in between the irregularities, or it collects in puddles, it is time to go to a tread with definite grooves. The grooves serve both to channel water out of the contact patch, and to reduce the total contact area for higher unit pressures between the rubber and the track. For extremely wet conditions, the tread may be as much as ½ inch high, and half its area devoted to grooves. These tires also have successively softer compounds, since they work at lower temperatures. If, for some reason, a rain tire has to be run on a dry track, there is a good chance of tread separation due to the heat, or at the least, rapid wear and poor laptimes.

WHEELS

Racing wheels are apparently another off-the-shelf item that everyone buys simply because they look right, or because they're wider, or because they're on a faster car. But again, to optimize a car's performance, and to take full advantage of the rules and what is available, you need a deeper understanding. Size is truly an important consideration, as mentioned in the section on tire widths. The rim diameter is fairly well limited by the suspension and brakes on any particular car, but rim widths are limited only by clearance, imagination, or racing rules. Most tires are designed for a specific rim width, plus or minus an inch or so, but it's safe to say—the wider the better. For a rim wider than recommended, or for very low tire pressures, some sort of mechanical retention is advisable for the tire bead. Some racers use screws through the rim, or more sophisticated clamping devices, which either prevent sudden loss of the seat or keep the tire on the wheel even if it goes flat for other reasons.

A third important dimension on race car wheels is offset, which is the distance between the centerline of the rim and the mounting face. Racing wheels are commonly available with offsets from +2 to −2 inches. The greatest offset would be best for minimum weight transfer and maximum cornering, except for a few other consider-

A new tire being mounted, showing the six retention screws in the rim which keep the tire bead seated even when pressure is lost.

ations. Even when it isn't necessary to keep the tires under fenders, more offset affects the suspension geometry and ride rate, and also creates more stress on the suspension. On the other side of the wheel, offset may be necessary to keep the tire from rubbing, or to provide room for brakes and suspension components. Some wheels are even designed specifically to clear disc brake calipers. Spacers are sometimes used to increase offset, but this also increases bending stresses on the lug bolts and allows more misalignment.

The construction of a wheel can be just as important as its size. A racing wheel has to be much stronger than a production wheel, because the traction loads are so much greater. Two-ton NASCAR sedans running on banked superspeedways, for example, are required to have reinforced steel wheels, which are very strong and very heavy, and allow little air to pass over the brakes. The conflicting problems in wheel design are strength versus weight and airflow through the center. For the weight, magnesium is currently the most common compromise, although filament-reinforced plastics show a lot of potential. Aluminum wheels are the street-racer's copy of the real thing, and frequently weigh more than the production steel wheels they replace. The strongest design in any material is a solid disc center, although that allows very little airflow to the brakes, unless inboard brakes are part of the package. Where solid centers can be used, they are made of spun sheet stock or honeycomb laminates. The most critical high-stress areas on a wheel are the bead seat, where high cyclical cornering stresses are resisted, and the hub flange, where bending and rotational torques are the greatest. Some well-known cast wheels have had the design error of spokes that were narrower at the hub flange than at the rim, and the centers frequently broke out. Lug nuts should be the ones designed for a specific wheel, especially with cast wheels, which require captive washers to prevent galling the alloy face.

The total weight of a wheel and tire combination is important for a number of reasons. It is well known that a low ratio of unsprung weight (wheels, tires, brakes, axles, and half the weight of springs and shocks) to sprung weight (everything else) contributes to good ride, or in the case of a race car, good traction. Unfortunately, the ratio is worse for a race car than a passenger car because of the size and strength required in unsprung components. Another reason for reducing tire and wheel weight is that the rotating mass has a rotational inertia which contributes to the effective mass of a vehicle—which must be accelerated or braked. In the case of typical race car tire diameters, this can account for an approximate additional ¾ pound for every added pound of tire or wheel weight. In other words, if a new set of tires weighs a total of 10 pounds more than the old ones, weight and rotational inertia account for a total of 17.5 pounds of additional mass that must be accelerated. Likewise, taking 10 pounds out of the wheels reduces the effective mass by 17.5 pounds.

Wheels and tires also have gyroscopic effects that are commonly feared even if not understood. Obviously, the greater the rotational inertia, the greater the forces on the chassis. For speeds of around 150 mph, with 10- to 18-inch-wide wheels and tires, the forces can be noticeable. In a hard turn at that speed, gyroscopic precession can cause 20 to 40 pounds to be transferred from the inside to the outside two wheels. In addition, this much more weight transfer can be added or subtracted on the front wheels alone, by a steering correction of one revolution per second at the steering wheel. Whether these forces work with the chassis or against it requires a complex analysis, but they do have an effect on vehicle control, and should be minimized. Rotational inertia can be measured by swinging each rotating component from a pendulum, and gyroscopic precession can be calculated from equations out of an engineering mechanics book, but the above estimates are true for most race cars in the 1500- to 2500-pound range.

DEVELOPMENT

There are three stages to the development of race tires, and all of them require a skidpad or a simple, accident-resistant race track. (The use of either is further covered in Chapter 13, but this section will include some basics on tires.) The first stage is to take a given pair of front or rear tires, not *four* tires, and change all the available variables until they are understood and optimized. This allows the racer to know when they are operating at their best, or if not, why not. The second stage is to obtain a number of tire designs or compounds, test each one completely as in stage one, and identify each as best for any particular condition. And stage three is for a driver to work with tire-company engineers to produce more extreme examples of the best tested.

Stage one alone is almost too much work for any but the most regularly sucessful teams—though beyond no one in cost. A skidpad should be used, since it simplifies testing, and one should be as available as a good race track. Most of the variables that affect the coefficient of friction, or Cf, as explained in the theory section, can be isolated and evaluated on the skidpad with no more than a steady driver, a stopwatch, and a tire temperature gauge. The most impor-

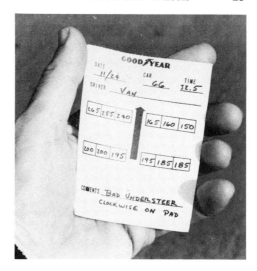

A tire temperature card, which shows temperature in three locations on all four tires after a hard clockwise cornering test.

tant point is that in a tire test the race car is no more than a tire-test machine and should remain a well-balanced constant factor except for changes in the test tires. Weight, driving technique, and path should be invariable. Second, the car's cornering power will be limited by either the front tires (understeer) or rear tires (oversteer) at any one time, and therefore that determines which tires are being tested.

The optimum temperature and camber angles should be determined first, since they have the greatest effect on the Cf. The tires should be broken-in, if necessary, and then allowed to cool. Assuming the front tires are to be tested first, the car is set up to understeer, preferably by using a very stiff anti-roll bar in the front. By following the driving and measuring technique as described in Chapter 13, the tire is pushed harder and harder, with laptimes and temperatures taken every few laps, until it's obvious that performance is dropping off with increased temperature or the car weight and cornering capability aren't great enough to heat the tires any higher. In conjunction with average tire temperature, the temperature profile should be taken in at least three locations across the tread. If it is noticeably uneven, the camber angle should be adjusted away from the hotter edge, to get the contact patch rubber working more evenly. Either camber or temperature can be studied independently, but it saves time and tires to work on both together. Finally, with the contact patch working evenly, the skidpad times can be converted into lateral acceleration in g's (approximately equal to the average Cf between left- and right-side tires), and plotted against tire temperature to identify the optimum point. If the Cf curve is still rising at the highest attainable temperature, simply pick an arbitrary temperature to use as a constant for further tests.

At this point, the proper camber angle can be rechecked. Evenness of the temperature across the tread is a good indication of the proper camber in skidpad tests. But since there may be other influences, such as better cooling on one side of the tire, or the fact that uneven temperatures can balance out somewhat in just the few seconds it takes to stop and take a reading, camber change should be compared to skidpad laptimes—but always at the same tire temperature. Vary the camber angle by plus or minus a degree, to see if either improves the Cf. If so, take that as the true indicator rather than temperature evenness. It's worth mentioning that the true camber angle—in action—is not known, nor is it important. All this test shows is the maximum capability of the tire, and the proper *static* camber angle setting for that suspension and tire.

Once proper temperature and camber are resolved, the less measurable effect of tire pressure can be checked—again trying to maintain a constant test temperature. If the first tests were run at some reasonable pressure—say between 20 and 40 psi—there should be small effect on a racing tire above those figures. However, advances in tire construction and lightness in vehicle weights make pressures worth looking at. So some extremes—say plus or minus 10 psi—should be tried to *see* if there is more to be gained. At the very least it will show what is to be lost if tire pressure must be decreased because of track roughness or increased to get more contact pressure on a wet track.

There are other variables in the performance of a tire, but they are less significant or less controllable. The rim width can be increased, with temperature, camber, and pressure held constant (or varied again to verify the optimum operating conditions). The question of maximum load effects on a tire are relatively unimportant, considering the fact that there is little that can be done about it. The basic philosophy of racing is to have the lightest vehicle possible for any number of other reasons. Besides, it is practically impossible to isolate the effects of total load on a race car tire test anyhow, considering the interaction with suspension geometry. This is also the case with the negligible effect of weight transfer on the diminishing average Cf between a more heavily and more lightly loaded tire.

If at any time during front tire tests, the front finally gains enough traction from the change of variables so that the car stops understeering or begins to oversteer, that's great! However, it does prevent further measurement of the front tires. At that point it is time either to go to a stiffer front anti-roll bar or to start improving rear tire traction until the car understeers again. The measurement of rear tires is more difficult because it is difficult to control a race car on a skidpad in an oversteering condition. As always, the objective is to be as steady as possible in throttle application, so as not to cause sudden breakaway. High engine rpm and a very smooth throttle linkage help a great deal.

As a final note on skidpad tests, remember that ambient conditions and the track surface can change during a day's hard testing, so it's a good idea to go back to the original baseline configuration and see how much, if any, it has improved on its own. Over a long period of testing, even tire wear can have an effect on performance. Without intentional tire tests, this wear can even indicate, over the life of a tread, something about the performance of a tire. If the wear pattern is grossly uneven, then it's time to make adjustments from insight and experience or by careful development steps.

Ultimately, what really matters is how fast the tires will go around a race track, or whether they'll last the required distance. But there are two ways to get to that point: by sophisticated and controlled test techniques, or by cut-and-try methods. A manufacturer may produce three tire designs, in three compounds each, with varying tire pressures, and run lap after lap around a complex road course to try and tell which produces the lowest laptimes—while assuming that all other variables, such as the driver and car, remain constant. This *may* be the most foolproof way to determine the best tire—for that car, on that track, on that day. But it does little for the state-of-the-art, or for a real understanding of what is happening, and how it is happening.

On the other hand, some sort of real-life test situation is valuable even after a long, careful development session. The previous tests were limited to steady-state conditions. For a given tire, rough track traction or sudden transient response in or out of a corner could be impossible to live with. If a standard, repeatable transient maneuver were possible, such as a controlled J-turn, it might indicate how sharp the breakaway point was, or how sharp the Cf versus slip angle curve was. But in the final analysis, a car is controlled by a very human driver, and what is comfortable for him can be more important than the highest coefficient-of-friction characteristics.

PREPARATION

Everything that has already been said about tires can be ignored if the driver is content to go out and circulate somewhere down in the pack with the also-rans. But the care and maintenance of tires and wheels can be a life and death matter. The first step is in putting it all together right.

Most race tires leak like sieves. In the interests of low weight and low rubber masses, the sidewalls have just enough rubber to hold the cords together. If immersed in water, they can be seen to simply ooze air. Air leakage shouldn't matter a great deal, however, considering the fact that a race tire's useful period of operation, or perhaps total life, can be measured in hours. Tubes are never used in a race tire because they store excess heat and add to weight and inertia. If a tire can be shown to be operating below its optimum temperature, a tube *might* be used to raise it, but anyone who has that knowledge probably also has the option of using a softer compound.

The mounting of race tires on alloy rims is best left to the people who sell the tires, although a persistent individual can do it with padded tire irons, a rubber mallet, and lots of soapy water or rubber lubricant. The consequences of a damaging mistake, however, such as a cut wall, or a nicked or cracked rim flange, may not show up until it is too late. Then again, once the tire is on the rim, it can be nearly impossible to inflate without some sort of clamping device to get the bead on the rim seat. Also, competition magnesium wheels have high casting porosity, and they can leak worse than the tire does. Some wheel manufacturers offer spray cans of a sealant that should be coated on the inside of the rim before mounting tires.

An alternative to fighting a tire onto its rim is to build the rim around the tire, as truck wheels are with split-rims. Some racing wheels are available in which the two sides of the rim are bolted to a common center section. This type of rim may be heavier for the same strength and more troublesome to assemble and seal, but it does have some advantages. Most of these wheels are available with many different widths of inner and outer rims, so not only can the total width be varied, but the offset can also. Another good point is their lack of a drop-center in the rim, which is otherwise necessary to drop the tire bead into during mounting. Having a relatively flat inner rim area provides more clearance for brake assemblies and cooling airflow, and helps keep the tire on the rim if air pressure is lost.

In any case, after the tire is mounted, it is a good idea to overinflate it at first by 20 or 30 psi, to make sure the bead is well seated, and to make sure the rim seat is not going to snap off, as often happens with truck rims. This *has* been known to happen on racing wheels, so it's wise to use an inflation cage. And finally, use valve core caps. Natural centrifugal forces on a spinning tire are in the proper direction to open the valve, but even if these forces aren't great enough, a small stone could do the trick.

The high and cyclical stresses on a racing wheel make it mandatory to inspect each one frequently for fatigue cracks, in addition to normal scratches, especially in the case of lightweight alloy wheels. The most certain and expensive method is by X-ray, which may have been done by the factory to detect casting voids. The more familiar practice is to use a penetrating dye and black-light inspection, which is more adequately covered in Chapter 11. The most common starting points to watch for cracks are: the spokes at the hub root, the lug nut faces if they are countersunk, and the inner bead seat. It is possible that a cracked casting can be welded by a certified aircraft alloy welder, but he will refuse to guarantee it because of the effect of heat on the surrounding metal, and the further stresses it causes. If a wheel cracked once, it will probably break completely the next time.

The balance of high speed racing tires and wheels is important, but not so critical now that construction techniques have made them more accurate and consistent in circumference. Ordinary static balancing, or bubble-balancing, is probably adequate on a heavy sedan, since there is so much mass to resist small vibrations. Static balance is also good enough for any solid axle rear end, because it's only when a wheel can pivot about its hub centerline that diagonal, or dynamic, imbalance will be apparent. But even on lightweight open-wheeled cars, with four-wheel independent suspension, there may not be a need for dynamic balancing. So little weight is ordinarily needed (it is added evenly to the inside and outside rims) that dynamic balancing is seldom important unless the driver still feels an imbalance. Most people who balance alloy wheels are aware of the stick-on lead weights, and also automatically cover them with racer's tape as insurance. It's up to the mechanic to see that inner wheel weights don't get knocked off by interference with the brakes or suspension.

Mounting new wheels and tires on a car may be the first opportunity to check for total runout, or out-of-roundness. If the tire hasn't been sitting with a lot of weight on it, there should be no reason for it or the wheel to have a total of more than .030-inch total runout as they are rotated on their axle. If there is more than that, there are three possibilities. The wheel may not have a centering hole which locates it on a matching surface on the hub, or spacers may have moved these apart. The wheel could have been machined out-of-round, though even a production steel wheel should be within .030 inch. Or the tire may be out of shape. The quickest solution is to mark the high spot, dismount the tire, and see how it compares to any high spot found on the rim. It may be possible to rotate the tire with respect to the rim to get two small tolerance variations to cancel each other out. When all else fails, if the tire has been paid for, and the out-of-roundness can be felt at high speed, the tire can still be ground true on machines found in some recapping shops.

One last word about bolting wheels to the car. What with increased hub thickness, and perhaps even wheel spacers, lug bolt thread engagement can be a problem. A good rule of thumb is 1.5 diameters, and more couldn't hurt unless quick-changes are required. As the bolt thread pitch should be known—say it is a $^7/_{16}$-20—then as the nut is screwed on, it should go ($^7/_{16}$ x 20 x 1.5) or 13 complete turns. The contact faces should be free of dirt, and each nut should be evenly torqued down. If spacers must be used, they should be carefully machined and fitted to prevent wheel wobble. Individual washers don't work well with alloy wheels, because they localize stresses and can wear into the wheel.

Most new tires require break-in before they can generate maximum traction forces. This may be due to a hard skin on the surface of the vulcanized rubber, or to a surface that is too smooth, but it should be anticipated on most tires, and especially tires with definite grooves and sipes. When spare tires are going to be needed during a race, they should also be broken-in, or feathered-in or scrubbed, beforehand. If a skidpad can be used, laptimes will indicate when they are ready. On a track it will be more up to the driver's feel, but probably not more than a few hard laps will be needed.

DRIVING

The last thing to consider in race tires—after everything else has been tried, tested, and understood—is finally getting them on the track. Temperatures and pressures are the only variable under control at this point, and these should be carefully watched. For long races, where tires will have to run for several hours—or the duration of their treads—it can't hurt to take pressures a few hours apart just to make sure that no tire has a slow leak. Since pressures rise 5 to 15 psi as a tire heats up, and the ideal running pressure is known from tests, make the proper allowance if they are checked while cold.

Most race drivers are aware that tires don't have peak traction when cold, and they use the warm-up lap for just that. Since the brakes and driveline usually need to be warmed up also, it is most efficient to accelerate and brake sharply—if no other cars are around. Another technique is to ride the brakes while maintaining moderate throttle in a lower gear. If the driveline and brakes are warm enough, or marginal in durability, simply swerving the car back and forth across the track may get the tires up to operating temperature. A tire can cool down quickly at high speed with no load, or while sitting still for a pitstop, so the driver needs to compensate for this when entering the next corner. It's not a bad idea to spin the rear tires freely when leaving the pits, as this warms them up rapidly and at least prevents a drastic oversteer condition.

When tire-company engineers are around, and pitstops permit, tires are frequently checked during fuel stops. The wear rate, or total tire mileage for a given car and track, ought to be known, but little things such as a change in ambient temperature or driving technique, or a spin, can change the wear drastically. Visual inspection can be good enough for an experienced person, but a tread-depth gauge is better, as it allows mathematical predictions. This, of course, just indicates average wear around the circumference. Tires are frequently lost because a wheel locks up in braking or the car slides sideways, and a flat spot is worn in one small area. The tire appears to have plenty of tread, and yet it wears to the cord in that one spot and blows out. In the middle of a race the person best able to discover a flatspot is the driver. Due to the practice of using greater front brake bias (explained in Chapter 5), and the known fact that a sliding tire has less traction, the driver can usually feel a flatspot at the steering wheel, if not see it happen on an open-wheel car. When a front wheel locks up—usually an inside front in a turn—it is often felt as a slight tug on the wheel to the opposite side. (Racing movies to the contrary, a skidding race tire seldom makes a sound that can be heard above the engine.) If that isn't enough of a signal, or there is still some doubt, a flat spot will create a noticeable vibration in the steering wheel on the next high speed straightaway—assuming that everything was in balance beforehand. And finally, on the next lap, all that lost rubber can usually be seen in a recognizable spot in one particular place. As for the driver identifying a tire that has been worn to the cord all the way around, things are a little more difficult. Drivers who have a lot of experience in this situation sometimes claim that the loss in traction can be identified when they get to the cords, and they can get to the pits on just one or two cord layers.

A slow leak during a race is less obvious and can be a little misleading. The first signal is usually a slow degeneration of cornering characteristics, most often a definite oversteer or understeer to only one side. A running check can be made in the next straightaway. If, under hard acceleration, the car pulls to the side in which it was oversteering, that side likely has a soft rear tire. If, under braking, the car pulls away from the side in which it was understeering, that side of the car probably has a soft front tire. Of course, abnormal cornering or handling can also be the result of broken or bent suspension components, which won't be cured by a tire change.

A complicated trick that is often used by racers is varying the compounds. It is not unusual in NASCAR or USAC oval races to change compounds all the way around on a pitstop, if it can be seen that the starting tires are running too cold, or are overheating and blistering. It is also possible to vary compounds from front to rear, to try and correct a handling problem, or even to vary compounds on the inner or outer side of the car. Even in a road race a car will, on the average, make one more complete 360 degree turn around the track in one direction than the other. Since the inside tires of the car will be doing less work, a softer compound may be used to keep them at optimum running temperature.

When a track starts to get wet, the decision to stop and change to rain tires is best made by computer and prayer. Some of the factors are: wet-driving skill of the driver, depth of the water, rate of evaporation or squeegee action of the cars, localized puddles and streams, and the immediate forecast. But most important is the tradeoff between: length of time for a complete tire-change pitstop, the difference in lap times between drys and wets, and the time remaining in the race. Even if a driver can run five seconds faster on rain tires, he can't make up for a fifty-second pitstop if only eight laps are left. Changing tires is a difficult decision, and the very best teams don't guess right more than half the time.

Although tires seem simple, they have an all-important and complex influence on the rest of the racing package, from the driver's technique to the selection of gear ratios. The next two chapters show how tire characteristics totally dictate the design, characteristics, and strength of race car suspensions and springs.

3

SUSPENSION GEOMETRY
AND ALIGNMENT °°°°°°°°°°°°°°°°

Once you understand the theory and function of racing tires, race car suspensions can be analyzed and modified to take full advantage of them. The design and construction of suspensions, especially race car suspensions, is so complex and so full of pitfalls, that it won't be discussed here. Most racers find it challenging enough simply to try to optimize what exists, whether on a production sedan or a factory-built formula car. A total redesign is beyond their comprehension. The broad subject of suspension geometry is so vast that it would take a book (which only a Detroit engineer could love), plus a dozen computer programs and a knowledge of advanced mathematics and engineering dynamics to cover it adequately. At that, there probably aren't a dozen race car designers in the world who could appreciate it. The best overall summary is provided by Harvey and Ressler.

The best bet is to modify what exists, or build and test, rather than try to design the ultimate suspension from advanced theory. Occasionally a designer has been convinced that he has discovered ''The

Truth,'' and when his brainchild was built on a race car it turned out to be too complex, or dynamically unstable—or even statically un-stable—because some minor effect was overlooked on paper. How-ever, it is quite possible that a person with a thorough knowledge of production suspension engineering could use the following specific information as it applies to racing, and the further references in the bibliography, to come up with a major advance. There *are* some new ideas that haven't been fully explored yet, but most of them are proprietary, and so can't be covered here.

THEORY

The first thing that has to be understood about any moving mecha-nism such as a race car suspension system is that six components of forces act upon it, and therefore there are six components of potential movement or restriction. Also, each of these six has to be analyzed in three modes: static position; dynamic displacement or travel; and transient movements or accelerations and direction changes. In addi-tion, there are highly complex interactions between various combina-tions. For example, consider the single wheel and hub carrier shown in Fig. 3. The longitudinal force Fx comes from braking or accelerat-

Figure 3. Forces and Torques on Each Wheel and Suspension

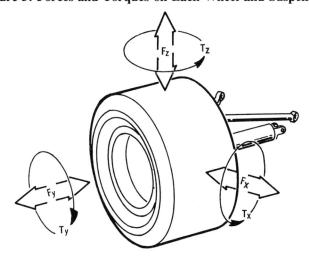

ing, the lateral force Fy comes from cornering, and the vertical force Fz is from vehicle weight and aerodynamic loading. Then there are the torques on the hub: Tx, which is generated by cornering forces at the ground; Ty, which is generated by bearing friction or brake torque; and Tz, which is steering or aligning torque. It is well known that in most suspension systems any force or movement in any direction will inevitably cause another force or movement in another direction. A vertical bump can cause a steering reaction or camber change, a brake application can cause a suspension deflection or steering pull, and so on. Each of the six will be covered separately—with some mention of its relationship to the others. In many cases, the most vivid way to understand a concept is to consider extreme examples of positions, forces, or movements.

FORCES AND DEFLECTIONS

Forces and movements in the vertical or z direction are known as tire load and bump/rebound travel. The magnitude of the forces is a combination of vehicle weight, tire load transfer, aerodynamic forces, and bump accelerations. The first three can be easily measured or closely estimated, but the last one depends on the track or the bumps a driver hits, and can only be guessed at. Race car designers frequently use a factor of three g's vertical acceleration, or in other words, a safety factor of three times the maximum of the other known forces. Other factors that enter in are the mass of the suspension components and the spring/damper rate, which are covered in the next chapter.

Tire load transfer, commonly called weight transfer, is the vertical force which shifts from one end or side of the car to the other, and depends solely on the g's of acceleration in any direction, the location of the center of gravity, and the wheelbase or tread width. If we assume the maximum g's in any direction to be a function of weight, aerodynamic downforce, and the maximum tire coefficient of frictions, then:

$$\frac{(\text{weight} + \text{aero downforce}) \times (\text{tire Cf})}{\text{weight}} = g$$

Simplified equations for maximum load transfer can then be given:

$$\text{lateral load transfer} = \frac{(g)\ (\text{weight})\ (\text{c.g. height})}{(\text{track width})}$$

$$\text{longitudinal load transfer} = \frac{(g)\ (\text{weight})\ (\text{c.g. height})}{(\text{wheelbase})}$$

This load transfer figure in pounds is then added to one pair of tires and subtracted from the other two. Another load transfer is found on solid-axle rear suspensions, when driveshaft torque tries to force the left rear tire down harder and lift the right rear tire. The measurement or estimation of aerodynamic downforce is explained in Chapter 6.

What a racer wants, obviously, is to reduce vehicle weight and load transfer, and to increase the aerodynamic downforce. There are no limits to these particular goals, and few negative interactions. The bump acceleration force should also be minimized, and could be zero for a perfectly smooth track. But since track (and off-track) bumps must be absorbed without structural failure, this force is largely a function of how much vertical movement can be tolerated. All race car chassis are as close to the ground as possible, to lower the center of gravity and to improve aerodynamics, so bump travel has to be compromised. Typical figures vary from perhaps half an inch of bump travel at maximum downforce on an Indy car, to over four inches on a large sedan on a rough road course. Rebound travel is limited only by spring/damper travel or driveshaft deflection.

Maximum lateral and longitudinal forces, Fy and Fx, are a direct consequence of the vertical force Fx, and the maximum friction capability of the tire. Since a tire can have a Cf of well over 1.0, this means that suspension forces in the horizontal plane are much greater than vertical forces. In addition, due to geometric leverage, lower suspension links carry much greater forces than the upper links. This is particularly important to realize because lateral and longitudinal movement of a tire should be essentially zero. Not only would these movements give the car a vague or loose feel, but they can cause a reduction in tire traction, or have major dynamic complications such as tire chatter.

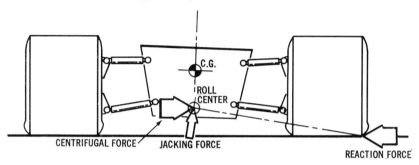

Figure 4. Jacking Effect Due to Roll Center Being Above Ground Level

Lateral forces have to be transmitted from the ground to the chassis, and the single point at which their resultant force vector acts on the chassis centerline is known as the roll center. The car has separate roll centers for the front and rear suspensions, which may be from a foot or so above the ground, to some inches below it. The car leans, or rolls, about those points—the roll axis—due to centrifugal force in a corner. If the center of gravity happens to be low enough to fall on that axis, however, there will be no roll. On the other hand, the roll axis should be close to the ground for other reasons. The higher these lateral force centers or roll centers get, the greater is the jacking effect. (See Fig. 4.) This is analogous to a pole-vaulter planting his pole at the location of the outside tire, and using the force and leverage to boost him into the air. That is definitely *not* desired in automobile suspensions. But the lower a roll center is, the greater the lean in a corner due to the leverage of the center of gravity above it. Or, conversely, the stiffer the springs required to resist roll. As if that weren't complicated enough, with most independent suspensions the roll center moves up or down and laterally as the suspension deflects, and usually in the wrong directions. As the car goes up, the roll center rises, and as it comes down, so does the roll center. For a description of how to locate geometric roll centers, see Ron Wakefield in *Road & Track,* June 1970.

In the same manner, longitudinal accelerating or braking forces can be put to use in intentionally jacking up the front or rear of a car. Under braking, tire load transfer to the front causes nose dive. But if the braking reaction force point on the chassis is above ground level, the pole-vault effect can be great enough to cancel out all nose dive. (See Fig. 5.) This is called 100 percent anti-dive, and is the basis of measurement for lesser percentages. The same principle works in reverse at the rear of a car when it is accelerating. Another way of visualizing this is to think of it as a ramp at the axle, resisting the longitudinal force. As the axle pushes against the ramp, it produces a vertical force to counteract load transfer. Using this analogy, it can be seen that the percent of anti-dive at the front, or anti-squat at the rear, is defined by the angle (from vertical) in which the tire patch moves as it rises and falls. In the case of linkage-controlled suspensions rather than ramps, the angle will usually change under deflection, or have a moving resistance point, as in the case of lateral jacking. The subject is covered in much more depth in an SAE paper by Winklemann.

It may seem as though 100 percent anti-drive and anti-squat would be desirable to maintain bump travel and aerodynamic ground clearance on a very low race car. However, there is another complicating factor at the front suspension. To get anti-dive means that the tire

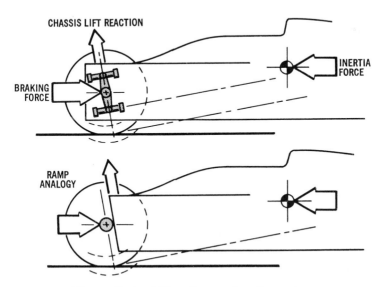

Figure 5. Anti-Dive Suspension Geometry

patch must move forward as it goes up. But to best absorb road bumps, the tire would ideally move *backward,* giving with the blow. Many passenger car suspensions, in fact, do just that, and *amplify* the dive in the search for softness. Obviously the higher the center of gravity, and the higher the percent of anti-dive, the harsher the ride. Few race cars can use more than 50 percent anti-dive because the harshness in braking is intolerable to drivers. Conversely, anti-squat in the rear is doubly beneficial, in that the desired tire patch movement is rearward, which absorbs bumps. An excess, however, can cause wheel chatter under hard acceleration.

TORQUES AND ROTATIONS

If suspension forces are straightforward, the torques and rotations are the secret of winning races—or disaster. Perhaps most important, and most difficult to control, are the camber angle and torques about the x axis. From tire characteristics described in the previous chapter, it's apparent that a race tire should always be perfectly vertical with respect to the ground, or perhaps cambered away from the direction of a turn by not more than one degree. What complicates this, is the fact that the car must usually turn in either direction, and it deflects both vertically and in roll. It's practically impossible to design a suspension that will produce the optimum geometry under all conditions, without its becoming too complex and heavy. If a wheel remains perfectly vertical over a one-wheel bump, then it leans in roll, and if it remains vertical to the ground as the car rolls, then it cambers over a bump. The suspension can't distinguish between roll and a one-wheel bump. Suspension designers have compromised back and forth for years, finally settling on two basic solutions. Most simple, and most familiar at the rear, is the solid axle, which of course has no camber at all—except perhaps half a degree in bending. In direct comparisons with independently-sprung rear wheels, in smooth corners, on heavy cars, there is no appreciable difference.

On lightweight race cars on bumpy tracks, however, the independent rear is superior, just as it is on almost every front suspension. In this case the most common solution to the compromise is to design the locating linkage so that the wheel cambers inward as it goes up,

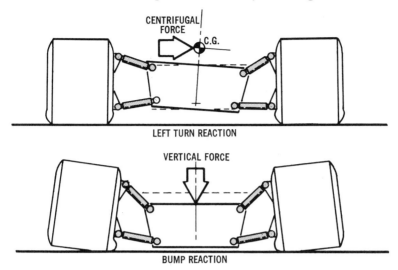

Figure 6. Suspension Camber Effects

and outward as it goes down, so that both the left and right tires tend to remain vertical as the car rolls. (See Fig. 6.) This means that both also camber when the car hits a bump while traveling in a straight line, but traction is not usually as critical then.

Any suspension which pivots while it is deflecting always has an instantaneous center of rotation, which is used to define its movement. With a swing axle, the center of rotation is obviously the inner pivot. When there are upper and lower lateral control arms, however, the center of rotation is at the intersection of lines projected from the control arm pivots. The reason the word "instantaneous" is used, is that the center of rotation moves with any suspension deflection. The center of rotation may be anywhere from a few feet from the tire patch in the case of very steeply inclined control arms, to infinity for perfectly parallel control arms. But in any case, the roll center of the chassis (center of lateral cornering force application) is at the intersection of this radius and the centerline of the car.

What is desired in either roll center height or swing arm length is not easily defined, since there are so many interacting factors. A relatively long swing arm radius is good in that it reduces lateral deflection (causing lost traction) in the tire contact patch as the tire moves up and down. It also reduces the dynamic camber change, which causes steering wheel kick from gyroscopic forces. And finally, the longer the radius, the less the geometry changes during suspension movement. However, as the radius approaches infinity, and camber change in bump approaches zero, the wheel is forced to remain parallel to the chassis—even during chassis roll. Since the chassis rolls to the outside of a turn, the wheels camber in the wrong direction. This can be eliminated by reducing roll, through moving the roll center close to the center of gravity or using high roll resistance from anti-roll bars. For many years drivers demanded some roll angle for an indication (feedback) of the limit of traction. But in recent years they have become aware that steering wheel angle and forces, and slow tire breakaway characteristics, are perfectly adequate indicators. Some current race cars may have a roll angle of less than one degree at 1.5 g's lateral acceleration. Everyone is realizing that the cost of high roll angles—used-up bump travel and undesirable camber changes—is not worth anything it may provide in softness or feel. Low roll angles also reduce the value of camber-eliminating solid or deDion axles. A fixed roll center at the center of gravity would eliminate roll, but a roll center at ground level tends to improve camber change and eliminate jacking. Getting the center of gravity down to ground level would cure everything, if it were possible, but it would take away all the fun and confusion.

The torques and rotations about the y axis, or axle, would seem to be irrelevant, since that is the plane of free rotation of the wheel. However, that is where some sizable brake torques—and perhaps some acceleration torques at the rear—may have to be resisted. Brakes themselves are covered in another chapter, but the suspension reactions are important in themselves. If the brakes are mounted to the chassis, with double U-jointed axles out to the hubs, the situation is simplified considerably. When the brakes are applied, all torque is resisted directly in the frame, so that the only extra forces carried by the suspension control arms are directly rearward at the hub center. This rearward force in itself was mentioned in a previous section, so now only the torque of a hub-mounted brake will be considered.

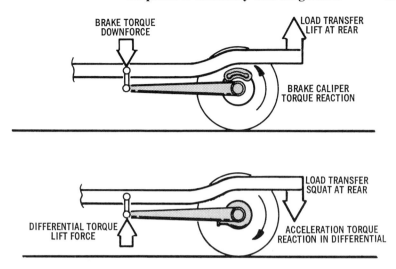

Figure 7. Anti-Squat and Anti-Lift with a Live Axle

If the brakes are mounted on a solid axle, as at the rear of most sedans, the torque reaction can be used to maintain a more constant ride height in braking. This can be totally independent of the ramp effect mentioned previously to prevent squat under acceleration, because it is dependent on pure rotation of the axle housing, and not necessarily fore-and-aft movement. For example, consider a short arm extending forward of the axle housing, with a link attached to the underside of the chassis. (See Fig. 7.) As the brakes are applied, forward load transfer causes the rear to want to lift. But at the same time, the brake torque is trying to pull the rear down. Depending on the amount of axle rotation that can be allowed, enough downward force can be generated to make the rear end actually squat under braking. The linkage is not that simple, of course, because of other control arm requirements and necessary bump travel.

Solid rear axles with integral differentials also have the opposite torque reaction under acceleration, due to the input gear (pinion) trying to climb up the axle gear (ring gear). If the axle is totally restricted from any rotation with respect to the chassis, there will be no lifting or downforce. But if it has an instantaneous center of rotation in front of it, where the longitudinal forces are transmitted to the chassis, an upward force will also be generated at that point which can be great enough to cancel out acceleration squat. This is further covered with mathematical examples in an SAE paper by Winklemann. It may be desirable to have 100 percent rear anti-squat and anti-lift in braking, but as usual, there are other complicating factors such as the effect these movements have on the steer angle of the rear axle, which will be covered later.

Another point which should be mentioned here is that a solid rear axle torque-resisting arm may be located off-center. This can help cancel lateral load transfer under acceleration, when driveshaft torque tries to rotate the axle housing to the left, and unload the right rear tire. If a torque arm projects forward from the right side of the housing, its action under acceleration will be to increase the load on the right rear wheel. However, under braking it will cause the right rear wheel to try to lift off the ground. There's no easy way out.

There are no reaction problems with independently sprung wheels with outboard brakes—as long as the upper and lower control arms are parallel. If the hub cannot rotate, it causes no upward or downward forces on the chassis. Although there are considerable forces in the links themselves, they all cancel out. But consider control arm axes of rotation which converge toward each other as in Fig. 8. This means that the hub will rotate as it rises and falls—or conversely—that as it is forced to rotate by brake torque, it will try to make the chassis rise or fall. The drawing shows that this convergence point forms another instantaneous center of rotation, which is the location of resultant upward brake torque reaction. As at the rear, this can be separate from the ramp effect mentioned for anti-dive. It may be possible to have a travel angle that is vertical at ordinary ride height to reduce harshness, with enough rearward control arm axis convergence to provide the desired anti-dive effect. However, it may have adverse effects on steering angles and torques.

Torques and rotations about the vertical z axis are commonly referred to as steering. But they aren't as simple as the mere act of intentional steering, since there are so many other movements and deflections that make other steering contributions. Even ordinary steering mechanisms include a number of factors such as steering

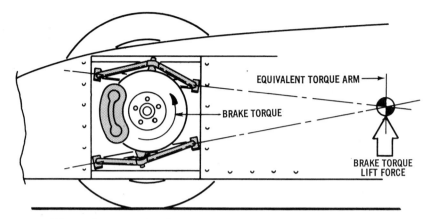

Figure 8. Anti-Dive from Brake Torque at Front Knuckle

ratio, variable ratios, total angle, force required, and feedbacks. In recent years, it has been discovered that very little steering angle is required—much less wanted—in a well set-up race car. When a car is balanced and driven correctly, total steering wheel movement may not be over one quarter turn throughout an entire road race. Of course, the steering ratio has a lot to do with this, but the driver is an amazingly adaptable machine, and a wide range of ratios are acceptable. Variable-ratio steering gears have been used in race cars with slow steering in the center for precision in control at high speeds, and fast ratios on either side to provide quick steering in emergency situations. It's worth noting that almost any steering geometry has some inherent variable-ratio, due to the conversion of rotary to linear to rotary motion, but in this case the effect is generally negative: the ratio is quicker in the center.

More important than steering ratio is the amount of force required at the steering wheel on very heavy cars and the kind of reactions the driver can feel at the wheel. As the driver approaches the front tires' limit of adhesion (understeer), perhaps his best information comes from the amount of force required to keep the wheel turned and how the car reacts when he moves the wheel the slightest amount. At the total limit of a tire's lateral adhesion, the steering force approaches zero and the car responds less and less to steering input. And *that* is

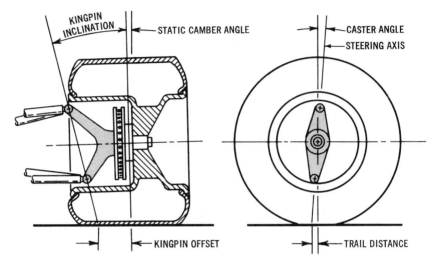

Figure 9. Front Suspension Alignment Considerations

what makes an understeering car so much easier to control than an oversteering car, in which the driver is less able to feel the approaching limit of rear traction.

The factors which affect steering feel—besides overall steering ratio—are caster, kingpin inclination, kingpin offset, tire width, tire pressure, and weight on the steered wheels. The last three are beyond modification with respect to feedbacks, but the first three are all-important in optimizing control. (See Fig. 9.) Caster is already well known. It places the tire's center of drag behind its steering pivot, for self-alignment at speed. Lateral kingpin inclination provides self-alignment even when sitting still, as it causes the chassis to rise when the wheels are turned in either direction so vehicle weight tends to keep the wheels straight ahead. Caster and inclination also provide some degree of camber change as the wheels are steered, although the effect is negligible for the small steer angle of race tires. Kingpin offset is the distance between the center of the tire patch and the center line of the kingpin at the ground. The offset is necessary to provide some steering feel, from the balance of longitudinal drag between the two front tires. Under braking, this can be felt as a pull away from the side that is losing traction or sliding a tire. In the case of a hard corner, where most of the load is carried by the outside wheel, the unbalanced pull created by that wheel's offset provides a strong understeering force at the steering wheel. A few inches of offset isn't uncommon, but when it gets too large—usually due to wide tires—the driver will have a constant wheel fight on his hands.

Ackerman steering is the geometry which causes the inside front wheel to steer at a greater angle because it is traveling in a tighter radius than the outside one. However, in the case of race cars, where it is desirable for a vehicle to have both front tires operating at about the same peak slip angles, Ackerman steering may be a disadvantage. As in the case of camber and inclination, though, there probably isn't enough steering motion to have any noticeable effect.

Then there are the factors of roll steer. In almost any suspension geometry there is some degree of unavoidable steering angle created as the wheel travels vertically. If it were merely a matter of symmetrical bumps during straight-line travel, it wouldn't matter, because the left and right wheels would steer in opposite directions and cancel each other out. At least it wouldn't matter as long as the wheels didn't go into toe-out, which is a relatively unstable condition. But as the car leans in a turn, it is important to have the roll steer working with the driver and not against him.

For example, a driver knows the approximate steering angle required in a given turn. But as he steers into a steady-state condition, the car's roll angle lags behind. When he finally reaches what he believes to be the final steady state, the car continues to roll more (or may even hit an asymmetrical bump), and it may provide still more steer angle at the front and/or rear. If it steers into the turn more at the rear than at the front, that's not too upsetting, because it gives the rear tires more cornering power, or understeer. But if the rear steers less into the turn, or even out of the turn, the driver is suddenly surprised by a loss of traction at the rear—oversteer—just when the car appeared to be stabilized.

There is no significant reason to have any intentional roll steer in a race car, assuming steer angle is parallel on the left and right sides. The driver can control the front or rear tire slip angles up to their peaks simply by basic chassis setup and the steering or throttle application in a turn. Any uncontrolled steer angle from rolling or deflections simply complicates his task. The most common reason for having roll steer in a suspension geometry is that it's so hard to eliminate completely. Due to all the previously described desirable conditions that are designed into a suspension, such as caster, camber, anti-dive, anti-squat, roll center, swing arm radius, and so on, a suspension designer may be hard-pressed to get roll steer anywhere near zero. Besides, quite often it's impossible to get suspension components in the right locations for precise geometry because of space considerations such as a tire, brakes, or engine being in the way. At any rate, if it can't be avoided, it should be developed to produce roll understeer instead of roll oversteer. If the chassis is going to surprise the driver, it ought to be with a more stable state, or understeer, even if it is likely to reduce total cornering power.

The final consideration in the theory of suspension forces and deflections is unintentional stress deflections or compliance. As rubber suspension bushings are eliminated from race cars, compliance comes mostly from the takeup in joint tolerances and the deflections in supposedly rigid metal components—but it is definitely there. Even if a suspension is designed on paper to have precisely the right camber angle in all positions, lateral force can cause an additional unwanted camber of over one degree. Compliance also affects the toe or steer angle of all four wheels just as much as it does camber. The only ways to cope with it are: anticipation in original design (very difficult), stress the components on a bedplate and measure the deflection (difficult), or develop the running vehicle on a track until everything seems to be working the way it was intended (less difficult).

At this point it ought to be clear that the design of a total suspension package is best handled by a computer. Fortunately, few production race car suspensions today are very bad, but unfortunately, few production passenger car suspensions are any good for racing—except the solid rear axle, which is very difficult to foul up. If the fanatic race car builder/mechanic *must* make radical changes from what exists, the safest route is to make some models first, out of some deformable plastic. This may help in seeing where the weak points are, and if it's possible to exaggerate the angles and deflections, it might even be possible to see where the inevitable interactions converge into confusion. Otherwise, the rest of the chapter is devoted to making the best of what exists.

HARDWARE

Types of Suspensions

If the ultimate suspension geometry has been built, it's only because half of its mechanical components are variable, and controlled in action by an onboard computer. There isn't a suspension on any production sedan or race car that doesn't have some non-optimum condition. There may be as many different types of suspensions as there are classifications in the Patent Office, so this section will deal only with those which are likely to be found on a race car: the upper and lower control arm independent, the vertical strut, the swing axle, the solid axle, and the deDion. Most of these have been well illustrated and described in great detail already (see Wakefield, *Road & Track*, June 1970), so this section will deal primarily with their racing characteristics or potential.

The first system, the upper and lower control arm linkage, is the most common layout in race cars of any size or purpose. Perhaps its greatest value is the almost unlimited range of geometry variations which can be designed into it. Practically all of the theoretical considerations previously discussed can be controlled—if not completely independent of the rest. The interactions can be either an advantage or an impossible nuisance, depending on the brilliance of the designer. Virtually any roll center or swing arm radius or anti-dive/anti-squat geometry is available, and it lends itself perfectly to steering control linkages. At the rear, for example, it's possible to have practically zero roll steer—except for perhaps compliance steer—by having a lower control arm with absolutely parallel inner and outer pivot axes. Non-linearity of the geometry, like interactions, is also either an advantage or disadvantage, depending on particular needs, so it is important to be aware of them. It is also important to be aware that most of the characteristic points—such as instantaneous centers—are not fixed, but vary with suspension movement. So perhaps the greatest

General suspension layout on a typical race car, with nearly horizontal arms, a shorter upper arm, and highly inclined coil-shock units.

disadvantage is in technical complexity.

It is also a very efficient suspension, from a strength/weight standpoint. The natural triangulation of upper and lower arms, with an apex near the center of the wheel, is a nearly ideal structure. The potentially wide attachment base on the chassis has excellent resistance to forces and deflections both laterally and longitudinally. Because of this efficiency and compactness, it is probably the lightest suspension possible, particularly in unsprung weight, and particularly when the brakes are mounted inboard. However, whenever a flexible driveshaft must be provided between the chassis and hub, extra complexity and weight is added in universal joints and some provision for plunge, or changing length in the shaft. In some cases the geometry is simplified by using a fixed-length driveshaft as the upper control arm, although this limits geometry possibilities and can have critical failure consequences.

There are some other disadvantages that should be mentioned. At the front, the desire to have good geometry and large, stiff control arms is limited by space inside the moving wheel. By the time a wide-rim wheel is vertically deflected and steered in full travel, there isn't room left for control arms—especially when brakes are also in the way. At the rear, rim width also makes it difficult to find space for the ideal pivot points. In addition, this sort of suspension is mechanically complex and requires a large number of precision parts, such as hub castings, control arms, extra suspension linkages, and dozens of adjustable pivots.

The next suspension, in which a vertical strut replaces the upper control arm, is relatively uncommon, although it is used on a number of production sports cars which have been quite successful in racing. This system has the upper locating point moving essentially in a straight line, while the lower locating point travels in an arc. Depending on the angle of the strut, and the angle and length of the lower control arm, it can be designed to approximate the geometry of a double control arm system, although it doesn't have quite the range in variability. This suspension is difficult to analyze in a short space, much less make generalizations about. Not that that matters a great deal anyhow, since modifying its geometry by moving points around is very difficult. The best that can be said about strut-type suspensions is that they are relatively inexpensive in mass production because of the reduced number of components—especially when a coil spring and damper are incorporated in the strut. But there are some definite disadvantages for racing. At the front, where the strut is the steering axis, greater tire width produces extreme kingpin offset. And at the front or rear, there can be wear problems because of the sliding surfaces, and it may be heavier than double control arms for the same strength.

The swing axle doesn't have much going for it in racing, except that it is light and simple. The camber change curves work in the right direction, causing both the inside and outside tires to lean in the proper directions. However, at the rear, where the inner pivot is commonly at the inboard differential universal joints, the short swing arm radius causes excessive camber change for wide racing tires. But by far the greatest disadvantage is that the roll center is very high, and there isn't enough freedom in geometry to get it lower. Swing axles have a drastic jacking effect, which is highly undesirable in race cars, if not all cars. At least they aren't complicated by having a lot of interacting effects, and they are quite inexpensive, as few components are necessary.

The solid axle seems to have little going for it in racing, and yet it is used on so many production cars that it is practically unavoidable. Its use is limited to the rear of front-engine cars for a number of reasons. It takes up a great deal of space for ride travel, and at the front it has almost insurmountable ride, steering, and gyroscopic effects. The greatest advantage a solid axle has is in keeping both tires flat on the ground most of the time. There can be a lot of slop and a lot of travel between the suspension and the chassis, without any undesirable camber effects. Because it is such a long component, it is easy to locate in any direction, by a number of possible linkages.

The lateral locating mechanism of a solid axle defines its roll center, which is relatively limited by ground clearance. The most common method—with the exception of leaf springs—is the Panhard rod, or a simple transverse link from the chassis to the axle. (See Fig. 10.) This is simple, light, and easy to adjust. The disadvantage is that it is asymmetrical. If it isn't as long as possible and always perfectly horizontal (as it can't be with suspension travel) it will change the roll

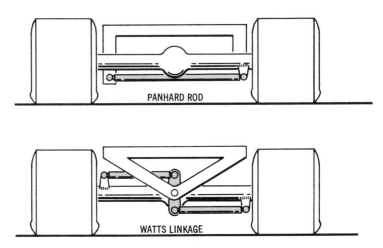

PANHARD ROD

WATTS LINKAGE

Figure 10. Live Axle Locating Linkages

center height differently in left- and right-hand turns. On the other hand, it seems reasonable that this asymmetry could be put to use in balancing out the inherent left rear wheel loading under acceleration with a live rear axle. If the Panhard rod is anchored to the chassis on the left, the roll center will rise as the chassis rolls to the right in a left-hand turn. This causes more load transfer to the right rear tire when accelerating out of a left turn than it would to the left rear tire when accelerating out of a right turn.

For perfectly symmetrical lateral location there is the Watts linkage or the roller-and-guide. These provide very definite fixed roll centers. One word of caution, however, is that the roller or center pivot should be fixed to the chassis and not the axle. Bump travel is perpendicular to the control links when they are parallel, and if they are attached to a chassis that has some lean, the chassis—or axle—will be moved sideways as it travels vertically in bump.

And finally, there is a more complicated method of lateral location. If four longitudinal control arms are used, as on many General Motors coil-spring rear axles, the convergence of any two to a point on the vehicle centerline defines a roll center. However, this is uncommon to race cars for a number of reasons, primarily excessive stress in the components.

The ideal longitudinal locating mechanism for a solid axle is a little harder to resolve, because of more interactions. Even if it were possible to get perfectly vertical movement of the axle, anti-squat requires a wheel to move longitudinally a slight amount as it travels vertically. And yet, if both left and right wheels don't move the same amount when the chassis rolls (one wheel up and the other down) the axle will have a steer angle. Since this is practically impossible to avoid, designers at least attempt to produce roll understeer, which is more stabilizing.

The strength/weight ratio of a solid rear axle must be the worst of any suspension. Unlike an independent suspension, the solid axle has significant forces and torques to be absorbed and transmitted to the wheels through its own unsprung structure. In addition, it is in the shape of a beam, rather than a space frame, which gives it poor resistance to bending from vertical load and cornering forces at the tire.

And, of course, the last criticism of a solid rear axle on a race car is its high unsprung weight and gyroscopic interactions between left and right wheels.

The deDion axle eliminates most of the worst features of the solid axle with integral differential. By mounting the differential to the chassis, and routing a dead axle beam around it, many suspension forces are reduced. Unsprung weight may be cut considerably, which reduces spring and damper requirements; the differential doesn't need to be supported between the wheels; and there are fewer torque problems at the wheel hubs (practically none if inboard brakes are used also). In addition, as with fully independent suspension, there is no lateral wheel load transfer due to torque under acceleration. Otherwise, the deDion is much the same as a solid axle, particularly in locating linkages.

One problem, of course, is that a deDion axle ordinarily requires two double-universal-jointed drive shafts, with some provision for plunge—as with most independent suspensions. In some cases, however, the need for changing driveshaft length is eliminated by making the dead axle variable in length, and absorbing lateral forces through fixed-length axles into the differential. The drawback in this, is that it places the roll center up where it would be with swing axles. With the acceptance of lower roll angles in the ideal desired suspension geometry, the need for connecting the left and right wheels for vertical stabilization has diminished. What advantage that had over double control arm independent suspension is now generally overruled by the disadvantages of higher weight and dynamic instability.

MISCELLANEOUS COMPONENTS

There are a couple of miscellaneous subjects that ought to be mentioned in the general category of suspension hardware. Whenever larger tires are fitted to a car, potential suspension stresses go up—maybe a little, but more probably a lot in the case of a production car taken racing. It may be of critical importance to strengthen the components which have to absorb lateral and longitudinal forces. On superspeedway banked tracks even vertical forces may be doubled. Most manufacturers of production cars are aware of the more strenu-

Production sedan suspension modified for racing, with solid eccentric bushings in the A-arms, and solid bushings and ball joints on the anti-roll bar.

ous uses their vehicles may be put to—whether as police cars or taxi cabs, in rallying or racing—and they often have optional heavy-duty suspension components available. Chevrolet, Ford, Chrysler, and American Motors all have separate catalogs or listings of these pieces, and as expensive as they may seem, they're hard to beat in value per dollar. Even if stronger components aren't readily available, racing rules usually allow the reinforcement of any chassis parts in the interests of safety. As long as there are minimum vehicle weight restrictions, any added weight for strength in the suspension is a good investment in survival.

The selection of suspension pivots is also important, and not just from the standpoint of ultimate strength. To get rid of excessive compliance, or deflection in components, all rubber should be eliminated from any production suspension. This includes control arm pivots, anti-roll bar mounts, and damper mounts. Rubber pivot bushings reduce ride harshness, but they also reduce the accuracy of geometry.

The purpose of a suspension pivot is to rotate freely, of course, but all too often, the wrong type of pivot will bind as if it were welded. For example, two inner control arm rubber bushings may be replaced with bronze bushings. But if there is any distortion along their axis under high stresses, the misalignment may lock them up solid, producing an essentially rigid suspension. At best, it will cause a great deal of friction and high wear, which results in looseness.

A spherical bearing should be used wherever there may be the slightest misalignment. But what is not commonly known is that even the best spherical rod ends produce a lot of friction when subjected to the kinds of loads a race car tire can generate. When a long control link is under compression—for example a rear radius rod during acceleration—loads in both rod ends can be so great that as the suspension deflects, the rod will bend rather than pivot at the joint. For the most critical and highly loaded bearings, nothing is good enough but teflon-lined spherical bearings. All-metal spherical bearings—with no teflon lining—are adequate only where misalignment rather than high load is the problem, such as throttle and shift linkages. Some catalogs list not only the loads that a bearing will carry, but the kind of rotation torques to be expected under given loads. When selecting a bearing size for a new application, these catalog figures should be carefully considered, using other known load factors explained in this book. At that, the bigger the better, within the limits of overall weight.

When mounting spherical bearings or rod ends, some thought must be given to *all* the forces they may have to carry. They are designed primarily for radial loading, and another force—say the spring load halfway out on a lower control arm—can cause an axial load on the ball. Catalog figures show that spherical bearings are only about 20 percent as strong along this axis, and can be pulled apart relatively easily. In some cases a high-misalignment bearing may be necessary, which has an axial strength of only about 10 percent of the radial strength. Where axial loads can't be avoided, an oversize washer should be provided on the mounting bolt to retain the rod end if it pulls part. This isn't necessary, of course, if the ball is mounted in double-shear, where it is supported on both sides—a structurally more efficient design anyhow.

MAINTENANCE AND SERVICE

At this point, without other absolutely necessary information—track development procedures, spring rates, aerodynamic loads, brake dynamics, handling, etc.—it is practically impossible to define the desired suspension geometry for a given car. However, some idea must be given of how to align and modify geometry. Later, with more information about other areas, the principles here can be better applied. For the time being, some very broad general assumptions will be made about desired alignment. If the chassis builder didn't provide some basic static alignment specifications to start with, the following estimates probably aren't too far off.

Ride height, if not defined by racing regulations, should be just enough to avoid scraping the track under the worst conditions. Two to three inches ought to be good for a starter, with more for heavy sedans and large aerodynamic down forces. Caster angle is perhaps least important, as the driver can live with an uncomfortable amount for a short time, and it has small effect on vehicle performance. Anywhere from two to six degrees ought to do it. Toe-in is just enough not to allow toe-out under any condition of deflection or braking stresses—from ⅛-inch toe-in on heavy, flexible cars to zero on formula cars. Camber angles are really unknowns at this point but tend toward zero to negative one degree (in at the top) at static ride height, with perhaps two degrees for heavier cars. The point here is that after the car is set up with specific figures for the first time, right or wrong, the driver *knows* what they are, and knows how to change them as development progresses.

The first thing needed in setting camber angles is some special equipment that most race mechanics don't normally have. For solid rear-axle cars, the very minimum is some sort of front camber measuring device. Professional bubble gauges which also read out caster angle are available for about a hundred dollars. For the beginner, a

Craftsman bubble-level protractor will give rough figures for a fraction of the price. To align a four-wheel independent suspension professionally and frequently, optical alignment gauges are available for two hundred to three hundred dollars, but a passable substitute can be assembled from some dial gauges and homemade stands. Finally, but most important, you need a truly level and flat surface on which to set the car. If the garage floor isn't flat enough, four spots must be shimmed up to within 1/8 inch of perfect horizontal, using a carpenter's level or a length of clear plastic tubing as a water level. More harm than good will be done if a car is aligned on an uneven surface.

BALANCE

The first step in static alignment is to set the desired static ride height and wheel load balance. Both should be adjusted with the anti-roll bars disconnected, as there is likely to be some asymmetrical pre-load in the bar. When the bar is finally reconnected, it should have no pre-load or torsion when the car is level. The shock absorbers should also be disconnected if they aren't the spring mounts, in which case they should be adjusted to full soft action. Good shocks have enough static friction to hold a car a half inch off the true spring balance point. Since suspension pivot friction can be significant even when the shocks are off, the car should be rolled forward and backward while bounding it lightly up and down from its natural balance height before any critical weights or measurements are taken. Caster, camber, and toe angles are all likely to change with any change in ride height, so it's mandatory to have an accurate reference point.

Wheel load balance for a road-racing car should be as equal from side to side as possible, keeping in mind that the center of gravity may be off-center when the engine or the driver's seat is offset. Oval track racers frequently use intentional asymmetrical loading since they only turn in one direction, but the same desired effect could probably be created by other modifications. Asymmetrical loading is certain to result in an instability under some condition or combination of cornering, accelerating, or braking. Ride height symmetry and wheel load balance are interrelated, so it is important to work on them at the same time, with constant rechecks.

Using a set of platform scales to balance the left and right side wheel loads, including the weight of a driver and fuel load.

A set of scales will be necessary to adjust wheel load. Since few race cars have wheel loads under 300 pounds, bathroom scales won't do the job. There are three options, rising in accuracy and cost. The simplest and cheapest is a spring-loaded lever arm that attaches to the rim and hoists it off the ground, but which changes ride height in the process. Next are platform spring scales which have some friction and inaccuracy. And finally are the platform balance feed scales. Two will work, but having four saves time in rolling or lifting the car. Unless total weight of the car is critical, accuracy isn't as important as equality between the left and right scales, which can be checked by weighing the same object on both. As with the alignment surface, it is mandatory that all scale platforms be perfectly level with each other.

Before wheel load balance can be set, the car must be loaded with a typical driver weight, full oil and water, and a known fuel load—commonly half full—and the tire pressures must be equalized. Roll and bounce out the suspension friction, and gently roll the car on the

Rear ride height adjustment screws in the back of a NASCAR sedan, showing extreme weight bias for left-hand turns on speedway banking.

scales. If the front wheel loads aren't within 2 to 4 percent of each other, one or more springs must be adjusted, depending on the desired height and attitude of the car. The method of spring tension adjustment varies, depending on the type of springs, from threaded coil spring mounts, to lever-arm screws on torsion bars, to variable shackle holes on leaf springs. If there is no adjustment, some must be made, as cutting or heating springs causes other serious problems.

The spring to be adjusted will not only correct imbalance, but it can correct variations in ride height. Say, for example, that the right front load is 50 pounds greater than the left front. Possible options are to decrease the tension in the right front or left rear spring, or to increase tension in the left front or right rear springs, or a combination of all four. If ride height is about correct and equal from side to side, tighten the right front and loosen the left front the same amount. If the front is too high, and yet level, loosen the right front and left rear. If the car has less ride height on the left, loosen only the right front. There are dozens of combinations of odd wheel loads, chassis tilt angles, pitch angles, and ride heights. Careful reasoning ought to indicate which spring ought to be adjusted in which direction, but if not, experience is also a good educator. If, after trying all alternate solutions with the greatest care, the chassis is still not balanced and level, it is probably due to unequal-rate springs or a twisted chassis. Once it is finally correct, variations in ride height or pitch angle can easily be made by carefully adjusting left and right springs the same amount in the same direction.

ALIGNMENT

When the chassis height and balance are set, a few alignment accessories can be made. With them, the car can be aligned while sitting on jack stands, without even having tires mounted on its wheels.

For alignment while the car is on the floor, a set of ride-height blocks are necessary. These are cut to just the right heights and located in just the right positions to hold the car the proper distance off the ground while making static suspension measurements. It is also useful to have a set of dummy shocks made from rigid pieces of steel, with the correct shock mounts on each end. These hold the suspension in precise position, even if the car is on jack stands or the springs have been removed. An even better idea is to make the links adjustable to three definite positions: full bump, full rebound, and ride height.

The next static alignment step in the sequence probably ought to be caster, and for double-control arm rear suspensions, rear upright inclination. The effect of these characteristics is slight enough that a tolerance of one degree might be adequate at first. Before beginning, both camber and toe-in should be set roughly where they ought to be, so that their own later alignment won't get the caster too far off. If an ordinary caster bubble-gauge is used, the standard procedure is adequate: turn the wheel 20 degrees in either direction, and read the caster angle. An alternate procedure for the front, and perhaps the only solution for the rear, is to use a bubble-level protractor between two ball-joints. On most front suspensions, caster is adjusted by moving

' **Application of a camber gauge (left hand) and caster gauge (mounted to hub) to check and align both simultaneously.**

the upper kingpin pivot fore or aft. If there is a choice, it should be moved by whatever method least affects the camber and toe. Record-keeping is particularily important here, in caster change per adjustment rotation, because it will probably have to be redone when everything else is correct.

Camber angle and toe-in are both critical enough to require precise measurement, and they usually interact to a degree that makes frequent rechecking necessary. Gross measurements can be made with a tape measure and bubble-level protractor—they would probably be adequate for amateur use on a heavy sedan. But for greater accuracy on light, responsive cars, better equipment is necessary. Toe-in can be set by comparing the parallelism of the left and right wheels to each other, although it is also important—especially at the rear—to reference the parallelism to the centerline of the chassis. If the rear wheels are perfectly parallel, and yet both steer off to one side by a few degrees, the handling will vary in left and right turns. The centerline of the chassis is best located from lower control arm inner pivot points, and should be permanently marked on fixed crossmembers. These points, and subsequent measurements, could also prove to be useful later in straightening a damaged chassis. A tight string stretched between front and rear center points establishes a centerline from which other parallel reference lines can be located. The parallel reference at the outsides of the wheels can be straight aluminum beams or string stretched between jack stands. A typical racer's ingenuity can produce any number of other rectangular frames of reference.

Toe-in and camber angles can be measured from any truly flat machined surface on a rim (check the runout by rotating it on the axle), or from a fine line scribed on the tread of a rotating tire. A machinist's scale is accurate enough to read the toe-in from front and rear reference points to the parallel surface. For front alignment, the steering rack or gearbox should be centered and held fixed while each tie rod is adjusted, so that there will be equal travel in both direc-

Using an optical alignment gauge for setting toe-in is somewhat faster and more accurate than using a tape measure and parallel reference lines.

tions. Camber angle is read directly from the camber gauge. In an emergency, angles can be obtained by measuring the relative distances from a vertical plumb line, and converting to angle by the following approximate equation:

$$\frac{(57) \times \text{(inches from vertical)}}{\text{(distance between measuring points)}} = \text{degrees}$$

This also applies if there is any reason to convert toe-in from inches to degrees. As with most other suspension geometry, toe-in and camber changes affect each other, and it will probably take a lot of going in circles to get both to the desired point.

With a solid rear axle, toe-in or camber can't be easily adjusted, of course, but a quick check will indicate whether the axle is in straight, or whether the housing has been bent. It is possible for construction tolerances to allow for a half-degree of misalignment. Some racers have attempted to take advantage of this by intentionally bending-in a degree or so of camber, but excessive wear on bearings and differentials has obviated any slight cornering advantages.

Independent rear suspensions are aligned much the same as the front, except that the alignment of axle shafts must also be considered. The goal is to have all four universal joints on a perfect axis when the car is accelerating (all deflections allowed for).

Ideally, toe-in would be zero under all conditions of bump, roll, acceleration, and braking. Any amount of toe-in causes some degree of tire scrub and drag, while any amount of toe-out, especially at the rear, will cause instability. Therefore, even on relatively rigid, lightweight cars, it's a safe bet to lean toward a slight amount of toe-in. Some toe-in also absorbs any toe-out caused by vertical travel, if it cannot otherwise be eliminated through procedures in the next sections.

DEVELOPMENT

There are two separate areas of development toward better suspension geometry. The first is to analyze and modify the geometry while the car is held fixed in a shop area, and the second is skidpad or track development. Each has its advantages, but neither is enough in itself. Knowing geometry theory and the approximate goals to be achieved permits a great deal of design and adjustmemt to be done in the shop. At the same time, the proof of the theories, and the last final degree of adjustment, can be found only in a real-life situation. Since track development has to include the areas of springs, aerodynamics, and test equipment, it will be covered in another chapter. Therefore, this section will be limited to shop development.

Assuming that the racing regulations allow suspension modification, there are enough pivot points, and enough adjustments, and enough directions of relocation to make the number of possibilities almost infinite. Camber change curves can't be improved without a firm knowledge of what they ought to be, but it will help later to know what they look like. On the other hand, there is a general consensus that roll steer ought to be nearly zero, or at least tend toward roll understeer.

To measure these curves, some special preparation and equipment are necessary. A pair of inexpensive dial gauges will improve accuracy and speed up the process, although a machinist's rule will do. If dial gauges are used, they should be mounted on a portable but rigid stand, and positioned so that they can contact a wheel face about a diameter apart, either horizontally or vertically. A large flat plate is bolted to the wheel or hub flange which the dial gauges contact as the wheel is moved vertically throughout its total travel. The chassis is set firmly on blocks or jack stands, the springs and shocks are removed (if they are not part of the locating linkage), and the suspension is moved vertically with a hydraulic jack. At the front, the steering gear is locked in its perfect center position. Of course, the suspension geometry has to have already been statically aligned to the desired specifications.

Each wheel is then jacked vertically through its total travel, while dial gauge or scale readings are taken at each inch. When plotted as shown in Fig. 11a, they give a vivid picture of the unwanted steer angles that come from suspension deflection. Then it is possible to improve the situation if it appears bad enough. The rear is the first problem to solve, since it is usually less complicated due to its lack

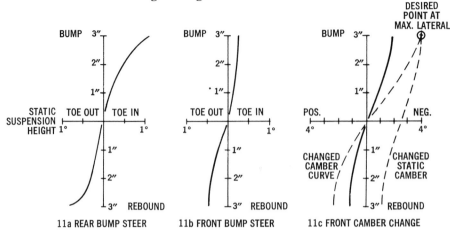

Figure 11. Dynamic Suspension Alignment Curves

of intentional steering geometry. If the lower control arm axes are horizontal and perfectly parallel, it probably won't steer. But if not, the goal is to get the steer near zero, or at least so that the wheels toe *in* as they rise, and toe *out* as they fall. The means of achieving this are as varied as the number of suspension systems available, but it should rapidly become obvious when major changes are made in radius rod lengths and mounting points. Then, however, the static alignment will probably be out of adjustment again.

When the rear toe is as close as possible, the front toe steer curve can be approached. The kingpins and steering hardware complicate the picture, but allow more options to correct a poor curve. If the rear curve had zero change, it would be nice to have zero change at the front also, but it at least ought to have *less* of the characteristics designed into the rear, as shown in Fig. 11b. Possible options for changing the curve include: steering rack or gearbox height and longitudinal location, steering arm height or angle, tie-rod length, and steering rack length. The effect of each of these changes, depending on the type of suspension and shape of the curve, is worth a chapter in itself, and better learned by experience.

Changes in control arms will also change roll steer, though there are fewer interactions in steering linkage change, which should only affect the static toe-in setting. Another important factor is whether the steering arms are ahead of or behind the kingpin axis. All else being equal, leading arms are more stabilizing because of lateral force suspension compliance. For example, in a hard left turn, the right front wheel will be forced toward the chassis a small amount. Since the steering link has less force on it, it deflects less, and being ahead of the kingpin, steers the car out of the turn—an understeering effect. Finally, where a compromise must be made in the toe-steer curves, the bump side is more important, since that wheel is obviously the more heavily loaded. Conversely, when a wheel goes into full rebound, it approaches zero loading.

Although not enough is known at this point to modify camber change curves, some mention is due. The curves can be obtained in the same way as the roll steer curves, only with the dial gauges aligned vertically, or with the use of a camber bubble gauge. The way to find the proper camber angle is to test the car on a skidpad and measure tire temperature evenness or laptimes, as discussed in Chapter 2. However, that produces only the correct camber at maximum roll angle. The final *static* camber angle required to give that roll camber may be ridiculous for straight-line running. If a static camber of three degrees is required for correct cornering camber, then it would be of value to try and change the curve. In this case, the extreme bump point of the curve is known, and it is desirable to get the ride height portion of the curve to pass through zero camber, as shown in Fig. 11c. Of course, the curve probably can't be changed without also changing swing-arm radius, roll center height, toe-steer curves, and so on. The complexity of the geometry increases exponentially. In the next chapter, springing and damping are added to the muddle.

4

SPRINGS, ANTI-ROLL BARS, SHOCK ABSORBERS

A spring is a spring is a spring. It doesn't matter whether it's made out of steel, titanium, rubber, silicone, air, or jello, as long as it has the required spring rate in pounds per inch of deflection. Of course, there are a few other considerations of importance which have fairly well limited the selection for race cars to metal alloys. The spring has to have a high value of energy storage per pound. It has to be durable under repeated stress cycles. And it is also frequently used as a locating mechanism. Over the years, racers have learned that to make a production car handle better, they have to install stiffer springs. They also believe in installing stiffer shocks, and stiffer anti-roll bars. Those are all over-generalizations that *may* be applicable in the conversion from street to track, but which can easily cause a loss in performance if there is no real understanding.

THEORY

SPRINGS

The whole idea is to keep the tires in the firmest contact with the road as long as possible. As a tire bounces over irregularities, its contact force averages out to be the load on that corner of the car. But the average doesn't count in a race car at the limit of traction. When the tire bounces up and unloads itself, *that* is the traction limit of the car. So spring rate is of far less importance than control of the tire, which is also strongly influenced by the damping action of the shock absorbers and the ratio of unsprung to sprung weight. Too high a spring rate or damping rate is just as bad as too low a rate.

The rate of a spring in pounds per inch, sometimes just referred to as pounds, is determined by design or test, and usually is a constant for a given spring. A 200-pound spring will deflect one inch if 200 pounds is placed on it, or 2 inches if 400 pounds is placed on it. If the rates of a car's springs are unknown, they can easily be determined in this manner. In addition to ordinary constant-rate springs, variable-rate springs are sometimes available. With these, the spring might deflect 1 inch with a 200 pound load, and yet only 1.5 inches with a 400 pound load. These are uncommon, usually quite expensive, and they cause unbelievable complexities in a race car's suspension. It's worth noting that variable spring rates usually only *rise* under deflection, which fortunately is the desired property in a suspension system anyhow.

What is not commonly known is that the geometry of the spring mounting system usually gives a vehicle a slightly variable spring rate even if constant-rate springs are used. If a coil spring could be mounted directly above the wheel, and if it deflected in a perfectly straight line, the wheel rate would be constant and equal to the spring rate. But since springs have to be mounted inboard of the wheel, and the connecting links travel through odd combinations of arcs, the spring operates at a disadvantage in leverage. (See Fig. 12.) Given a set of engineering drawings, the leverage, or mechanical ratio, could be calculated. For an existing vehicle, however, the ratio can be found by a more straightforward method, due to the fact that the force ratio between the tire and the spring is the inverse of the displacement ratio. Say, for example, that when the wheel is deflected 2 inches, the spring deflects 1 inch. The displacement ratio between spring and wheel is 1 : 2 and the force ratio is 2 : 1. In this case, the spring force is twice the wheel force. However, it's important to

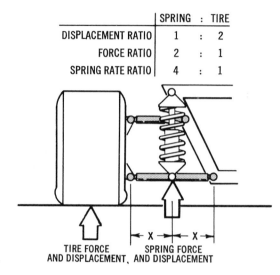

	SPRING	:	TIRE
DISPLACEMENT RATIO	1	:	2
FORCE RATIO	2	:	1
SPRING RATE RATIO	4	:	1

TIRE FORCE
AND DISPLACEMENT, SPRING FORCE AND DISPLACEMENT

Figure 12. Geometric Consideration in Spring Rates

distinguish that the spring *rate* in pounds per inch will be *four* times the wheel rate, since both force and displacement change by a factor of two. If this ratio is carefully measured in one-inch increments over full suspension travel, the variability in rate can be plotted. It isn't uncommon for this changing rate to decrease with deflection, due to undesirable spring geometry. The leverage ratio also accentuates the interaction of offset wheels on ride rates with some non-parallel independent suspensions. The further out the wheel gets, the greater the leverage it has on the spring, and therefore, the lower the ride rate, the lower the chassis sinks, and the lower the roll rate.

The ride rate is also linked to the chassis roll rate from lateral forces in a turn. Because the chassis center of gravity is usually above its center of roll, something must be provided to keep the roll to a minimum. If single suspension springs were located in the center of solid front and rear axles, the chassis would literally fall over. Obviously, then, the further apart the springs are, for a given spring rate, the greater the roll resistance. Since it is desirable to have a race car's center of roll very low, more roll resistance is required than can be provided by the relatively soft spring rate and narrow spring base. This is the reason for anti-roll bars.

Coil and leaf springs for a racing sedan. Note that two coils have been close-wound and ground flat, and the eyes are centered on the main leaf.

With the ability to control roll angle relatively independently of the vertical ride rate, race car spring rates have gotten considerably lighter over the years. Although a complex analysis would be necessary to study the total effect of spring rates, experience has proven that the softer the better—within certain limits. The lower limit of spring rate and/or travel is the point at which the chassis hits the track on hard bumps or high banks, or the point at which moving suspension components contact each other. Although it is possible to provide relatively soft contact points for suspension components (to prevent stress failures), most racers prefer to have the absolute limit be the chassis hitting the ground. Whichever part hits the ground—body or frame—is probably less critical than the highly stressed suspension, and it can safely take some wear. In addition, in the search for maximum lowness, positive stops on the suspension may eliminate some valuable travel. For example, positive suspension stops which just keep the chassis off the track in pure bump may restrict the bump travel too much in roll. Finally, and possibly most important, when the suspension bottoms suddenly, its spring rate rises instantaneously to infinity. This causes that particular tire to have a sudden loss in traction capacity (assuming a less than glassy-smooth track), and therefore a sudden handling change—which at the rear creates critical oversteer. The chassis striking the track at the same rate will unload a wheel somewhat, but the effect is far less. That is not to say that either is a desirable condition. Suspension travel and spring rates should be selected so they just approach that point but do not allow contact under normal track conditions.

When selecting travel and rates, there are a number of factors to consider besides roll and bumps. Wheel load transfer under braking and accelerating would use up wheel travel too, if 100 percent anti-dive and anti-squat were not designed into the geometry. In addition, a lateral force jacking effect will cause a change in wheel travel as the chassis rises. The interaction of all these variable forces and displacements is beyond reasonable analysis, which means that the final selection must be made from track test experience. Theoretically, it may be possible to combine the geometry effects of anti-dive in braking with lateral jacking as the car enters the corner and anti-squat as it accelerates out, to maintain a relatively constant suspension travel for bumps. The problem is that these geometry requirements have other more serious negative consequences.

BARS

An anti-roll bar cannot rightly be called a sway bar since it neither causes nor reduces sway. Nor can it be called a stabilizer bar since it may very easily cause the car to be unstable. All it is supposed to do is resist vehicle roll angle in a turn. However, the distribution of roll resistance between the front and rear wheels has a great effect on the cornering stability of a vehicle. The explanation has usually been dependent on a previously mentioned characteristic of tires: the total cornering power of two equally loaded tires is slightly greater than the cornering power of one tire with twice the load. In other words, the end of the car with the greatest load transfer to the outside tire has slightly less cornering power. This is true, and it works in practice— but there is also another significant factor.

The major effect of anti-roll bars may be seen from a consideration of torques on the vehicle about its center of gravity, as shown in Fig. 13. The diameter of the circle around each tire represents the load on that tire, and therefore its traction capability in any direction. If the front and rear cornering forces and the left and right longitudinal

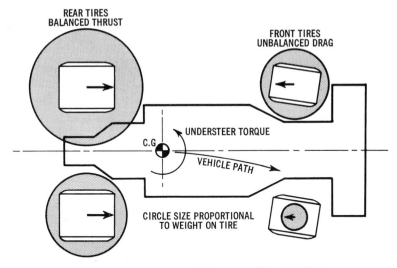

Figure 13. Anti-Roll Bar Effects on Chassis Balance

forces all balance perfectly around the center of gravity, then the car is perfectly balanced in that condition. However, the circles in this example indicate that there is greater load transfer at the front, reducing front cornering power, and resulting in a counter–clockwise torque, or understeer. But we must also consider the cornering drag of the two front tires, and enough forward thrust from the two rear tires to balance that drag. As front lateral load transfer increases the drag on the outside tire and decreases drag on the inside tire, there is again a counter–clockwise torque about the center of gravity. At the same time, increased front load transfer reduces rear load transfer and causes forward thrust to be more centered on the chassis centerline and contribute less to a clockwise torque, or oversteer. This is especially true of cars with an open, or unlocked, differential, in that forward thrust is supposed to be perfectly balanced between the left and right rear wheels, regardless of the load carried. An accurate mathematical analysis of both tire depreciation effects and tire drag effects depends on a large amount of other variable data on tires, load transfer, roll resistance distribution, differential type, and so on. But it is safe to say that both effects are important, and fortunately both

Two types of anti-roll bar ends. The perforated end is more rigid than the bent bar, which can bend in addition to its normal twisting action.

work toward the same result. A distinction between the two is not irrelevant, however, since the latter helps to explain other stability effects from power application, braking and differential action.

At either end of the chassis, the effectiveness of an anti-roll bar is dependent on a number of geometric factors. Of course, the diameter of an anti-roll bar is all-important to its roll resistance, all other linkages remaining equal. But for the installation or relocation of a bar, the mechanical force ratio between tire travel and bar lever-arm travel must be considered. As with finding spring rate ratios, this can be done from engineering drawings, or experimentally on an existing suspension. The force ratio is the inverse of the displacement ratio between tire travel and bar-end travel—and is also likely to vary with movement. Another complication to be aware of is deflection in the anti-roll bar lever arms. If the bar has relatively rigid arms attached to its ends, and they are close to the bar pivots, there is probably little unwanted deflection. But if the arms are merely bent out of the same material as the shaft, then the arms will have some bending which will reduce the effectiveness of the bar.

The lowering of a race car center of gravity toward the roll center, and the use of a very stiff anti-roll bar, can bring the maximum roll angle down to one or two degrees on a modern racing car. At one time some drivers claimed that a significant roll angle was necessary to provide information about cornering forces. But high roll angles have so many other disadvantages—taking up bump travel, causing camber changes, and causing roll steer—that other feedbacks have replaced roll in importance. On the other hand, a stiff anti-roll bar has a noticeable drawback in one-wheel bumps, as it increases the single-wheel spring rate as though there were an additional torsion-bar spring in the suspension. As in everything else, there has to be some trade-off between the advantages and disadvantages.

SHOCKS

Shock absorbers are more appropriately called spring dampers, since they reduce the suspension spring oscillation to zero relatively rapidly. The ideal spring has practically zero friction in its movement, which allows it to keep oscillating for a long time. So some sort of controlled friction must be supplied. Mechanical friction, as between two solid surfaces rubbed together, is not desirable, because it is relatively independent of velocity or displacement. It treats little bumps as firmly as large, high-speed bumps. On the other hand, viscous or hydraulic friction increases as a function of velocity, and its force/deflection curves can be modified precisely to any desired performance. The problem arises in deciding what that performance ought to be—a complex and little-understood area. Some of the factors to be considered in damper design or selection include: total travel, maximum resistance force, rise of the resistance force curve, total energy to be absorbed, ratio of bump/rebound force, internal mechanical friction, jerk, and weight. Since few racers can build their own shock absorbers, the factors will be merely described, as relating to selection. (See Fig. 14.)

Total travel is a simple factor, but often ignored. It is very important that suspension travel not be limited because of bottoming in the shocks. Adjustable shocks in particular have delicate valves which can be pounded to pieces. As with springs and anti-roll bars, the shock travel and force is seldom equal to that of the wheel but has

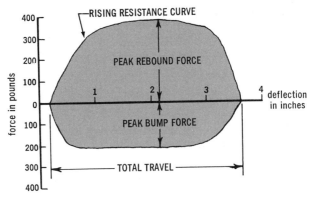

Figure 14. Shock Absorber Force-Deflection Curve at an Arbitrary Cycling Speed

some mechanical ratio. Even with a solid rear axle, inclination of the shock absorber reduces its travel and, therefore, its effectiveness.

Maximum resistance forces are generally referred to as stiffness and are always related to a specific test velocity of piston travel. Some manufacturers of racing shocks can provide graphs with a series of curves showing force as a function of travel for various cycling speeds. The more that compression and extension forces increase, the faster they bring a suspension oscillation to zero. This can be overdone, however, to the point of critical damping where the suspension doesn't cycle at all but slowly returns to its original ride position without overshooting. Even if this were desirable—it tends to hold the tire off the ground too long—the forces it would transmit to the chassis would be intolerable. As it is, shock absorber forces are probably many times greater than spring forces and should be respectfully considered in bracket design.

The rise of the force/travel curve from zero is an indication of absorption ratio between small and large bumps. A gradual curve avoids harshness over minor bumps such as tar strips, without reducing the maximum bump absorption capability. However, a gradual rise also decreases the total area inside the force/travel curve, so that total energy capacity is decreased.

Bump/rebound ratio is the comparison of peak forces in either direction. Most passenger cars have traditionally used a 30/70 ratio, meaning that 30 percent of suspension travel is resisted in bump, and 70 percent resisted in rebound—over a series of cycles to zero. On the other hand, racing shock absorbers commonly have a ratio closer to 50/50, with some having the capability of adjustment to other ratios. It has not been conclusively proven that a 30/70 damping ratio is better than 50/50 in any respect, all other factors being equal. In fact, a shock absorber with an uneven ratio has a feature that can be a definite disadvantage on a race car. Over a series of bumps, a 30/70 resistance ratio will have a tendency to cause the wheel to rebound a little less on each cycle. In other words, instead of the wheel falling, the chassis will fall, decreasing suspension travel. It might be said that the suspension is being pumped down. If the effect is known and anticipated, a desired height change might be possible, such as a 70/30 shock absorber which pumps the suspension up. In fact, this sort of action is designed into some kinds of automatic load levelers.

There are other performance characteristics of shocks that have less application to racing. Jerk, or the instantaneous change in acceleration, is an important consideration in ride comfort. It has not yet been applied to the improvement of tire traction but there are possibilities. Heat absorption and dissipation are also factors. A shock may generate a great deal of heat over a long, rough surface, and if it can't get rid of it fast enough, the fluid may boil, or aerate, and lose its damping ability. For test data on a number of high-performance shocks, see Dinkel, *Road & Track,* October 1974.

HARDWARE

SPRINGS

Since most springs have the same type of characteristics regardless of material or configuration, the type of spring used is decided primarily by original design requirements. Current race cars are most commonly supported by coil springs, torsion bars, or leaf springs, plus the occasional air/oil spring and sometimes even rubber. The major points of selection are space requirements and the use of springs as locating mechanisms. A coil spring and a torsion bar are essentially the same in performance, because the former is no more than a torsion bar which has been wound into a different shape. However, there are places where either cannot be used because of space limitations or the accessibility of mounting structure. The coil has shape and displacement characteristics similar to a shock absorber, which makes them convenient to mount closely, if not concentrically. On the other hand, the torsion bar takes up far less volume, especially when it can be mounted parallel to, or inside, frame members. The leaf spring doesn't have much volume in itself, but it often requires a great deal of space for bounce travel.

More important in a lightweight race car is the ability to also use the spring as a suspension locating device. In this case the coil spring is practically useless, since it has little structural rigidity and in fact may have a problem in buckling. The torsion bar, which requires a lever arm and pivot, is a natural selection to double as a suspension control arm. And the leaf spring, of course, does a fairly decent job of locating a solid rear axle in practically every direction. Transverse leaf springs have also been used as control arms on the independent suspension of lightweight cars, though the combination of loads can cause a lot of trouble.

If spring friction is important because of ride harshness, coils are the best selection, with virtually no sliding or rotating surfaces. Torsion bars are next, with a couple of easily lubricated pivots. And leaf springs are the worst, with a large amount of sliding friction between leaves. In some cases, this has been eliminated with single-leaf springs, but they are not common because of construction and stress problems.

Weight, and especially unsprung weight, favors the torsion bar. Some part of every spring has to be considered a part of the unsprung suspension mass. In the case of a torsion bar, less than half the weight of the lever arm alone is considered unsprung, while half the total weight of a coil spring is. Leaf springs come out worst of all, with the largest mass usually being centered about the axle. There is

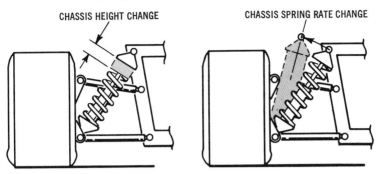

Figure 15. Choices in Spring Adjustments

further potential for coil or torsion springs, in using hollow wire, or tubing, for the spring structure. For a cylinder in torsional stress, very little of the core material is used effectively, so by hollowing the wire and increasing the diameter slightly, the same performance is available at a lighter weight.

A final consideration which can be very important in a highly tuned race car chassis is the ease of spring adjustment or replacement. There are two separate variables here that must be distinguished. Any suspension can be adjusted in either wheel spring rate or ride height, or both. For example, if an independent front suspension coil spring mount is moved vertically along its axis, the ride height will change, but not the ride rate. On the other hand, if the chassis mounting point is moved outboard, the ride rate will increase without necessarily changing the ride height. (See Fig. 15.) On race cars, where efficiency of space and chassis material is important, it is often more convenient to change springs, rather than the mechanical leverage, for a change in rate. Ride height, however, is often easily adjusted by screw mounts on a coil spring base, by anchor screws on a torsion bar, or by relocating holes in leaf spring shackles.

Variable rate springs should also be mentioned, although on a race car their action is too complex to be understood easily. Disregarding the potential for rate change in the suspension linkage, intentionally provided on a few race cars, only leaf and coil springs are easily applied to variable-rate. The leaf is obviously and easily changed by varying leaf thickness and length in the stack. The coil spring has to be built intentionally—and expensively—to have a variable rate. It can be done either by using tapered wire or winding the spring with varying coil spacings so that coils bottom progressively instead of all at once.

This leads to the consideration of rubber components in a steel-spring system. Rubber may be used in series with the spring or as spring mounts to absorb minor vibrations before they reach the primary spring. This is in effect a variable-rate system that is common to production cars, but which reduces desired spring control on race cars. At the extremes of suspension travel, bump rubbers are used to prevent metal-to-metal contact by providing a very rapidly increasing spring rate instead.

As simple as bump rubbers appear, they can have a large influence on the suspension and can be put to good use if understood. Although production bump stops are usually mounted between the frame and axle or lower control arm, race car bumpstops are commonly mounted on the shock absorber shaft. Some manufacturers provide production bump rubbers to fit their shocks. However, they are simple enough that a racer can modify the stock bumpers or build his own. The material used affects the force/deflection curve and the impact absorption or rebound, and varies from butyl rubber on passenger cars to polyurethane on race cars. When available, different material densities can also be used to get different characteristics. But by far the greatest effect comes from the shape of the rubber. Production shock-mounted bumpers usually are of a hollow conical shape, which gives a smoothly rising rate as they are compressed. The rate curve can be found by slowly compressing the rubber in measured steps on some sort of a scale, such as a valve spring compression tester. If the rate change seems too steep, it can be modified by carving material off the circumference and re-testing. This is an area for considerable experimentation, both in the desired curve and in how to obtain it—but the materials are cheap. For those who want to start out with some engineering data, Kruse and Edwards have the best available information.

Bump rubbers are sometimes used to produce a variable-rate sus-

A lightweight adjustable racing shock absorber, with adjustable spring perches on the threaded housing, and a urethane bump stop (top right).

pension in normal travel instead of just at the limit of bump. But this is undesirable from two standpoints. The rate change is very much unlike a variable-rate spring—which is already too complex for accurate suspension analysis—in that it has more sudden changes. And, the durability of bump rubbers can't compare with a steel spring—if *one* of them fails or drops off, the handling will become unlivable.

BARS
An anti-roll bar is a fairly straightforward device that doesn't allow much choice in shape or layout. For passenger cars, which aren't expected to need much adjustment, they are bent out of a single length of bar stock, with fixed lever-arm holes in the ends. However, since the lever-arm length as well as the shaft diameter can have a major effect on race car handling, arms are often made easily adjustable. Lever-arms may be provided with a number of holes, or have a sliding mounting block. They may also be made removable, so that they can be fitted to any number of different diameter shafts. The bars themselves must be mounted in low-friction bearings which are as

Two types of anti-roll bar adjustments, the sliding end to vary roll resistance, and the variable length link to balance wheels loads.

close to the arms as possible, to minimize two-wheel ride rate effects or bending of the shaft. All linkages should use spherical rod ends to eliminate any possible binding under any extremes of suspension travel.

SHOCKS

Shock absorbers are like tires, in that a few manufacturers have tied up the racing game so securely that there isn't much choice. But there also isn't much chance for anyone to have a far better shock absorber than everyone else. Unlike tires, the difference between the best shock and a mediocre shock isn't great enough to have a major effect on ultimate performance. But that doesn't mean that the *best* shock, properly tuned to a car's suspension, won't improve it's handling.

The most important selection criteria are length and total travel. These figures are easily measured from chassis drawings or the vehicle itself, and a tolerance should be added to allow for a change in ride height without bottoming. Damping characteristics of a shock absorber aren't normally a purchase option, with manufacturers ordinarily designing force/travel/velocity curves to fit a particular vehicle. Sometimes they advertise the bump/rebound ratio, however, since it is a simple quantity to relate to. Some shock absorbers have adjustments which vary the bump or the rebound force without the necessity of disassembling the shock. In the typical case where only the rebound is adjustable, this means that not only total damping but the bump/rebound ratio will change. Methods of adjustment vary from a simple knob on the body, to disconnecting one end, compressing it totally, and rotating the shaft. Other characteristics can be varied only by complete disassembly, modifying valves, springs and/or orifices— assuming a person knows what effect he wants to produce. Factory representatives are experienced in this area and can quickly produce a modified damping action to suit whatever a driver asks for. Although there is no consensus on what characteristics make up the perfect racing damper, over-the-counter shocks aren't bad. For the theorist, a paper by Speckhart and Harrison provides an extensive bibliography on the more general aspects of shock absorbers.

Mounting a shock absorber is a simple task, but a few principles should be kept in mind. First, the end forces are quite high, and mounting brackets should be in double shear and well reinforced. Rubber grommets may be good enough for passenger cars and sedan racers, but the fastest formula cars all use highest quality spherical bearings. And it is worth mentioning that a shock, whether it is mounted inboard or outboard, has to be mounted rightside up. There is a fluid reservoir inside which won't work if it is mounted horizontally or upside down. One last word about shock absorbers for the ultimate racer—some are available with light alloy components instead of steel, for those last few pounds of saved-weight at any cost.

DEVELOPMENT

SPRINGS

It is practically impossible to explain the racing development procedure for springs, anti-roll bars, and shock absorbers without a knowledge of many other areas of vehicle dynamics. But chassis development has to be broken down into manageable bits, recognizing that each section may be incomplete with respect to later chapters. At the end of the book it should all fit together.

Spring selection can be approached fairly closely in original design if the engineer is willing to make the calculations. All he needs to know is the leverage ratio between the wheel and the spring, total travel desired, total loads on the chassis, and an estimate of maximum vertical accelerations expected. From there it is a relatively simple matter either to select the spring from a catalog or design one from scratch. However, even the best designers usually have to make some later modifications in spring rate or height on the running vehicle so this section will concentrate on changing characteristics rather than original design.

The essential criteria for springs, with respect to race car handling, is that they be as soft as possible, without allowing bottoming, and that they be relatively well balanced from front to rear. Preventing bottoming means that the suspension should not hit the frame, the chassis should not hit the ground, the shocks should not collapse completely, and the spring coils should not stack solid (in the case of coil springs). Bump rubbers will protect things at the last fraction of travel but they shouldn't be considered a part of normal spring action. With all the possibilities for bottoming, especially considering the variation from smooth tracks to bumpy or hilly tracks to high-banked ovals, the only way to know is by testing on each particular track.

In the absence of sophisticated instrumentation to record suspension travel, any bottoming will have to be felt in the chassis, or heard as parts hit. Clay indicators may be attached to suspiciously close surfaces, or wear strips attached to the bottom of the chassis. If nothing is even close to touching, then either the chassis or the spring rate aren't low enough. Any given suspension is probably set up not to bottom under the worst anticipated track conditions. But if those conditions aren't encountered, ground clearance is being wasted. As mentioned previously, the chassis bottoming on the ground is probably the least undesirable condition. Spring height is the easiest factor to change, at least as a test. If lowering the suspension by an inch causes metal-on-metal contact, remove or relocate those pieces and try again. When the chassis just barely touches the track under the worst possible conditions—full fuel load and maximum aerodynamic downforce over the hardest bump—that's low enough (assuming there are no minimum ground clearance rules). At this point there is the option of raising the ride height slightly and trying a lower rate spring. There are no definite rules to follow to decide between minimum ground clearance and minimum spring rate. There has to be a trade-off between better aerodynamics and lower center of gravity with the former, to better ride and tire traction with the latter. Only testing will tell—if all other factors such as alignment and roll stiffness are optimized in both cases.

At least it is possible to estimate some things about a spring change. For example, if the front wheel ride rate is 200 pounds per inch and the chassis just barely touches the ground with three inches of ground clearance, that means there is a bump of about 600 pounds force. Therefore, if the ride rate is reduced to 150 pounds per inch, 600/150 or 4 inches of ground clearance will be required. Of course, this is a gross simplification, which ignores a lot of other factors such as shock absorbers and front/rear roll resistance, but it gives ballpark figures for faster changes.

It is also valuable to know how to identify springs by their rate, how to modify them if necessary, and how to select a different rate. Of course, it is possible to load a suspension spring and measure its deflection, and that may be the most accurate method. But some springs would require a great deal of weight, and it makes things a lot easier to know some of the simple mathematics of spring rate.

The basic equation for coil spring rate is a function of the coil diameter (D), the wire diameter (d), and the number of active coils (n). The rate is found by:

$$\text{lbs per inch} = \frac{1{,}500{,}000 \times d^4}{n \times D^3}$$

Using this equation, a new spring can be designed, or it can be seen how a change will affect its rate. For example, if the wire diameter is increased by 10 percent, then the rate will increase by: $(1.10 \, d)^4$ or $1.46 \, d^4$ or 46 percent. Similarly, it can be seen that a 10 percent increase in the number of coils will decrease the rate by about 10 percent, and a 10 percent increase in coil diameter will decrease the rate by $1/(1.10 D)^3$ or 25 percent. In practice, the coil diameter is usually difficult to vary without modifying spring mounts, so wire diameter and number of coils are most often altered. Free height, ride height, and solid stack height are also important to consider in the winding of a spring. Free height may end up shorter than full rebound travel, allowing the spring to become loose during rebound. Even worse is a condition where the bump travel is limited by all coils bottoming at once, causing destructive stresses in the spring and suspension components.

The material a spring is made from can have a slight effect on rate, but the previous equation is applicable for most spring steels. More important is the effect of material on durability and yield strength. It isn't uncommon for a spring to be stressed beyond its yield point, and to sag to a different ride height. Most spring builders are aware of the proper steel alloys to use, the calculation of stress limits, and the best method of heat treatment after winding. A final suggestion for the selection or construction of coil springs is the type of ends. Passenger cars usually have spring seats designed to accept an inexpensive "open-wound" spring end. Race cars, however, usually require ends which are "close-wound" and ground flat, to better distribute their load on the spring seat—particularly in the case of shock-mounted coils.

The basic equation for torsion bar spring rate is a function of the bar length (L), the bar diameter (d), and the lever arm length (l). Its spring rate is derived by:

$$\text{lbs per inch} = \frac{(2,200,000) \times (d^4)}{(L) \times (l^2)}$$

Using this equation, it can be seen that a 10 percent increase in bar diameter will increase its rate by 46 percent, just the same as with a coil spring. Similarily, a 10 percent change in length will change the rate by about 10 percent, and a 10 percent change in arm length will change the rate by about 20 percent. Torsion bars don't have the same space and height problems as coil springs, but material and stresses are just as important. For those who want to build their own bars, nickel chrome-moly (4340), or chrome-moly (4130) steel are satisfactory. Use 4130 if there is any welding. After welding, or heating for bends, bars must be heat-treated to a Rockwell C hardness of about 35. In making any calculations, it is important to note that the above equation is for spring rate at the arm end in pounds per inch— which is *not* the same as pounds-feet of torsion in the bar. The spring rate is also not the same as ride rate, which will be some fraction thereof, based on the square of the mechanical force or deflection ratio between arm end and tire travel.

Leaf spring calculations are a mess because of the possible variations in the length, width, thickness, and number of leaves, not to mention spring arch and location of the axle. Any calculations would be far more difficult than actual physical measurement of the rate, with changes made by adding or subtracting leaves. However, to give a rough idea of how changes will effect the rate, a basic relationship can be shown, where leaf width (w), thickness (t), and length (l) are considered:

$$\text{lbs per inch} = \frac{(\text{constant}) \times (w) \times (t^3)}{(l^3)}$$

This isn't enough information to design a spring from scratch, but for a symmetrical leaf spring, with evenly spaced leaves, it indicates the effect of changes. If the width of all leaves is increased by 10 percent, the rate will increase by 10 percent. However, if the thickness or length of all leaves is changed by 10 percent, the rate will change by 25 to 33 percent. The selection of materials and heat treating, with respect to stressing and sag, are the same as for coils and torsion bars.

BARS

When selecting or modifying spring rates in a race car, it isn't enough to merely consider ride rate and ground clearance. Any change in the ratio of front/rear spring rate will naturally affect the front/rear roll rate, and therefore the oversteer/understeer characteristics. However, the handling can usually be brought back to balance with properly selected anti-roll bars. Without a definite knowledge of what the amount of roll resistance ought to be at the front and rear, it is useless to try to pick the proper anti-roll bar for a car without road testing. Therefore, a simple consideration of the effects of modifications ought to be sufficient. Since an anti-roll bar is simply an unanchored torsion bar, the same sort of equation applies, at least in geometric relationships. Of course, even the exact desired change in bar stiffness is unknown, but the equation gives some relative magnitudes:

$$\text{bar roll resistance} = \frac{(\text{constant}) \times (d^4)}{(L) \times (l^2)}$$

Length (L) of the bar is relatively difficult to change, but it can be seen that changing arm length (l) is more effective, and that the slightest change in bar diameter (d) can have a major effect. Because most of the chassis roll resistance is ordinarily provided by the suspension springs, however, the percentage in roll change will be far less than the percentage change in the bar's roll resistance alone. For cars that need an extremely stiff anti-roll bar, or where ultimate lightness is a factor, hollow anti-roll bars are often used.

Installation of an anti-roll bar is straightforward—with a few notes. All rubber should be eliminated from mountings and linkages, to provide the most direct-acting roll resistance. Linkages should also be checked for binding throughout total travel. All anti-roll bars should be checked for parallelism between the arms before installation, and the links adjusted for zero preload in the bar with the chassis sitting on a perfectly flat surface and all four wheels at ride height. If the handling develops an asymmetry between left and right turns after some time, the bar may have twisted. A recheck of arm parallelism will quickly answer the question. Unless a bar is overstressed, it shouldn't twist to the point of yield, especially if the right material and heat-treat are used. As with springs, chrome-moly 4340 steel (or 4130 if welded) is best, with a heat-treat to Rockwell C 35 hardness.

There is so little interaction between anti-roll bar stiffness and any other chassis components or characteristics that its selection or adjustment is usually the last step in controlling oversteer/understeer. As was explained in the Theory section, changing the ratio of anti-roll bar stiffness from front to rear usually has a great effect on handling. Ordinarily, whichever end of the car has a reduced roll stiffness will have greater lateral traction. A stiffer front bar produces more understeer, and a stiffer rear bar produces more oversteer. Usually. In some cases the effect has been indistinguishable, or even worked the opposite. This could be dependent on the type of differential, the braking distribution, or even driving style. It may even be that the chassis is so weak in torsion that the springs and anti-roll bars have no effect at all. Only skidpad testing—confirmed by track testing—will tell for sure.

The current consensus in racing is that the best handling comes from a very low spring rate with high roll stiffness—whether from stiff anti-roll bars, a wide spring base, or by keeping the center of gravity and roll center close together. Soft springs, however, require some degree of anti-squat and anti-dive geometry to keep the car off its bump stops.

The primary reason why variable-rate springs are so difficult to deal with on a race car, is that they also provide a variable roll-rate. With linear-rate springs and anti-roll bars, the front/rear distribution of roll rate is relatively constant, making the handling fairly constant and predictable. However, when the roll rate changes with suspension deflection and/or roll angle, anything can happen. If the suspension design has the springs totally removed from any roll resistance—if their center of support is at the roll center—and the anti-roll bar takes care of all roll resistance, *then* variable-rate springs may be more tolerable. In fact, such suspensions have been used, but not too successfully, for unknown reasons. It may be that variable-rate suspension springs aren't that desirable under any circumstances.

Once the car is developed and on the race track, it would seem that the suspension was beyond consideration. However, very finely developed race cars are so sensitive to changing conditions that they can have a critical change in handling over the length of a race. Reduced fuel loads or a track surface which becomes oily can cause a car to oversteer or understeer excessively. If pitstops are long enough, the anti-roll bar can sometimes be adjusted—if a tire compound change won't produce the desired result. Oval track racers frequently use the

One method of altering anti-roll bar resistance from the cockpit is to use a sliding bracket with manual control cable to vary the arm length.

technique of diagonal weight-jacking for really quick and rough changes. More recently, the variable anti-roll bar has become popular. By providing a hydraulic or mechanical linkage to change the length of the arms or the spring rate in the arms, the driver can modify the handling at any time or place. It's even conceiveable that the handling could be changed from corner to corner, if any driver could tell exactly what he wanted and where he wanted it.

SHOCKS

Shock absorbers don't ordinarily get much development time. They're either too hard or too soft, or right or wrong for the driver's taste. However, it isn't commonly known that they can have a direct effect on handling characteristics other than ride. Shock absorbers may not provide any roll resistance or pitch resistance in a steady-state condition such as a long curve or accelerating or braking. But they do resist suspension movement in short-term transient conditions. As the chassis rolls to one side in a turn, the roll is resisted not only by springs and anti-roll bars but by some damping rate. If the rate is not equal at front and rear, the shocks will affect oversteer/understeer for a short time. This can have a positive or negative effect, but the most desirable case is probably to have zero effect. Next best may be to have an increase in understeer as the vehicle approaches steady state. This would imply that the front damping rate should be less than the rear. In other words, the rear roll resistance decreases as the chassis rolls and the rear shocks deflect more slowly. It probably takes an extremely aware test driver to make this distinction, but on the other hand, an intolerable inverse condition may be cured by the application of this knowledge. Especially since it is so easy to adjust the damping rate on some racing shocks. This also makes it important to be certain that the rate is equal from side to side at both ends of the car.

A final point on shock absorbers is that they may be used to control other than vertical oscillations. Some dampers are designed for the steering system—to absorb unwanted steering wheel kickback. This tends to be a quick fix for poor design, but it may come in handy if the kingpin offset is excessive for other design reasons. Dampers are also used to control other solid rear axle oscillations, whether in rotation or a longitudinal direction. Many passenger cars have the shocks staggered fore and aft on the rear housing. By having one mounted ahead on one side and the other mounted behind, high-frequency housing rotation can be reduced. Specially-designed horizontal dampers are sometimes used to reduce any longitudinal movement which may be the cause of rear brake hop.

LOAD LEVELERS

Load levelers are a special case in suspensions which can include the areas of springing, damping, and roll resistance. The idea is to balance any changes in load, or changes in suspension travel, by some separate and controllable force. The principle is fairly common to the rear of passenger cars and trucks but it presents some difficulties to finely balanced race car handling characteristics. Another important distinction is that a race car cannot be stopped and adjusted for changing conditions as a passenger car can, but must respond very rapidly and automatically. Still, a load leveler is highly desirable in racing, considering the large changes in fuel load and aerodynamic downforce. It would simplify the design of all suspension geometries if some reliable system could be built in to provide constant suspension travel and chassis attitude under all conditions. Many of the important problems of roll center height, anti-pitch, lateral jacking, and aerodynamic loading could thus be reduced or eliminated.

The solutions fall into two categories: force balancing systems, in which the spring rate is increased, or deflection balancing systems, in which the springs are jacked up.

Force balancing systems are quite difficult to design for use with metal springs, since their rates are largely fixed functions of original spring design. The most probable possibility would be adjustable leverage on the spring, perhaps by making the chassis mounting points move horizontally. Most force balancing systems use air or hydraulics as either primary or booster springs. In this case, the spring rate can be changed rapidly and at any time by simply changing the static fluid pressure in the spring. The primary disadvantage in this is the same as for variable-rate springs. Changing the spring rate is apt to change the roll-rate distribution and, therefore, the handling characteristics.

Deflection balancing systems would seem to be simpler, and adaptable to any type of springs. In this case, the chassis mounting points are made vertically adjustable, and can be moved by hydraulic or pneumatic cylinders, or even by electric power through motor-driven screw jacks. This method reduces the effect on handling, since for constant-rate springs, the ride rate or roll rate distribution shouldn't change with deflection. The primary disadvantage is that a great deal of extra spring and shock absorber travel is required.

Then there is the problem of a power source, as it does take some power to raise a chassis on its suspension in a short time. In fact, it would take half a horsepower to raise a 1650-pound car 2 inches in 1 second. While that doesn't seem like much compared to engine output, it isn't a simple operation to tap it from existing power trains or to generate it independently. Possible options are: existing oil pumps for hydraulic power, an auxilliary engine-driven pump, or the pumping action of the shock absorbers. The latter device actually exists, and seems to be a source of free power, but it is undependable on smooth roads. Pneumatic forces are available, as with brake boosters, but race engines just don't produce enough vacuum. Electric screw jacks have time lag, reliability and weight problems, although they may allow simpler control systems.

The sensing and control system is the real problem. For either force or position devices, the sensor should probably be sensitive to position, since that is the quantity to be corrected and it is usually easier to measure than forces. The advantage of a suspension travel sensor on each wheel is that it can distribute a corrective change to each wheel separately, whether the deflection is due to load transfer, cornering forces, fuel consumption, or aerodynamic loads. The difficulty comes in trying to filter out the deflections that *shouldn't* be corrected, such as ordinary bumps or dips in the road. An improper sequence or frequency of bumps could cause the suspension to get out of synchronization, causing the chassis to leap up and down. The system may require an on-line computer to control it under all conditions.

5

BRAKES ○○○

From a safety standpoint, the brakes are just about the most critical system in a race car. And yet, paradoxically, there is little to be gained in lowered laptimes by development or engineering improvements. Brakes are generally bought as a package, and there is little choice or variation from race car to race car. If a racer follows all the rules of setup and maintenance, the brakes are about as close to their maximum theoretical performance as any part of the car. Stopping performance is currently limited by tires and aerodynamic downforce, not by the state of the art in brakes. Of course, developments in automatic anti-skid brake systems—covered briefly at the end of the chapter—promise some gains in performance. However, even if there were a lot to be gained, so little time is spent braking that improvements don't have a great effect on total laptimes.

THEORY

REQUIREMENTS

The desired characteristics of a race car brake system are: 1. reliability or fail-safety, 2. ultimate stopping power, 3. balance or proportioning, 4. feel or modulation, 5. durability or fade resistance, 6. pedal pressure, 7. life of the friction material. As long as the driver can hold all four wheels at the verge of lockup from top speed to the minimum speed, and the brakes will maintain that consistency for the length of a race—both of which are reasonably possible—then there are no further gains to be had, unless perhaps a reduction in weight. But there will always be a trade-off between one-lap performance and durability. Anything that improves performance—whether increased tire traction, increased downforce, or decreased brake mass—will increase the demands on the system and decrease durability. Decreasing the mass of the entire vehicle, of course, is all gain, but that is taken for granted in race cars. As with wheels and tires, the rotating components of a brake system have a double contribution to mass. Their rotating inertia can add about another 50 percent to their total effective weight which must be accelerated or braked.

The idea of testing brakes by locking up all four wheels and sliding to a stop isn't too sensible. Stopping power is generated by two friction surfaces transforming energy into heat and, if the wheels are not rotating, then the friction is generated exclusively between tire and ground. This works, of course, but not more than a few times before the tires get flat spots and/or blow out. Meanwhile, the brakes do practically no work at all. In addition, as discussed in Chapter 2, a tire has its maximum traction at a point just short of lockup, or at about 5 to 10 percent slip. So the car can theoretically stop faster with unlocked wheels—if the driver can modulate them that closely. In practice, race tires are so sensitive that a race car may stop in a shorter distance with all four wheels locked up. That's worth keeping in mind for the critical emergency when loss of steering control is no problem—or is already lost.

HEAT ABSORPTION

The energy that a brake system must absorb is mostly a function of the weight of the vehicle and the change in speed. The equation for this energy is:

$$\text{ft-lbs} = (\text{weight}) \times (\text{top speed}^2 - \text{minimum speed}^2) \times (.0335)$$

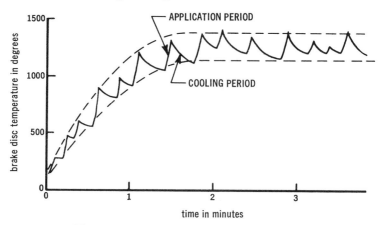

Figure 16. Brake Cycling Temperatures

For example, a 2000-pound race car braking from 200 to 50 miles per hour must absorb and dissipate 2,500,000 foot-pounds of energy. Even more amazing, it will probably generate it in a period of less than seven seconds. Fortunately, aerodynamic drag adds some braking force, and the faster and less streamlined the car is, the more it helps. Depending on the average speed and shape of a race car, from 10 to 20 percent of braking energy comes from air drag on the body. The drag force is a function of the square of velocity, making it far more effective at high speeds. It is not uncommon for air drag on a race car to provide 0.5g deceleration at 140 miles per hour with no brake application at all. And at 200 miles per hour, the deceleration will double to 1.0g. Race cars intentionally have the lowest possible drag, which further adds to the load on the brakes.

The rest of the energy has to be absorbed by the four brakes and stored until it can be dissipated into the air stream. The fact that even a race car takes far longer to accelerate than to brake means that the brakes have some reasonable time to dissipate this heat. Still, there is a limited amount of metal in the brake discs in which to store heat, and a typical racing application can raise their temperature 200 to 300 degrees in a matter of seconds. If that energy can't be dissipated before the next application, there will be a net temperature rise. The average operating temperature will rise until it stabilizes where braking input equals cooling output (see Fig. 16) and can be anywhere from 1000 to 1500 degrees at the disc face. At those temperatures the friction material decomposes rapidly, not to mention the changes in the metal at the disc face. If the mass of the discs or the cooling air are not adequate, temperatures will rise to the point of lost friction capability (fade), where the brake material burns, the brake fluid boils, or the discs themselves crack and fly apart.

FORCES

The ultimate one-stop force that can be produced is a function of a number of mechanical design factors—and the force available from the driver's foot. The design factors are friction material coefficient (k), tire- radius (R), brake disc application radius (r), and mechanical force ratio (f). Therefore:

stopping force = (pedal force) × (f) × (K) × (r) × (1/R)

Since most of the factors are relatively fixed, the stopping force is most easily controlled by the mechanical force ratio between the pedal and the braking device, although the others may have some small positive or negative effects, and must be considered. The maximum stopping force required for a race car will be the point at which the tires are on the verge of sliding—with peak aerodynamic downforce. For a 2000-pound car, with 500 pounds of downforce and a tire Cf of 1.4, the stopping force required is (2500 × 1.4) or 3500 pounds. Assuming a peak pedal force of 100 pounds, a friction material coefficient of 1.0, a brake application radius of 0.5 foot, and a tire radius of 1.0 foot, then the force ratio (f) will be found by:

3500 pounds = (100) × (f) × (1.0) × (0.5) × (1/1.0)

or a force ratio of 70 to 1.

The problem is that the force ratio and the travel ratio are inversely proportional. In other words, to get a force ratio of 1 to 70 between the pedal and the brake discs, the travel ratio must be 70 to 1, or 7 inches of pedal travel for every 0.1 inch of pad travel. It doesn't matter whether the force ratio is from mechanical linkages, different hydraulic cylinder sizes, or a combination of the two. When pedal force or travel limits are reached, an assist will be necessary. Fortunately, light race cars are usually below the point where a force boost is required, but 4000-pound sedans with tire coefficients of 1.2 can be marginal in required pedal effort. When necessary, force assist is available in two ways—power booster or servo-action. Servo-action brakes, whether drums or discs, use a wedging action to increase the force of the friction material against the rotating surface. The reason why they aren't usually applied to racing or even to disc brakes in general is that the action is relatively hard to control. The force multiplication is non-linear and tends to cause wheels to lock— and to be hard to unlock. Vacuum power boosters are rare on race cars but have been used on some large American sports cars and sedans. The first drawback is the lack of vacuum generated by racing engines, which requires a large vacuum reservoir. But power brakes also cause some loss of response and feel between the pedal and the wheels.

BALANCE

When reliability and stopping power are adequate, balance or proportioning must be optimized. Distribution of braking forces to each wheel is fixed. But the load on each wheel is not, so there comes a time when one wheel is more lightly loaded and will lock up more easily. The most common example is the inside front tire when braking into a turn. When the load transfers away from it, the limit on braking will be that tire, unless it is to be skidded and flat-spotted. This is less of a problem at the rear, where a drive axle—and usually a locking differential—connect the inside and outside wheels.

The effect of longitudinal load transfer is even greater since maximum braking is ordinarily done in a straight line. It is well known— often from personal experience—that if the rear wheels lock up first in braking, the car will be highly unstable. So it's important that under all circumstances the front wheels should lock first—and yet not so much sooner that the rear brakes don't do their full share of stopping also. At the same time, neither the left or right wheel should lock before the other, which could cause swerving or instability. But that is more often a maintenance and proper functioning problem than one of design or development.

Proper longitudinal braking distribution is an important design consideration and is a function of center of gravity height (h), the wheelbase (b), the total weight (W), the front and rear weights (Wf and Wr), and the tire coefficient of friction (Cf). The equation for the ideal front/rear ratio is:

$$\frac{Ff}{Fr} = \frac{Wf + (W) \times (Cf) \times (h) \times (1/b)}{Wr - (W) \times (Cf) \times (h) \times (1/b)}$$

The tire coefficient will probably be slightly less at the front for smaller front tires, but this complicates the balance equation and the effect is less than the accuracy of other quantities. This simplified equation also assumes that aerodynamic downforce is balanced the same as the weight from front to rear, that Wf and Wr are constant, and that tire diameter is equal front to rear. In fact, this is far from reality. Varying tire diameters can be an important problem or solution to front/rear brake balance. Also, Wf and Wr can change considerably, not only from fuel consumption, but from the common practice of having higher aerodynamic downforce at the rear—which changes the load distribution with velocity.

It is important to remember that the tire coefficient varies with the track surface and is not a fixed quantity—as the brake distribution is. For example, when the track becomes wet, the coefficient can drop to a fraction of the dry track value, changing the optimum balance by 10 to 20 percent. Fortunately, the change in Cf works in such a way that the slipperier the surface, the more likely the front wheels are to lock first. In other words, if the balance is set for perfect brake proportioning on the maximum traction surface, the car will always brake stabily on a wet or oily surface—although with reduced efficiency, since the rear brakes are under utilized.

Obviously the optimum brake balance is a very complex problem. Although an equation can be written to include all the changing factors, it doesn't make much difference as long as the balance can't easily be changed in action. The problem is minimized by placing the fuel load at the center of gravity, by keeping the center of gravity low, and by distributing front and rear aerodynamic downforce properly. But the only solution to variable tire coefficients is to have an electronic anti-skid system or an easily varied proportioning valve.

A final important influence on front/rear brake proportioning is the effect of engine drag at the rear wheels during deceleration. At one time, when brakes were less durable, that was a valuable contribution to braking. But now that brakes can work at their peak for the length of a race, engine drag simply upsets the balance. A 7-liter engine can add over 200 pounds of brake force at the rear tires—which will cause lockup and skidding if the balance was otherwise ideal. On the other hand, if engine inertia is very great and the car is decelerating very rapidly, the brakes may also have to drag the engine down, which *subtracts* rear brake force. The actual figures require some heavy calculations but it is apparent that the effect is undesirable in either case and should be avoided. If declutching during braking isn't practical, leaving the transmission in the highest gear as long as possible will minimize the problem.

FADE

The theoretical consideration of brake fade—or total loss—can't compare with the actual experience on a race track. At such times, the importance of durable and reliable brakes can make a definite, life-long impression. Any brake system can be faded if the energy input is great enough or frequent enough, or if there isn't adequate cooling air. For a given race car with limited power to get it back up to speed, however, if the brakes don't overheat and drop off in 15 minutes of hard racing, they'll probably last the life of the pad material. When brakes *do* go away, there are three possible reasons or types of fade.

First is mechanical fade, where the temperature increase causes metal components to expand or deform excessively. Drum brakes could expand away from the shoes or warp the friction surface. Discs have less of a problem in this area, but they can still warp out of a flat plane. And the expansion in calipers, cylinders, and lines displaces fluid that would otherwise be applying some force.

More common is the chemical fade in friction materials. There is a coefficient of friction curve for each different material, which usually rises with temperature, has a relatively constant value over a wide range, and then drops rapidly at a critical temperature. The peak friction may never come back again if the material has been permanently glazed. But there is also the possibility of vaporization in the bonding material. In this case, some of the bonding material in composition pads is vaporized, and it forms a layer of high-pressure gas between the pad and the disc. This is the type of fade which occurs on new, unburnished pads, and is referred to as green fade. Preventative measures—beyond careful break-in—include air grooves in the friction material or holes in the disc surface.

The last kind of fade can come from boiling brake fluid. The fluid comes very close to the red-hot disc, and is in direct contact with the caliper and pistons, which can be over 500 degrees themselves. When the fluid boils in the caliper, air bubbles form, and being compressible, they use up all-important pedal travel. The pedal may go all the way to the floor while producing only half the pressure required at the caliper. The best solution for this, aside from better caliper cooling, is to have a number of insulators between the disc and fluid. Usually, a Bakelite insulator on each piston will suffice. Insulation also comes in handy at other locations, such as the disc mounting flange. The thinnest layer of chemical or composition insulation, or even a firmly bolted interface, can make a difference of 100 degrees. This can mean life or death for wheel bearings where the disc is bolted to a front wheel hub.

HARDWARE

Because of the emphasis on racing applications, this chapter will concentrate on disc brakes only instead of including drum brakes. Although drums are used on the rear of some production sports cars and racing sedans—and on all four wheels of nearly all NASCAR sedans—they are not highly stressed in such applications. When drum brakes approach their limit of racing performance, they are inevitably replaced with discs. The advantages of disc brakes in a racing application are: less flex or expansion problems from braking forces and heat, perfectly linear force multiplication (no servo-action), less sensitivity to water, ease of maintenance and replacement, and most important, far better heat dissipation characteristics. The relatively minor disadvantages—higher forces required and disc warpage—are tolerable or easily overcome. A discussion of the hardware breaks down into six categories: discs, calipers, master cylinders and lines, brake fluid, pads, and accessory devices.

DISCS

There usually isn't much choice in discs for a given car. The racer takes whatever comes bolted to the hubs. If there is a choice, it is probably between a solid disc and a ventilated disc, and perhaps also the thickness. A ventilated disc has far better heat dissipation capabilities per pound than a solid disc and can run a few hundred degrees cooler, although a solid disc may be perfectly adequate for relatively slow and lightweight race cars. All else being equal—in ventilation and dimensions and material—the heavier the disc, the more heat it can store without building up to destructive temperatures. When everything else fails to improve brake life, the last step is to increase disc thickness or mass.

The most common material for brake discs is cast iron or Meehanite, although a number of other alloys show a great deal of promise in better heat conductivity and lighter weight. Bendix (SAE paper 700137) has made some studies of aluminum and copper alloys, and beryllium has even been used for brake discs in some aircraft applications and a few race cars. However, the problems of strength, durability, and cost have made cast iron the most practical choice. Although beryllium can do the same job at a quarter the weight, as it wears it generates a poisonous dust.

In cost per pound of weight reduction, it makes sense to stick with ventilated iron discs. A halfway solution is to replace the non-wearing center of the disc with an aluminum hub. This cuts weight and yet provides enough cast iron in the friction and ventilated areas to absorb and dissipate the heat. A further advantage is that the bolted interfaces prevent some heat from passing to the hub bearings. One innovation which has shown up on a European disc is friction surfaces with intentional deep V-grooves. When the brake pads are grooved to match, this provides much more contact area and cooling surface for the same size pad and disc. While it hasn't been positively proven superior, at least it suggests that accidentally scored discs aren't necessarily ruined—as long as the pads are burnished-in to match.

Calipers

The choice of caliper can be all-important, from considerations of strength, piston area, and cooling. The primary criterion is the total piston area, since that is the major factor in pedal force multiplication and front/rear proportioning. With all else being equal—master cylinder, tire, and disc size—the ratio of piston area from front to rear is the braking distribution ratio. Using previous equations, the total required force ratio between master cylinder and wheel cylinders can be calculated. This defines total caliper piston area. Then, calculation of the proper longitudinal force distribution will give the ideal distribution of that piston area between front and rear calipers. For example, assume a required force ratio of 80 to 1 between calipers and pedal, a 1-inch-diameter master cylinder, a mechanical leverage at the pedal of 4 to 1, and 60 percent of the vehicle weight on the front wheels during peak braking. The piston force ratio will need to be 20 to 1, requiring a total caliper piston area of at least 16 square inches, with 60 percent or 9.6 square inches at the front and 6.4 square inches at the rear. It isn't likely that calipers are available in exactly those sizes but it provides a first approximation in selection and the ratio can be further modified with master cylinders or tire diameters.

The greater the piston area per caliper, the lower the pedal force and the hydraulic line pressure will be. However, as mentioned previously, this requires more travel at the pedal. Another disadvantage is that more piston area, and/or more pad area, means less disc exposed to the air, and less cooling. In some cases, two pairs of calipers have been used on the front discs, but they usually cause such severe overheating that it is necessary to go instead to higher hydraulic pressure with single calipers. When hydraulic pressures get well over 1000 psi, then caliper stiffness becomes critical. Any spreading of the caliper, even a few thousandths of an inch, can use up valuable pedal travel. The deflection is easy enough to check with a dial gauge and a heavy foot, but it may be impossible to reduce without adding material and further shielding the disc.

Due to the natural flex and movement between caliper and disc, something must float, or have a built-in allowance for relative movement. If the caliper has interconnected pistons on both sides of the disc, they can float from side to side. Otherwise, either the caliper or disc must be mounted loosely enough to move laterally and yet have no freedom in any other direction. Sometimes the caliper slides on bushings on the mounting bolts, but more often the disc is located freely on the wheel studs.

MASTER CYLINDERS

Although it is possible to get by with a single master cylinder, there are some very good reasons for using two, or at the least, a common production tandem cylinder. The advantage in fail-safety is obvious and in some cases required. If one system loses all its fluid, the other independent system will still slow the car—although at a drastically reduced rate. The tandem cylinder does this by having a floating piston isolating the two fluid systems in the same cylinder bore. When fluid leaks out of one system, the piston bottoms at one end and allows the other system to keep functioning. A pair of parallel master cylinders has the same effect, except that the two pistons are connected by a variable balance bar. This can be used to modify the force ratio to either one, an adjustment not possible with the two equal tandem pistons.

Previously discussed force ratios between the pedal and the caliper must take into consideration the mechanical leverage between the pedal and the master cylinder. This is the ratio between the measurements from pedal to pivot and from master cylinder rod to pivot. The ratio may vary anywhere from 6:1 to 3:1, and is relatively constant with travel. The fact that the ratio is not perfectly constant makes it possible to use the variability to advantage. By careful location of the pivot points and travel arcs, the ratio may be made to vary from large travel multiplication with low force multiplication at the beginning, to take up the slack, and little travel with high force at the end. Just as at the caliper, even the most minor flex from extreme pedal forces must be avoided. And it is important to check that the pedal isn't unnecessarily limited in travel by bottoming on the floor when everything deflects under pressure.

Master cylinders and their fluid reservoirs are frequently mounted with an extreme rearward rake. When they are being used, the deceleration will cause the fluid to flow forward, and settle at an angle of over 45 degrees from the horizontal. So it's important that the cylinder angle and/or capacity be adequate so the drain hole into the cylinder isn't uncovered. The reservoir should also provide enough capacity not to run dry when the pads are completely worn and the pistons are at full travel. Reservoirs must be vented to the atmosphere to allow the fluid to drain. But free access allows the fluid to slosh out, and allows destructive moisture to enter. The only solution is a rubber diaphragm or bellows to seal the vent and yet allow atmospheric pressure into the reservoir.

All brake plumbing must use the highest grade steel tubing, preferably with aircraft nuts and fittings. Flexible hoses should be of the braided-stainless-wire and teflon type to prevent pressure expansion from using up pedal travel. All lines and hoses should be carefully routed and shielded to protect them from any bending, impact, heat, chafing, crimping, or vibration. They are very definitely the driver's lifelines.

Fluid

Brake fluid is usually taken for granted—until it boils from excessive heat and causes brake loss. Actually, it is hard to find a fluid that is practically incompressible and that will boil at over 550 degrees—a few racing brake fluids will meet these criteria. There is also a liquid silicone fluid available that is supposed to have an even higher boiling point but it hasn't been conclusively proven in racing yet.

Moisture is a critical problem with brake fluids, since they have a strong tendency to absorb it from humidity in the air and the water has a drastic effect on the boiling point. An absorption of even *one* percent of water can drop the boiling point over 100 degrees. It is apparent that the brake system—and all brake fluid containers—should be kept well sealed at all times, especially in humid or rainy weather. A leak in the brake line is bad enough in that it loses fluid and pressure. But at the same time, air leaking back into the system has the same effect as boiling the fluid, and will probably be noticed much sooner than fluid loss during a race, if the leak is very small.

PADS

Developing the friction material for brake pads is a black art beyond the racer's capability to modify. Selection is simply a matter of buying and trying until the best is found. Of course, it is important to keep all oil off the pads because once it soaks in, the pad is ruined. Most racing pads are very stiff, to prevent deflection or warping under extreme pressure and temperature. But some pads derived from passenger-car designs have relatively weak steel backing plates and may therefore be reinforced with a flange.

Heat insulation between the disc and the caliper pistons is perhaps as important as rigidity. There is a very small distance between the disc, which may be over 1200 degrees, and the brake fluid, which must be under 550 degrees. One type of brake pad has an air gap between two thin metal backing plates, but extreme forces on some heavy cars could cause the plates to bend and collapse. While passenger car brake pads have a relatively constant coefficient of friction up to perhaps 1000 degrees, they decompose or fade rapidly above a certain temperature. Racing pads have somewhat the opposite effect in that their friction coefficient is constant at much higher temperatures but drops off below 800 to 1000 degrees. On some race cars there isn't enough friction to lock the brakes until they have been brought up to operating temperature.

VALVES

A number of brake proportioning valves have been designed in an attempt to provide a better, or variable, brake balance between front and rear wheels. Most common is the pressure relief valve for the rear brakes on cars with a tandem master cylinder. There is no way to vary line pressure between the front or rear brakes with such a cylinder. If the rear is slightly over-braked and the next smaller calipers are too small, then a valve must be provided to limit the brake pressure to the rear. This is simply a spring-loaded piston installed in the line, with the spring load adjustable for the desired pressure limit. There are two disadvantages to such a valve. First, the rear braking force is non-linear—although that characteristic might be put to good use if carefully thought out. And secondly, the valve uses up some valuable fluid displacement or pedal travel.

Another alternative, particularly for cars in which the rear load changes drastically due to fuel consumption, is a proportioning valve in which the limiting spring pressure is controlled by axle deflection. The less the axle deflects because of reduced loading, the less the pressure spring force and the less the brake line pressure at the rear brakes. Conversely, the greater the downforce at the rear—say from aerodynamic loading—the greater the line pressure and braking force available at the rear. Although this sort of valve is available on some passenger vehicles and trucks, it could be adaptable to race cars—if there are no serious dynamic problems to be solved.

Finally, on cars with front discs and rear drums, some sort of residual pressure valve is necessary to hold pressure in the rear lines. Otherwise the rear brake return springs would apply a reverse force in the hydraulic lines, which would cause the front brake pads (which have no return springs) to drag on the discs.

INBOARD BRAKES

There are a number of advantages in having the entire brake system mounted on the chassis, with flexible axle shafts out to the wheels. Modern racing wheels are so wide that there is seldom enough cooling airflow when the brakes are mounted deep inside. It is also difficult to find adequate space for suspension or steering travel with the brakes in the way. Also, unsprung weight is reduced by having the brakes inboard of the suspension and the stresses in suspension components are reduced by not having to resist brake torque. When double universal-jointed axle shafts are already present, as with an independently-sprung rear end, it seems to be an obvious advantage to mount the brakes on the differential housing. Even at the front, it may be desirable to add the weight and complexity of the shafts and universal joints just for the inboard brakes alone. At the front the only drawback is the added weight, but at the rear there are some problems. First, the brakes, the differential, the transmission, and the engine or exhaust pipes all contribute heat to each other. Their closeness can make cooling as difficult as in the wheels. Second, oil could get on the brakes from the engine or differential. And finally, there is the possibility of axle failure causing loss of the brake force at any one wheel. At the front, axle torque acts only in one direction: braking. But at the drive axles, there is a complete and severe stress reversal with every change from braking to acceleration, and axles have been known to snap. The consequences of losing one brake can be as critical as the loss of two because of the effect on braking stability.

DEVELOPMENT

PROPORTIONING

Since most race car brake systems are already optimally developed to handle any forces that current cars and tires can generate, the only areas of potential development for the racer are in proportioning and cooling.

Proportioning is the first consideration, since it has such a great effect on stability and on the generation of heat between front and rear brakes. The idea is to have the distribution of forces such that the rear brakes will never lock first even under the most severe possible racing conditions. Fortunately, those conditions are also the best racing conditions, or in other words, maximum braking on the highest coefficient surface—and with minimum fuel load if the fuel tank is toward the rear. Because the previously mentioned aerodynamic downforce bias to the rear is greatest at high speeds, it is also wise to test the brake proportioning at relatively slow speeds—say under 80 miles per hour.

With the above fixed conditions—typical coefficient road surface, minimum fuel load, and minimum aerodynamic downforce—the test

A brake balance bar, with clevises and rods leading to front and rear master cylinders. As the central pedal pivot is moved toward either cylinder, that end of the car receives more braking force.

procedure is as follows. First the brakes and tires are warmed up to typical racing temperatures by practicing pedal modulation with many high-deceleration stops. Wheel lockup can be determined by using electronic instrumentation, as discussed later, or by an outside observer to watch the tires. It isn't easy for the driver to detect which tires are locking first without a long, tire-destroying skid. The driver accelerates to 80 or 100 miles per hour, shifts into top gear, and then gradually applies the brakes harder and harder until he can feel or hear a lockup—hopefully right in front of the observer—and then he immediately backs off. At this point, all that has been found is which end has the greater braking force. It is still necessary to find the force distribution at which the other two wheels lock up.

On cars with parallel master cylinders, it is simply a matter of adjusting the balance bar between the two pistons and the pedal arm. Moving the pedal arm pivot closer to the front or rear system cylinder increases the force distribution toward that end of the car. On cars with a single tandem master cylinder, the adjustment is a little harder. In the first place, if there is a pressure relief valve in the rear brake system, it should be plumbed out, to learn just how far off the basic proportioning is. Then, whichever end of the car locks up first is ballasted with known weights, and retested until the opposite end begins to lock up first. The proportion of ballast weight compared to the dynamic load on that end of the car is the approximate percentage of overbraking at that end. Say the front wheels lock first and it takes 200 pounds of ballast directly over the front wheels to make the rear wheels lock first. If the static front weight is 1500 pounds and there is about 500 pounds of calculated load transfer to the front, then the front brakes have approximately $(200)/(1500 + 500)$, or 10 percent, too much braking force. At this extreme, or if the balance bar on parallel master cylinders is too far off-center, it will be necessary to correct the brake balance by some major component changes.

There are many possible options for correcting a misproportion in braking, such as changing weight distribution, tire coefficients, disc diameter, center of gravity height, or wheelbase. But the only practical means of modification on a given race car are tire diameter, caliper piston area, or, in the case of parallel master cylinders, a variation in their piston diameters from front to rear systems. Even changing tire diameter can have an effect on other vehicle characteristics and a variation in master cylinders is also complicated. So the most professional solution is to change the brake caliper piston area.

In the example of the front being overbraked by 10 percent, this would require a corresponding reduction in front piston area, or an increase in rear piston area, depending on whether the over-all pedal force was desired to be greater or less.

When the front/rear brake ratio has been developed as closely as possible by major component changes, *then* it can be fine-tuned with other devices such as the balance bar or rear pressure relief valve. Since the relief valve doesn't have the correct action for early lockup at the front, it is important that tandem master cylinder systems have a basic over-bias to the rear before fine-tuning. The balance should then be altered back and forth between front and rear, until it is ever so slightly greater on the front on the highest traction surface. Still, it should always be remembered that any change in tires or track coefficient will probably upset the balance again.

This production sedan has had all lights replaced with duct openings to the brakes, carburetor, and oil cooler (headlight location).

COOLING

The brake discs and calipers have a great deal of heat to get rid of in a very short time between brake applications. The three means of doing so are: conduction through the mounting surfaces to the hubs, wheels, or suspension components; radiation to nearby components; and convection to the moving airstream. Only the last is either very effective or very easily improved. There have been some attempts to water-cool brakes but such systems have been too heavy or inefficient compared to the relatively free use of natural airflow.

Before any effort is made to improve cooling efficiency, it is a good idea to know whether there is a problem. For open-wheeled race cars there may be adequate air flow. If there is no fade and the brake pedal remains firm throughout a race, then there is nothing to be gained from adding brake scoops or ducts. But on a heavy race car with full fenders and wide wheels, durability is sure to be marginal without some directed airflow. At best, high temperatures will probably cause rapid pad wear. In such a case, it is hard to get too much brake cooling, but the air scoops and ducts could increase air drag. When it rains, of course, it is possible for the brakes to run too cool and ducts should be closed off.

The energy input to the brakes is largely proportional to the load on the tires during deceleration. That can be from about 50:50 for a rear-engined race car, to 65 percent on the front of a front-engined sedan. This means that the front brakes of a sedan can generate about twice as much heat as the rears and are usually the limiting factor. Fortunately, they are closer to the frontal air flow and are easier to get cooling air to.

For a measure of the problem in degrees, it is useful to record brake temperatures during the most severe applications and therefore be able to measure the effectiveness of cooling improvements. Even without complex electronic instrumentation and thermocouples, it is still possible to get peak temperatures by applying thermo-changing materials. Welding-supply shops carry wax sticks and paints which melt or discolor at certain specific temperatures. A more accurate—and expensive—method is stick-on indicators called Temp-Plate which are available in various increments between 100 and 1100 degrees. If they are attached to a brake caliper or piston and the dots blacken up past 500 degrees, then big trouble can be expected.

Cooling air is most effective on the disc, since that has the highest temperature differential and the effective airstream velocity is greater than at the caliper. It is not enough just to have a lot of air—it should be distributed evenly to both sides of the disc. A disc which consistently runs hundreds of degress cooler on one side than the other will have destructive thermal stresses if not permanent warpage. The situation is poor, considering the fact that the natural airflow inside a wheel is usually in one direction, depending on the shape of the wheel spokes and the air pressure under the chassis. It is possible to increase the natural airflow, and in the proper direction to reduce pressure under the body, by designing a centrifugal blower as part of the wheel spokes or as a hubcap. This has a pumping action which is proportional to velocity but which does cost some power in the process. At worst it might amount to a few horsepower at top speed and

This plastic "hubcap" has spokes designed to pump cooling air through the wheel from the brakes. The wiring is for an electronic test speedometer.

yet it does improve the aerodynamic downforce.

When air is ducted to a solid disc, the best solution is to run it into a fabricated can which directs it equally to both faces. For ventilated discs, with a natural centrifugal airflow due to the internal vanes, the best duct location is to the center or eye of the disc. The best source of cooling air is any positive pressure area at the nose of the car. On sedans this has commonly been the former location of headlight lenses, and on sports cars with headlights the highest pressure area is usually the under-nose spoiler lip. The greatest difficulty is in getting large duct hoses—the bigger the better—from the nose to the disc, with all the suspension hardware in the way. Although smooth fabricated aluminum or fiberglass ducts are the most efficient, wire-reinforced flexible hose (such as 4-inch dryer ducts) passes a lot of air and yet will give way if the wheel contacts it. Front spoilers prevent a lot of useful air from reaching the front discs, but as a last resort, what air does pass under the nose can be directed toward the discs by canvas shields fastened to the suspension arms. When all else fails, it is time to find heavier discs and calipers.

There are a few other areas in which braking performance can be improved, such as reduced component weights, increased aerodynamic drag during braking (when allowed by the rules), and perhaps

An air scoop and duct leading to the eye of an inboard rear disc, which would otherwise be shielded from any cooling airflow.

anti-skid systems. But the payoff in reduced laptimes is hardly worth the cost or effort. It is far more practical to try and increase tire coefficients and aerodynamic downforce so that existing brakes will have more traction to work with.

ASSEMBLY AND RACING

Since the brake system is so critical to the life of a race car and driver, its assembly and maintenance should be handled with more care and intelligence than any other area. Mounting discs is more than a simple bolt-up job, as any wobble or runout will cause the caliper pistons to knock back at high speed, using up pedal travel. The disc, flanges, and hub mounting faces should be clean, free of burrs, and perfectly parallel. When the disc is bolted up, a dial gauge should be used to measure the runout at the friction face. If it is over .010 inch, then it will be necessary to rearrange or grind components until it is the absolute minimum. It is frequently possible to eliminate runout by rotating parts with respect to each other until production tolerances cancel each other out. Play in the wheel bearings also appears as runout, so they must be adjusted with some slight preload to insure zero play under extreme hub heat and stresses. Live rear axles are especially prone to end-float which can push the disc and pistons around. It may be necessary to open the differential and use spacers under the axle keepers to pre-load the axles in position.

Mounting of calipers is also critical, since the braking force at that radius is more than twice the braking force at the tire patch. Mounting brackets can't be too stiff, and all mounting bolts must be of the highest grade, carefully torqued, and safety wired. The caliper should be shimmed until the disc is centered and parallel. The caliper may be toed-out a few thousandths, to allow for torque deflection in the direction of rotation during braking. For proper pad wear it is important that the pads be perfectly aligned with the caliper pistons, although they can be shifted in or out, or rotated slightly with respect to the *disc* without any harm. It can't hurt to file and polish the edges of the pad backing plates and the stops on the caliper where they contact, to insure smooth sliding movement under high forces. Before filling the system with fluid, it is a good idea to check piston and pedal travel at the master cylinder—and to allow some extra pedal travel to make up for stress deflection.

Brake system bleeding is one of the messiest and most difficult jobs to do properly. Especially with four-wheel disc brakes, balancing valves, and a tandem master cylinder. The calipers are such a maze of pistons and passages that the only positive way to get every last air bubble out, is to bleed them before mounting. The best way to do this is with a long flex hose attached to the caliper—preferably the flex hose to be used between caliper and chassis—and a glass jar of clean, fresh, moisture-free brake fluid. If the caliper has four pistons, it helps to have blocks of wood cut the right thickness to hold the pistons in the caliper, in either full compression or full extension. The caliper is filled by looping the flex line up and over into the fluid jar, and sucking the fluid in with piston movement. Compressing any two pairs of pistons—by hand—forces the air out, and return springs or siphoning action draws the fluid back in. Using the glass jar makes it possible to see when air bubbles are no longer being expelled. Having the caliper off the car makes it easy to rotate it into every possible position of air-up in even the most torturous passages. When the air bubbles diminish, a little rest or tapping with a mallet allows the remaining micro-bubbles to consolidate. When *no* foam or bubbles can be forced out of the flex hose, it will be practically impossible to tell whether there is flow at all, except for the rising fluid level in the jar. At that point, all pistons should be blocked in the fully extended position and the hose carefully removed from the jar with the caliper well below the fluid level. Until the free end of the hose is attached to the vehicle lines, it should be treated like a brim-full container of acid. If no fluid spills out, no air will get in. When the front or rear calipers are filled and plumbed into the system and that respective master cylinder reservoir is filled, then that end of the car's lines can be back-bled into the master cylinder. It is very important that back-bleeding be slow and careful and steady, with no let up on the caliper pistons until every last air bubble pops out through the master cylinder bleed screw and it is closed. Otherwise, air may be drawn back into the lines or calipers. It might even be desirable to run a hose from the bleed screw to the fluid jar, as further insurance. When the system is back-bled, the pistons should be blocked in their fully-retracted position until the caliper is fitted over its disc. As a last measure it can't hurt to check the system by very careful pressure bleeding.

When one end of the car is finished, it might be a very educational experience for the driver and/or mechanic to see how the car stops with only one brake system working—with rear-only being the worst possible condition. In the first place, it will show whether there is enough pedal travel for that system to function at all with no fluid in the other system. But even with full force available at the rear, it can be a shocking discovery to learn how much worse and how much more unstable the car's stopping performance is. It makes perfection worthwhile.

With all the previously discussed preparation and precautions, the actual racing performance is mostly a matter of treating the brakes with some respect. First, as was explained, new pads or discs must be broken-in carefully before they can be pushed to their limit. This is especially true of spare pads if replacement is necessary during a race. For long-distance races, it is important to have good records as to how many miles a set of pads will last under the most extreme conditions. It also helps to know how far this range can be extended, if necessary, by reduced braking effort. The wear is non-linear with temperature, which means that backing off just a little can save a lot. Or conversely, a small increase in stopping requirements can shorten pad life a great deal—not to mention the effect that extreme temperatures can have on caliper seals.

Reading the wear profile on a set of well-used brake pads can be as informative as reading tire wear, if something in the brake system is out of line. To get maximum life, ideally the pads would wear down perfectly parallel with the backing plates. However, if there is taper-wear in any direction, or rocking-wear, then something is not positioned quite right or is flexing. Taper wear can be reduced by shimming one end of the caliper to counteract stress deflections in the mounting brackets or by moving the pads with respect to the caliper pistons in the direction of maximum wear. This repositions the application force to where it is more needed. Relocation is relatively easy, by grinding away locating faces or redrilling the mounting pin holes. Rocking-wear is more apt to be caused by flex in the pad backing plate and is hard to cure without the manufacturer's help.

When pads must be replaced during a race, racing teams spend a lot of time and effort to reduce the time required. The biggest problems are heat, retainers, and piston displacement. The easiest brake job can be practically impossible when the components are between 500 and 1000 degrees. Asbestos gloves can really be cumbersome. The retainers have to be fail-safe in operation, and yet quick-release when necessary. And the pistons have to be displaced back to their original position before new pads will slip in. The quickest device is a vacuum source connected to the master cylinder, which the driver can switch on to retract all pistons at once. Of course, it must be precisely regulated so that air is not sucked into the system past piston seals.

When the brakes do fail, it can be either slowly and with some warning—or with a bang when a line fails or a disc cracks apart. Small, beginning disc cracks can usually be felt as a definite vibration in the brake pedal, and are a strong warning that the disc may be ready to go. At best, any crack will probably be shaving material off the brake pads at a rapid rate. If the failure is slower, as with fade or fluid leakage, disaster may be delayed a little by pedal pumping. The pumping can build up pedal height by bleeding some of the air up through the master cylinder reservoir or by making up some pedal travel with more fluid per bite. Still, it's not conducive to confidence or low laptimes for the driver to be pumping with the left foot while the right foot is hard on the accelerator down a long straightaway with no escape road at the end.

At the end of a race or even after a hot practice session, the cool-off lap should be used for cooling the brakes the same as anything else. If the car is stopped with blazing hot discs, the exposed portion cools much faster than the part covered by the pads. This can cause heat-checking or cracking of the disc—not to mention the effect it has on the pads and calipers.

A final trick, which has occasionally been used on otherwise well-developed brake systems, is to install a proportioning valve next to the driver. In the first place, it is more accessible if it is advantageous to quickly change the brake balance for wet or oily track conditions. But it is also possible for the driver to change the balance himself while driving—to account for fuel consumption or rain—if some sort of simple lever is provided. However, the correct lever position for correct balance under any condition must be well-known in advance, because a race is no place to experiment.

ANTI-SKID SYSTEMS

At this writing there is no anti-skid system being used on any known race car. However, since a few racers have been experimenting with them and a number of different types are in limited production, some mention should be made of the problems related to race cars. Although the potential of anti-skid brakes is limited—on a race car with a skilled driver on the best surface in a straight line—there is something to be gained. In transient braking, or braking into a corner, such a system will prevent early lockup of the inside front wheel. In the rain or on a slippery track, it would probably modulate the brakes better than any driver could. And finally, it would automatically compensate for a change in load balance due to fuel consumption or unequal front/rear aerodynamic downforce.

Production systems in use on passenger cars are well-developed for their purpose and are well covered in a number of SAE Papers mentioned at the end of the book. However, that doesn't mean that they are easily adaptable to racing use. In 1972 Mark Donohue tested such a system for Porsche, and although he was enthusiastic about the performance potential, Porsche felt it wasn't sufficiently fail-safe for racing then. Carroll Smith also wrote a very good article (*Sports Car Graphic,* February 1971) on applying anti-skid brakes to race cars which pointed out many areas for consideration.

For anyone contemplating adapting a production system to racing, the following problem areas should be anticipated. Race tires have about half the percentage of slip at maximum traction, which requires a change in the electronic logic which controls modulation. High-rate suspension frequency may interfere with the modulation cycling and set up destructive vibrations or get out of phase and *reduce* braking effectiveness. There may also be difficulty in finding the power to modulate with. It should be from a hydraulic pump, since there is little engine vacuum available. Racing generates heat and vibration conditions which can be destructive to any electronic equipment associated with brakes, and high-power ignition systems can generate enough radio-frequency interference to confuse the computer or logic unit. A driver may want to lock up the car's brakes intentionally, so there should be a pressure over-ride. And finally, there should be adequate fluid capacity for high temperature and pressure expansion, and the system should revert to normal manual operation in case of failure or dysfunction. With that list of potential problems with anti-skid, it may be a long time before there is much more improvement in existing manual brake systems on race cars.

6

AERODYNAMICS ०००००००००००००००००००

THEORY

Nothing has had as great an impact on race car design in the last decade as aerodynamics. And it seems that it has been the subject of more technical articles than any other area besides engines. But because you can't see or touch aerodynamics, very few automotive people have a firm understanding of the subject. Perhaps that's why so many people write about it. It is very difficult to prove someone's theories wrong—until a faster race car comes along with a different approach. The basic principles of air flow can be picked up from a fluid mechanics textbook, which will give an engineering explanation of such terms as viscosity, turbulent flow, laminar flow, boundary layer, density, and so on. However, for this chapter to make sense all you need is a basic awareness of the flow of air and the fact that air forces generally increase with the square of velocity. In other words, when speed is doubled, the forces increase by four times. For a better background, one of the best hardcover references is *Fluid-Dynamic Drag* by Hoerner.

A great deal is known about aircraft aerodynamics, from all the government-financed work by NACA, and a lot of it is applicable to race cars. However, there is a major difference in free air at aircraft heights and air in the earth's turbulent boundary layer where natural obstructions cause uneven airflow. Another problem unique to race car aerodynamics is the ground effect, which causes objects to have radically different airflow characteristics as they approach the ground. Therefore, most aircraft data, with the exception of some airfoil tests run close to the ground, must be used with caution.

To assist in understanding airflow, a few general comments should be made. First, at current racing velocities, the air is seldom compressed to any great degree, and actually flows very little. What happens is that the moving body displaces each air particle perpendicular to its surface, and in the absence of skin friction the particle would

Yarn tufts taped to the body of a race car indicate the direction of air flow—in this case, over the nose at 100 miles per hour.

return to its approximate original position after the car had passed. Second, when the aerodynamic profile of a race car is considered, particularly open cars and open-wheeled cars, the *total* area touched by the airstream has an effect. That includes tires, wheel wells, cockpit, radiator ducts, and even the smallest odd obstructions. As with any other moving object, there are six components of aerodynamic forces or torques on a race car. But since lateral force and roll inputs are insignificant on a race car, only drag, downforce and its front/rear distribution, and lateral stability will be considered here.

DRAG

Air drag is broken down into profile or shape drag which is a function of frontal area; skin friction drag which is a function of surface roughness; and induced drag due to lift. All of them have a varying relative importance depending on the speed and shapes considered. With the shape that race cars are in today, profile drag is by far the most significant. When profiles start improving, then skin friction drag may become important enough to consider, primarily in controlling turbulence in the layer next to the surface (the boundary layer). Induced drag depends on lift, and it increases at a much faster rate than lift (or downforce) does. On race cars with wings or with large downforces in general, induced drag can be considerable.

Since profile drag is the most immediate problem, the basic overall shape should be considered first. Generally speaking, better results can be expected from streamlining applied to the rear of blunt objects. This is apparent from the realization that it is much easier to push air than it is to pull it. That is, air which is trying to compress at the front of a body tends to follow smooth streamlines, while at the rear, airflow separates from the surface and becomes random, without a solid object to push it back into place. When air can no longer follow the body, it breaks away in a wave which curls under and rolls like an ocean wave, creating a series of alternating high-drag vortices. Therefore, disregarding all other effects, it would seem that the maximum body volume should be moved well to the front to permit the most gradual convergence angle at the rear of the body. Various theories and experts suggest that the convergence of the body should never exceed 10 to 15 degrees to avoid separation of the flow. However, this figure depends on the condition of the boundary layer and flow around and under these relatively narrow shapes, so it can be found with any accuracy only experimentally.

This airflow breakaway at the rear of a body which can't converge gradually enough, or can't have a long enough tail, is the reason for the abruptly cut-off rears on racing cars—the Kamm theory. The idea is that if the airflow has separated at some point, there is no reason to continue the body any further, regardless of the shape, as it will have little effect on air drag. However, if the body is smooth enough so the streamlines are still attached all the way to the trailing edge, as with a well-profiled wing, then the cut-off will have a noticeable effect.

With a really clean shape, even the volume-forward generalization can be disregarded. If the contour is correct and there are no body seams, lips, or projections, a fully attached flow may be possible in which the air has a much greater tendency to follow the body. But in practical application, dents, nicks, dirt, or uneven airflow from another car encourages the flow to separate. The individual drag from mirrors, struts, or other protrusions is insignificant when considered separately. However, when placed on or near any body surface, not only are they in a much faster airstream, but they can critically affect the airflow on the vehicle as a whole by their turbulent wakes. The wake is assumed to spread out like a boat wake at about a 15-degree angle behind the disrupting object. Even major bumps, scoops, and bulges are likely to break up the airflow if their trailing surfaces aren't converged gradually enough.

Wheels and tires are a special drag problem on race cars, especially on open-wheeled cars. Not only because they are relatively blunt and have a tremendously large frontal area, but because they rotate and the front ones must be steered. Drag increases with the square of velocity, and the top of the tire has an air speed of twice the speed of the car. And at the bottom front quarter of the tire, the airflow is trapped between the tire and the ground. This, plus the vortex created by the spinning wheel and brake assembly, can upset the airflow all along the side of a car and can be the greatest contribution to drag. All else being equal, a well-enclosed race car has much lower air drag than an open-wheeled car. Where race sanctioning bodies prohibit fenders, even the most modest fairings ahead of and behind the tires probably can help.

When a complete vehicle is designed, air scoops and ducts are usually an afterthought. The only really necessary high-pressure areas are on the nose of the body and downward on the tail. The creation of positive pressures for air induction anywhere else on the body is a waste of air drag and apt to be an upsetting influence on air flow elsewhere. The currently popular NACA submerged-type duct inlet, however, has good over-all efficiency. It is designed to counteract the slow-moving boundary layer by pulling in high-momentum free-stream air without disrupting external airflow or creating a high-pressure area on the body. It is primarily used when an air inlet is needed at a specific location on the body where there is no natural positive pressure. If there is room for ducting, however, a full-frontal nose inlet is somewhat more reliable.

Internal airflow is needed to cool the engine and drivetrain, the brakes, the driver, and for carburetion. Although a water-cooled engine may be heavier, it is better for aerodynamics in that heat can be taken to the air instead of vice-versa. If properly located, the radiator has a small effect on drag, and in some cases could theoretically reduce drag. A heat exchanger in a duct can be considered as a ram jet. A tapered diffuser duct slows the air and builds pressure; the heat exchanger (radiator) expands the air, and a smooth discharge nozzle accelerates the air with some added thrust energy. To prevent the radiator from blocking the flow excessively, however, the diffuser must slow the incoming air smoothly and evenly. And it must be well sealed to prevent loss of pressure.

Since almost all braking power is dissipated in heat to the air, and mostly while the car is accelerating between brake applications, a smooth passage of air both to and from the brakes ought to be as important as radiator ducting. More care in the weightless air-cooling of brakes permits lighter discs and calipers and should reduce wear.

The engine and driveline radiate a great deal of heat from their walls—especially from the exhaust pipes. An engine compartment can't be totally enclosed without raising radiator requirements. So it's a good idea to have some circulation around these components regardless of the cost in air drag, or seals, gaskets, and wiring can suffer heat damage.

Engine induction requires the coolest, fastest moving air available. Theoretically, a horsepower increase of about 1 percent can be expected for each 10-degree drop in inlet temperature and a 2 percent increase is available for an inlet airstream velocity of 150 miles per hour. However, an inlet velocity that varies with speed may disrupt intake ram tuning pulses which could be more valuable, and an unusually large inlet may cost more in air drag than it is worth.

Driver comfort is every bit as important as vehicle performance. If radiator or brake heat spills into the cockpit, it can easily cost a race of any great distance. Most heat sources have been moved to the rear on race cars, but where the radiator or engine are still up front, cool air ducting to the driver is critical. Also, the intakes ought to be placed as high as possible to avoid pavement heat, dust, and exhaust fumes from the car ahead—especially where a lot of close drafting is expected. Wherever auxilliary ducts and scoops can't be avoided, it is important not only that they have a well located inlet and smooth duct flow, but that the controlled exit be in a negative (or relatively less positive) pressure location.

The mathematics of aerodynamic forces are quite straightforward, even if measuring the necessary quantities is not. The influencing factors are frontal area (A) of the body in square feet, the *air* velocity (V) of the body in miles per hour, and a non-dimensional air drag coefficient (Cd) which is based on the shape of the body. For standard air temperature and pressure, the equation is:

$$\text{force} = (.0025)\,(Cd)\,(A)\,(V)^2$$

Some typical values for Cd will give an example of what to expect. (See Table 1.) The equation shows that a reduction in frontal area is as valuable as a reduction in the shape coefficient, although the latter isn't as easy to measure. The corresponding equation for horsepower required is:

$$\text{horsepower} = (.0027)\,(\text{force})\,(V)$$

Shape	Air Drag Coefficient
Flat plate	1.15
Corvette Stingray	.40
Sphere	.15
Land Speed Record Car	.11
Airfoil (typical)	.05

Table 1. Examples of air drag coefficients

So it can be seen that forces increase as the square of velocity, and horsepower required increases as the cube of velocity.

DOWNFORCE

In recent years aerodynamic downforce has proven to be of far greater value to reduced laptimes than low drag on high-powered race cars. In some forms of racing, however, fuel economy has recently gotten more emphasis, so the compromise between drag and downforce has become harder to make. And while there is no question that the lowest air drag is best and the greatest downforce is best (assuming that the suspension can handle it), the proper distribution of downforce between front and rear wheels can be hard to resolve. Since the downforce increases with velocity, it is possible that it can cause the handling to change from understeer to oversteer, or vice-versa, as the speed increases.

Finding or increasing downforce is not simply a matter of inverting lift theory and shapes from studies of aircarft in free air. A non-lifting airfoil in free air has negative pressures acting over much of its surface—both top and bottom. But a relatively blunt race car body has very little underside airflow because it is so close to the ground. A large part of the air passes over the top of the body, creating extreme negative pressures which try to lift the body. At one time it was assumed that raising the nose and smoothly contouring the underside would create a venturi, which would generate low pressure and draw the car down. This works quite well with airfoils—which have low-profile drag, and don't have wheels. The combination of high pressures in front of the nose of a race car and wide tires which block part

Front aerodynamic spoilers are made low enough to just touch the ground under the worst conditions of cornering and braking, and as wide as possible—except where limited by the rules, as in NASCAR.

of the ground flow actually creates high air pressures under the nose, which can migrate well back under the car. If the underside is raked forward at an extreme angle, the effect is minimized, because the pressure will decrease all the way back from the mimimum clearance point. In fact, experiments by Cornish have shown that completely blocking the underside flow at the front allows the naturally negative pressure at the rear to act forward under the entire vehicle. This more than counteracts the lift generated by flow over the body and creates considerable downforce. Total blockage is impractical on a vehicle which requires suspension travel, although race cars have closed the gap until the nose drags over bumps and during braking. There is a problem, however, in that the downforce generated by a surface close to the ground is unstable. In other words, the closer the nose gets to the ground, the more downforce it generates, until theoretically the force would be great enough to grab the ground and bottom the springs. Some tests have shown the force to increase as a function of velocity cubed.

Considering the entire body, however, downforce is generally a function of velocity squared, the same as air drag. Therefore, it can be seen that total horizontal area is as important as the shape coefficient of downforce. Identical airflow over a body that has twice the surface area would have twice the downforce at the same speed. The problem is in getting the airflow to do what it is supposed to.

At the nose, any available positive pressure (dynamic head) is helpful in forcing the body down, but at the same time it is harmful in increasing air drag. It should be apparent that the problem is not so much a matter of where the air flows as it is one of what the air pressures are on any given surface. For example, NASA studies show that a wing works very well when close to the ground, in having lower pressures beneath it. But if it is mounted just ahead of a blunt nose or tire, the wing may end up with positive pressure behind and below it, canceling any downforce it would have had by itself.

Moving back across the body, the problem of countering lift becomes essentially unsolvable. If air must pass over the body at a high rate, it is going to generate low pressure. There is no way to avoid it without creating a lot of air drag. The best that can be done is to

Two examples of rear spoilers: the adjustable NASCAR version which is limited in height by the rules, and the Porsche version which also supplies air pressure for an oil cooler duct.

reduce the cross-section area, so that high-speed airflow is minimized, but the effect is hardly worth the effort. Where the pressure is negative on top of the body, the less body the better. In locations where the pressure is really low, as at the crests of fenders, it can help to ventilate the bodywork—to reduce the surface area which pressure acts on, and to let any high pressure out from below. On the other hand, if a relatively well blocked underside has negative pressure, the larger and better sealed it is, the more downforce it will provide. It is all a matter of knowing where and what the pressures are.

At the rear it is not enough to simply converge the body at the proper angle to minimize drag. At best that would merely reduce the upper negative surface pressures until they were neutral at the trailing edge. Instead, it is again a problem of generating high pressures above and low pressures below any surfaces, without having high frontal and low trailing pressures. A large board mounted at 45 degrees off the tail would have a very high pressure differential between the top and bottom, but it would be just about as great in the forward direction. It would have almost as much drag as it did downforce.

The simplest solution is to mount a vertical lip at the extreme rear edge of the upper body surface. This has the effect of generating a high pressure area ahead of it, which acts downward on the body. But surprisingly, it doesn't necessarily add drag to the body as a whole, unless it adds to the frontal area. If there is a rearward-sloping body surface ahead of the lip, the positive pressure area can also act to push the car forward. So the lip contributes both to increased downforce and decrease drag until it reaches a height where the negative pressure at the rear cancels out those effects.

The second and more effective answer—where it is permitted—is the separate wing. Modern wings have amazingly high ratios of downforce compared to drag. So much so that it seems like a real something-for-nothing situation to get 500 pounds of extra downforce at a cost of less than 150 pounds in drag. However, it is necessary to know how to get all the theoretical force that a wing is capable of. Before a lot of time is wasted in finding the most efficient airfoil shape, the wing had better be mounted a long way from the nearest

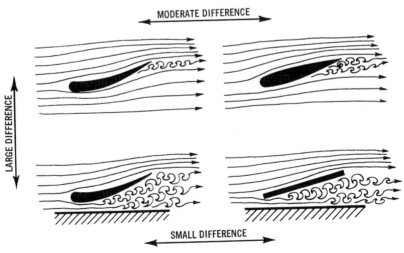

Figure 17. Wing Performance — Free Air versus Surface Interference

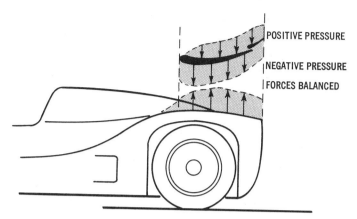

POSITIVE PRESSURE

NEGATIVE PRESSURE

FORCES BALANCED

Figure 18. Interference of Body-Mounted Wings

body components. If there is any obstruction within one or two chord lengths (distance from leading to trailing edge) of the wing, there will be pressure interference. As Fig. 17 shows, free flow is needed on both sides of a surface to make it a wing. If the wing is placed near the body's boundary layer or if it is tilted to a high angle and stalls out, a piece of plywood would work just as well. Another problem in mounting a wing closely above a body surface is that the pressures can cancel each other out. Negative pressure on the bottom of the wing creates a negative pressure on the surface below it (see Fig. 18), and the wing might as well be a huge spoiler mounted on the body. If the wing is stuck way out in back with nothing below it, the negative pressure acts directly at the ground. Of course, mounting the wing high enough above the body would accomplish the same result and provide smoother air to the wing. But even if sanctioning bodies hadn't ruled that out for safety reasons, the height created problems of high center of gravity and high drag pitch forces trying to lift the nose.

Exposed wheels and tires are also a problem in lift, according to Fackrell and Harvey. The primary problem is that the frontal air pressure wedges itself against the bottom front quarter of the rotating tire and is squeezed into the tire contact patch. If there are grooves in the tread where the air can escape, there is little effect on traction. But perfectly smooth racing tires may be losing some traction by having a direct stream of air acting on them. Fortunately, the upper portion of the tires has an opposite effect. In moving forward at a high velocity (dragging a boundary layer with it), it has a reduced aerodynamic lift at the top. Not that it makes much difference, as little can be done for open-wheeled cars anyhow.

As a sidelight to aerodynamics, it should be mentioned that innumerable suction-cup tread designs have been invented to reduce the air pressure in the tire contact patch. The advantage is obvious—a potential increase in contact pressure of over 14 pounds per square inch (and some race cars have over 100 square inches of tire contact) without an increase in weight or inertia. The problems aren't all solved yet, though—like what to do with water and dirt, the high rubber contact loading, how to compensate for wear, and most important, how to get the tire to let go enough to rotate.

The ultimate in suction-traction devices use auxilliary pumps or blowers to reduce air pressure below a vehicle, as the General Motors Chaparral did in 1970. Unfortunately, that system was too complex to be completely developed before it was outlawed. There are a number of other methods which can be used to reduce the pressure— exhaust extractor systems, filtered engine intakes, or fan blades on the wheel spokes—but they are much less effective. The skirt which is necessary to seal off the underside would have to be even more novel and efficient than the one which was used on the Chaparral.

Radiator ducts can hurt or help aerodynamic downforce. The duct inlet must be in a positive pressure area to get enough airflow, or a positive pressure area must be created. When the radiator is in the nose, the inlet is obvious and the outlet is the problem. If it is ducted underneath the body, the air pressure creates lift, and if it is ducted upward to generate downforce, it cooks the driver. Most nose outlets are directed laterally around the cockpit whenever possible. Centrally-mounted radiators appear to have unnecessary frontal pressure areas, although a submerged entry on the top of the body may create valuable downforce on the body. But there is still a problem of what to do with the outlet air. If it is directed up for downforce, it interferes with airflow to the rear wing, and if directed rearward it may return some of the heat to the engine. An extreme rearward radiator location may be best for low drag but then there is the problem of getting air into the inlet duct.

The last and perhaps greatest consideration of aerodynamic downforce is what to do with the force. It usually increases as the square of velocity, which means that as the speed quadruples from 50 to 200 miles per hour (common for a road race), the downforce will increase by *sixteen* times. With aerodynamic systems capable of 1,000 pounds of downforce at top speed, it is very difficult to design a suspension that will work right at the highest and lowest speeds. In the absence of automatic load-leveling systems, racers have tried a number of fixes. They have designed suspension systems for minimum camber change with deflection, or tried to compromise between high- and low-speed setups, or tried to make variable-rate springs work, or simply pre-loaded the springs to take the maximum load at speed. None of these solutions is without serious faults, so aerodynamic downforce is currently limited in potential until some means is found to balance the forces at the suspension.

STABILITY

Two primary sets of aerodynamic forces affect stability in race cars— the ratio of downforce from front to rear and the ratio of lateral gust force from front to rear. In taller passenger cars and trucks a rolling force from gusts can cause instability, but race cars are usually low enough to avoid this problem. Downforce stability is of major importance because of the high forces available and the fact that they change drastically with speed. Assuming that the car is mechanically stable, or that it would have the same degree of steady state understeer at low speed and high speed if there were no air drag or downforce, the problem is to make it aerodynamically stable also. In other words, mechanical instability should be corrected with mechanical solutions which are relatively independent of velocity, and aerodynamic instability should be corrected with aerodynamic solutions which are a function of the square of velocity. The distribution of downforce that would be most comfortable to the driver in terms of stability is one where the rear force is proportionally much greater than the front, so that as the car went faster it would have a greater tendency to understeer. However, this wastes potential front cornering power, limiting the cornering speed to whatever the front tires can handle, and subsequently creates unnecessary aerodynamic drag from the excess rear downforce. So the ideal downforce ratio from front to rear might be approximately equal to the weight distribution from front to rear, or have a net force vector acting at the center of gravity.

But the problem has other complicating factors. First, as the car goes faster and air drag increases, more tractive effort is required at the rear wheels just to maintain a constant speed. This tractive effort detracts from cornering force available at the rear, creating a potential for oversteer. However, this may be balanced by another effect from air drag. This drag acts at a point some distance above the ground, which causes an overturning torque above the rear tire contact patch. (This is true only under power. When the car is coasting, the drag torque acts around the center of gravity.) For example, if a total drag force of 400 pounds is centered at a point on the body 2 feet above the ground and the wheelbase is 8 feet, then even without downforce, $(400) \times (^2/_8)$ or 100 pounds of tire load will be transferred from front to rear. (See Fig. 19.) For a fixed drag force height and vehicle wheelbase, these two air drag effects can only balance each other at one specific speed, since they don't increase at the same rate with an increase in speed.

Another problem is the fact that the mechanical load on the tires changes with load transfer under braking and accelerating. During acceleration the rear tires gain load. But if the center of aerodynamic downforce (which may be much greater than load transfer forces) stays at the center of gravity, then the rear tires will be too lightly loaded and the car will have a tendency toward aerodynamic oversteer. During braking even more load is transferred forward, and if the center of downforce doesn't also move forward, the front tires will be more prone to lockup under braking at higher speeds. At least in this case it is a stabilizing condition, but there is still lost ef-

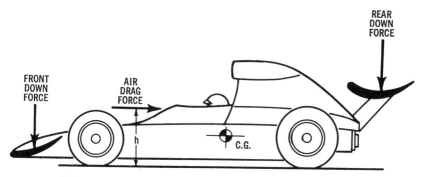

Figure 19. Effective Location of Aerodynamic Forces

ficiency in braking unless there is some sort of variable brake proportioning.

If it were acceptable under racing rules, it might be possible to provide variable aerodynamic surfaces to move the net force vector forward under braking or rearward under acceleration to maintain a more neutral aerodynamic stability. In fact, that is approximately what happens when the nose lifts under acceleration (reducing aero downforce at the front) and dives under braking (increasing aero downforce at the front). But when these conditions aren't adequately known and allowed for, it is safer to have a somewhat higher downforce toward the rear to prevent any possibility of oversteer at top speed.

Another complication is in the fact that aerodynamic downforces aren't generated exactly at the front or rear wheels. To get better airflow and efficiency, the front spoiler or wing is mounted well ahead and the rear wing or spoiler mounted well to the rear of the wheels. Each by itself not only adds leverage loads to its own end of the car but subtracts weight from the other end. So it is apparent that downforce stability can be changed considerably by simply moving wings or spoilers fore and aft.

It is possible for any number of these factors to work together, for or against the desired result. When everything goes against the driver, the results can be disastrous. Say, for example, there comes a time when the front load is lightened from: acceleration rear load transfer, body drag rear load transfer, rear wing downforce behind the rear tires, reduced downforce at the front from a nose-up attitude, the car goes over a rise and turbulence from another car combines with a wind gust—and up it goes. It is not that unlikely, either, as over a dozen race car drivers have learned from direct experience as their cars flipped over on their backs.

The same sort of philosophy in downforce applies to the center of lateral pressures due to side winds on the body. The center of pressure should be at the center of gravity and yet vary with the change in load transfer from front to rear. The lateral forces from gusts are usually far less than downforce, and yet at the limit of cornering traction at high speed, they can have a critical effect. Unfortunately, the lateral center of pressure on a high-speed body is about one fourth of the overall length from the front. With race cars tending to a rear weight bias, then, there is a great torque trying to turn the car away from the wind. Ideally, to minimize lateral displacement (off the edge of the track), perhaps the lateral pressure should turn the car *into* the wind so as to give it a corrective lateral force from the tires' slip angle. In practice, however, that would be felt as oversteer by the driver and it could be tragic at the wrong moment. So it may be best to have the center of lateral pressure a little forward after all—but less than it usually is because of excessive understeer effects.

The most effective methods for moving the center of pressure rearward are to increase the lateral area at the rear or to improve lateral streamlining at the front. This fits well with the practice of low, rounded noses and large tail sections with huge fins and end plates on wings. For maximum efficiency, fins must be located in relatively clean air flow and not in the wake of a "dirty" body or spinning tires. But since fins add to the total side force, the ideal design would be a very small fin at a long distance out behind the body for clean air flow and high torque leverage. Another aspect of fins is their effect on lift. As with end plates on wings, laterally mounted fins will tend to increase whatever pressure differential exists above and below the body. Downward pressure on the front or rear body will be increased by fins as they prevent vertical flow over the sides.

HARDWARE

The basic hardware component of aerodynamics, of course, is the body, which in most cases can't be altered very much because of production rules or structural considerations. Even when it can be modified, there isn't a great deal that can be done between the front and rear wheels. A certain amount of air has to pass over a volume that has already been reduced as much as possible, so it is simply a case of keeping airflow interferences at a minimum. Improved streamlining in this area will do little more than improve the airflow to whatever downforce devices are used at the rear. Otherwise, the hardware can be broken down into front or rear spoilers (for full-fendered race cars), front or rear wings, and ductwork.

SPOILERS

The function of front or rear air spoilers has already been covered: they keep air from passing under the nose and develop pressure on the upper rear bodywork. Anything that accomplishes these ends and satisfies the race rules is advantageous, no matter what it looks like. Many devices have been built and marketed for passenger cars with appearance as the primary objective, and in many cases they do make a contribution to reduced drag and increased downforce. But understanding the previous theory will indicate the more useless designs, such as trunk-mounted airfoils, hood-mounted vortex generators, and airfoil-shaped bumpers. Many production trunk spoilers and under-nose spoilers are stylish and do a good job as far as they go, but they don't do anything that a similar-sized flat plate wouldn't do in the same position. The object in such cases is to stop the airflow, and the contour of the device doesn't make much difference.

At the front, production under-nose spoilers usually don't come close enough to the ground, because they have to contend with curbs in parking stalls and steep driveways. In addition, they may be so effective, compared to rear downforce devices, that an unwary person could easily produce a high-speed oversteer condition. Where the maximum amount of downforce can be tolerated at the front, however, the idea is to build whatever aluminum or plastic device is necessary to block airflow as completely as possible and as far forward as possible. For production bodies, one of the best materials has been Lexan, a practically unbreakable translucent plastic. If the spoiler is mounted vertically below the nose, a $^3/_{16}$-inch thickness is adequate to resist deflection. As for height, it can be made slightly oversize and then worn to the proper clearance by contact with the ground. However, Lexan *can* be broken by a high velocity impact on its edge. If it is necessary to angle the spoiler forward, it is better to leave more clearance and extend narrow sections of thinner Lexan down in front of the $^3/_{16}$-inch panels. The small sections tend to roll under instead of breaking on contact, and the loss of one or two can be tolerated. It also helps to have a rolled flange at the body mounting surface to help avoid breakage around a sharp edge.

If the spoiler is made from aluminum or fiberglass, it could help to give it a scoop shape which curves around the sides ahead of the tires. This helps to channel some of the deflected air to the side of the body instead of over the top where it contributes to lift. However, a rigid plastic or metal spoiler had better be *very* strong to cope with inevitable contact against the track or the ground during some off-course excursion. A final note is to be wary of sharp, forward-projecting bottom edges. This particular shape is highly sensitive to ground clearance and the closer it gets to the ground, the harder it pulls the car down. In other words, the downforce will be unstable and sometimes unpredictable.

The rear spoiler lip is pure simplicity as long as it's strong enough and has been proven not to contribute too much drag.

WINGS

The subject of wings has been researched very thoroughly and with great precision because of all the years of aircraft development. There is enough test data on every shape and size of wing (even some in close relationship to the ground), to make the proper choice a simple, scientific matter—if the requirements are known. One of the most complete sources of data on airfoil shapes and performance is *Theory of Wing Sections* by Abbott and vonDoenhoff. For data on short wings close to the ground, NASA Technical Note D-926 by Fink and Lastinger does a pretty good job.

Technical reports from NACA or NASA also provide a lot of valuable data on wing flaps and slots. Their purpose is to keep airflow attached to the wing at high values of downforce (or lift). By very careful design and construction of multiple-flapped and slotted wings, it is possible to bend air a long way around a curve without its separating and causing a high-drag turbulent wake.

With all that information available, it still takes some interpretation before the desired profile can be selected. For those without a background in engineering or aerodynamics, David Reilly explains the process fairly clearly in *Road & Track,* June 1969. One point was not made clear, however (probably because the article was written when it was still acceptable to have a moveable wing that could be trimmed out to zero downforce and minimum drag). With the necessity of running wings at a fixed angle, the selection requirements are simplified. What is most important is to find the maximum ratio of downforce to drag (or *lift* to drag ratio, as it is reported for aircraft) at the highest values of downforce. After the most efficient shape is found, then the wing area can be selected to produce any amount of force for a corresponding cost in drag. However, all lift and drag coefficients are presented for an ideal wing or one which is infinitely long and therefore has no tip effects. As a real wing becomes very short, its aspect ratio (AR), or span/chord ratio, must be considered. The actual drag coefficient is:

$$(C_D) + \frac{(C_L)^2 \ (chord)}{(3.14) \ (span)}$$

Obviously, the shorter the chord and the wider the span, the better. Where the span is limited by the rules or the width of the body, the drag due to lift is by far the predominant effect.

One wing shape that probably won't be found in government publications is the Liebeck, or banana wing, which has been quite successful on the rear of many race cars. This profile is based on the fact that race cars don't have to face the aircraft compromise between minimum cruising drag and takeoff/landing requirements. All that is important in race cars is to have minimum drag at the greatest down-force condition. The Liebeck airfoil does this by essentially having no upper aerodynamic surface, which would normally have some negative pressure acting on its forward portion. Instead, it acts as a tremendous high-pressure air bucket with great concentration on maintaining attached flow on the highly curved lower surface. Also, by keeping the leading edge as high as possible, little of the high-pressure air on the top can act in the forward or drag direction. A computer analysis of boundary layer theory and potential flow theory gives the optimum shapes, relative size, and location of the airfoil and its flap. The result is a claimed record coefficient of lift of over 4.0, with a low (but unknown) coefficient of drag.

Because of the precision in design and construction, airfoils such as these are particularly sensitive to external disturbances. It is possible that surface roughness (from tape, dents, paint nicks, or excessive dirt) anywhere on the lower surface could upset the entire flow and destroy over half of the downforce capability. Wing strut fairings and end plates may be necessary, but they are also major contributors to disturbed airflow, with the standard 7- to 15-degree wake in which the downward-acting negative pressure is destroyed. The struts themselves don't add much to over-all vehicle drag, but the interference effect in an airfoil's high-velocity area can be critical. It may be very important to have well-designed airfoil shapes, smooth seams and well-filleted intersections in these locations. Further improvements have been made by Pershing, in using non-constant airfoil cross-sections to take advantage of local airflow variations.

One other related piece of aerodynamic hardware is the Gurney flap, or the vertical tab at the upper—or high pressure—trailing edge. According to Dr. Liebeck, this adds a great deal to the downforce with an immeasurable increase in drag—as long as the flap is not much more than one percent of the chord length. Both the Liebeck airfoil and the Gurney flap are being patented in cooperation with the McDonnell-Douglas Corporation.

It would appear that the construction of a wing is fairly simple, using familiar riveted aluminum construction as is common to most race car builders. But there are a few hazards to be aware of, such as

A good rear wing such as this one, with flap, "Gurney lip," and end plates, will still be inefficient because of all the airflow interferences ahead of it.

precise shape, smoothness, and strength. To maintain the proper smooth airflow, the cross-section profile must be held to very close tolerances with the given airfoil coordinates. At the same time, surface roughness can either hurt or help, depending on its location and the airspeed. For example, a wing with perfectly laminar flow may have no airflow separation at low angles and generate no turbulence. And yet, if the wing is in a high-lift condition and airflow has separated from one side, intentionally created skin turbulence can cause the airflow to separate later. This is the purpose of the vortex generators or vertical tabs mounted on the top of some aircraft wings. The need for, size, and placement of intentional roughness is a job for an aerodynamicist—and a lot of experimentation.

The strength of a wing can be critical to the driver, and some constructors just aren't aware of the loads that a wing may be carrying. It isn't unreasonable for a large race car wing to be able to generate

This Liebeck wing has a very strong and streamlined supporting strut, which improves airflow on the deeply curved and critical lower surface.

over a *thousand pounds* of downforce above 200 miles per hour. And yet some are constructed as though all they had to support was their own weight. Just the fact that the load is distributed evenly over the surface and yet has to be carried by two or four specific points is enough to create structural problems. Most wings are constructed with the standard aircraft technique of riveting a sheet aluminum skin over stamped aluminum spars and ribs. Plastic wings, however, have proved to have smoother surfaces with greater strength for a given weight. Most of them are constructed with a fiberglass skin bonded over a rigid urethane or honeycomb core, which may be reinforced with some sort of spar to provide stronger attachment points. It ought to be apparent that a fairly good wing can be designed and built by a competent race car builder, but to produce a really professional wing takes a lot of knowledge and experience.

Mounting a wing can be just as important as its basic design, considering the loads involved. The failure of a wing or support strut at speed can cause an instantaneous loss of traction and stability. It pays to know what the loads are and to test-load the assembly well over what is expected, to account for vibration and bump acceleration overload.

Of course, the loads won't be there if the wing isn't mounted in a good location. At the front, the only consideration is to avoid high-pressure areas (or body surface) immediately below or behind the wing. The farther ahead the wing is, the better it will work. And the closer it is to the ground, the harder (and more unpredictably) it will press down. At the rear, it is hard to find clean, non-turbulent, free-stream air. Upstream disturbances include the cockpit, roll bar, engine inlets, turbochargers, mirrors, and so on. A wing *will* work in turbulent air but nowhere near as efficiently as it will if some thought is put to streamlining—or eliminating—everything ahead of it. Again, the farther it is from the body, the better it works.

OTHER DEVICES

A few other devices that can reduce drag or increase downforce should be included under hardware. Although not currently used on race cars, they have shown great potential in bending airflow to make it go where it is wanted and to keep it attached to rapidly converging rear surfaces.

Boundary layer vacuum or booster devices delay airflow separation by moving air through strategically placed holes or slots in the body. The slow-moving air can be sucked off the surface or high-velocity air can be blown out and downstream to counter skin-friction drag. Of course, it is difficult to determine just where and what needs to be done, and it does require some power to move the extra air. The power source might be the inlet to a supercharger, or a separate suction/blower air pump might produce a net advantage in critical situations such as on an airfoil.

Another device is the guide vane. If properly located, such vanes can move the air around sharp corners or blunt tails by turning it in small slices. Still, their own form drag and interference drag, plus the drag of the necessary supports, may negate any advantage.

A high-speed rotating cylinder which is located at the rear edge of a body may generate enough airflow on its surface to draw a large amount of free-stream air around a corner. The cylinder takes up a great deal of space and weight, however, and must have a surface velocity many times the velocity of the vehicle. Driving such a cylinder would require some complicated mechanism and would consume a small amount of power. Another disadvantage is that it may be an illegal moving aerodynamic device under current international racing regulations.

A final device is another suction system which reorganizes the turbulent separation airflow at the rear of a body. As the air separates from the body, it forms cyclically alternating vortices which spread out in the wake and dissipate drag energy into the air. By sucking the heart out of the first vortex, and pumping it out longitudinally behind the body, Cornish has eliminated successive vortices and improved the trailing airflow. At the moment, it hasn't been demonstrated that the reduction in drag is greater than the power required to pump the necessary volume of air. The extreme example, of course, would be a gigantic pump to remove all air from the front of the body and push it out the back—in other words, a jet.

DUCTS

Ducts will be considered aerodynamic devices—although they are internal and consist largely of empty space—because they are most often a last-minute add-on. To get the maximum air into the duct with a minimum of frontal pressure or external interruption, it is necessary to keep the slower boundary layer out. The entire duct opening can be raised above the body surface with a splitter plate below to deflect the boundary layer out, but the submerged NACA duct opening may have less effect on vehicle drag. David Reilly explains the operation and construction of NACA ducts in layman's terms in *Road & Track,* March 1970.

Even after high-speed air has been drawn into a duct, it must be carefully routed. Rough, corrugated ducts can reduce the flow, and sharp turns can almost totally destroy it. Sometimes turns are necessary, such as from horizontal flow to vertical carburetors, or to dis-

The radiator duct on this sedan is carefully sealed to insure efficient airflow to the radiator. A deflector keeps hot air from the carburetor.

tribute the flow evenly across a radiator face. In such cases, one carburetor or one edge of the radiator core may get most of the ram air effect, which starves the rest of the carbs or core. A common solution for engine inlets is to make the inlets bell-shaped and to surround each inlet with a filter or porous foam to even out the flow. Removing this element may increase total flow but it has been known to cause some of the cylinders to misfire at high air speed.

Airflow through radiator cores can be distributed more evenly by guide vanes in a large radiator duct. These ducts usually have a small opening which must rapidly expand in one or more directions to a much larger core size. If any wall slopes away from the free-stream airflow direction by more than 5 to 10 degrees, the air will probably keep going straight. A vane, or group of vanes, perhaps extending all the way to the core, will be necessary to keep any airflow divergence angle below the separation point.

DEVELOPMENT

The development of aerodynamic race car shapes should go all the way back to original vehicle design since the arrangement of components is so closely related to the external form. In such a case, the scale model wind tunnel is the most valuable tool in that it allows cheap and rapid experimental changes to be made. If anyone really knew how all the particles of air would flow about a body, that wouldn't be necessary. Since most designers think they know—and don't use wind tunnels—it becomes necessary to develop the final shape and various accessories by on-the-road testing. Full-scale road testing isn't all bad, however. The forces are usually much greater and much easier to measure, and there is no question whether they can be directly scaled up to the real car from a model.

MEASUREMENT

Aerodynamic development is usually concentrated on lowering air drag, increasing downforce, and improving internal airflow. In the reduction of drag, the primary means of measurement is the coast-down, which is explained in more detail in Chapter 13. By applying the theories previously discussed, making intuitive changes, and recording the rate at which the car decelerates, it is relatively easy to find some improvements. It isn't even necessary to get the actual drag figures in pounds or horsepower as long as the tests are accurate and repeatable enough so the data can be believeable. It usually takes a great change in configuration, however, to show up in reduced air drag, and a little air drag doesn't count for much in reduced laptimes except on the high-speed banked ovals of USAC and NASCAR.

When drag figures are calculated, one of the most useful means of reporting them is in pounds at 100 miles per hour, instead of in drag coefficients, which neglect the possible change in frontal area. A figure of 280 pounds drag at 100 miles per hour is a real figure that means something to everyone. If someone needed to know the drag at 150 mph, all he would have to do is multiply the drag by the speed increase fraction squared, or $(150/100)^2$, to get a figure of $2.25 \times 280 = 630$ pounds at 150 mph. The same applies to any aerodynamic downforce measurement in pounds at the front or rear wheels—as long as suspension deflection doesn't change the increase to some other than a square function.

The most important figures to get are the aerodynamic downforces, and if there are any compromises to make between them and drag, downforce usually is the more valuable—up to a point that can only be determined by laptimes. A reasonable estimate for high-powered race cars on road courses, however, is that a 1 percent increase in downforce is more valuable than a 10 percent decrease in air drag. For example, reducing drag from 280 pounds to 250 pounds is less important than increasing wing forces from a total of 280 pounds to 285 pounds at 100 miles per hour. As ridiculous as that seems, it shows why streamlined road race cars have never been able to keep up with ''dirty'' winged and spoilered cars.

Downforce is usually easier to measure than air drag if precision is not important—and with the size of the figures in pounds, it usually isn't. The forces are most useful when measured directly at the front and rear axles, and with a constant rear tire thrust to include air drag rear load transfer. Fortunately, that is also about the easiest way to measure them—by using the suspension spring deflections and holding the car at a constant high speed while recording data. Even if an elaborate electronic or mechanical recorder (as discussed in Chapter 13) is not available, it is often possible to mount visual suspension deflection indicators where they can be seen by the driver at speed. The deflection, of course, is irrelevant except that it is related to the number of pounds it takes to deflect the suspension an equal amount at rest—and also that total suspension travel should not be used up.

BALANCING FORCES

So there is no need to know the exact force figures, except to know their balance between the front and rear wheels. With the static weight distribution known, it is fairly easy to balance the front and rear aerodynamic downforce in pounds in about the same proportion, with a slight bias to the rear. The most accurate data available, however, won't account for dynamic and transient conditions during acceleration and braking, and the final balance must be determined by the driver's acceptance. Still, it is important to remember that an aerodynamically stable (understeering) race car is limited in cornering by front wheel traction, and at that point no increase in rear downforce will have much effect—except perhaps to make it feel better and go slower due to increased air drag. During development it can be an educational experience to find out just where the car starts showing high-speed oversteer characteristics and to try to keep the force balance just under that point. The problem is that the driver may find the car tragically uncontrollable at that point.

Another problem is that it may not be easy to get enough downforce at one end to balance the other, and therefore the other will have to be reduced. Obviously, an increase in downforce is preferred, at any cost within the rules. Using the previous theories, this means ridiculously large spoilers and/or wings or minimum ground clearance must be tried at the lesser end of the car. It can even be worthwhile in development to try things that are *not* legal, just to find out what extremes might be necessary. In NASCAR, where bodies and spoilers are very explicitly regulated, about the only thing that can be changed to affect the front/rear downforce is the rake angle of the chassis. By lowering the nose and raising the tail, downforce can be increased at both ends. Where rear spoilers are not regulated, it is more efficient to keep the entire chassis low and raise just the rear spoiler.

The optimization of wings is a little more complicated, even assuming a given airfoil profile and size has been selected. The first step at the rear is to get clean air to the wing. Cotton tufts mounted to wire uprights can show which directions the air is flowing over the body, if it isn't apparent from the location of upstream interferences. If the car has been raced, dirt and oil streamers on the body, wing, and supports often give the picture even more graphically. Long streamers of a colorful lightweight thread can be seen from the cockpit and can give a good visual indication of turbulence or flow detachment. If it exists, there are only two choices: eliminate whatever is upstream, or find a more aerodynamic shape for it.

For both front and rear wings of any design, the maximum downforce occurs just before stall, or the angle at which airflow can no longer stay attached to the bottom surface and separates. Downforce drops sharply at that point, and drag rises at an even faster rate. Standard airfoil data cannot be relied upon to give the maximum wing angle at the rear because the angle of the oncoming airstream cannot be accurately determined. The stall point should be obvious in performance, especially if it happens at the rear wing first and causes an oversteer condition. But it is possible that a race car wing may stall gradually due to other interferences such as bodywork, airstream turbulence, or attachments causing some wing surface areas to have early airflow separation. In such a case, downforce instrumentation or tufts attached to the lower wing surface will show the condition at any wing angle. It is a good idea to allow a couple of degrees of margin to allow for gusts or the deflected airstream from another car. When a wing is accurately tested and doesn't seem to be producing the maximum forces that were predicted, it may be necessary to change the flow conditions on its surface. If it isn't smooth enough, a new wing is called for. On the other hand, a glassy smooth wing surface might be improved by a boundary layer tripper strip consisting of no more than a span-wise length of tape. However, the need for, or location of, a boundary layer transition can only be determined by long and careful testing.

Another problem at the rear is that the struts will always have some amount of flex due to loads, and the flex is in a direction to trim the wing, or reduce its angle and downforce. This can be an advantage if the wing loads become too great at peak speed. At least it should be considered, as it could cause aerodynamic oversteer at high speeds. If after the most careful development a wing still doesn't generate enough downforce at either the front or rear, or both together, then it is time to find a better profile or to build a bigger wing.

Since current racing rules prevent the application of aerodynamic loads directly to the wheel hubs, it is necessary to allow for the loads in the suspension springs at high speeds. This was discussed in Chapter 4, but another technique might be mentioned. On high-speed USAC ovals, where vehicle speeds are relatively constant, the springs may be pre-set for those speeds. In other words, the springs are designed to hold the suspension at a specific ride height with a large amount of aerodynamic downforce—even though the springs will raise it against the rebound stops at very low speeds.

PRESSURES

The development of airflow, whether on bodies or wings or in ducts, can be simplified by the measurement of pressure distributions and velocity profiles. Pressure distributions come from recording air pressures at many points on a surface at a given air speed and averaging them out over a larger area. The most common method of measurement is to drill tiny holes in the surface, bond in tubes connected to a multi-tube manometer, and read the relative water level heights at speed. More equipment detail and procedure is given in Chapter 13. The data can then be plotted on a profile of the body in pounds per square foot, as shown in Fig. 20, based on the relationship that 1 inch of water level change equals about 5.2 pounds per square foot of air pressure. If the pressure were known over every square inch of body surface, it would theoretically be possible to average them all out—both positive and negative, on top and bottom—to get the total aerodynamic forces in any direction. It is much more useful, however, to apply the knowledge of pressures to locate ducts, vents, deflectors, and undesirable interferences. For example, it is useful to know the pressure on the body close to a wing. If the pressure changes very much when the wing is removed, then the wing and body may have harmful pressure influences on each other. At the front of the body, identification of positive and negative pressure areas will show which

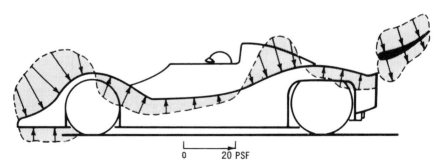

Figure 20. Pressures on Body at 100 mph in Pounds Per Square Foot

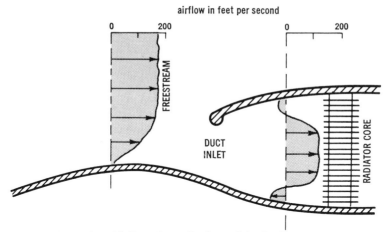

Figure 21. Airflow Over Body and in Radiator Duct

surfaces and curvatures contribute to downforce and which should be modified. Once the pressures are known, any number of productive changes can be found.

Velocity profiles are the measurement of the airstream velocity at various distances from the body and across air duct cross-sections. The same multi-tube manometer can be used, except that it is connected to rows of parallel tubes, or a "rake," which is placed in the airstream to be measured. When placed behind a protuberance or on the rear of a converging body shape, it can show at what level the airstream may have separated. The most common use is to measure the airflow in a duct, of which a typical measurement plot is shown in Fig. 21. In this case the data is better represented by velocity in feet per second, which is equal to the square root of the manometer water level in inches times 66. If the average velocity across the duct is estimated and multiplied by the duct area in square feet, the result is flow rate in cubic feet per second at a given vehicle speed. That in itself doesn't mean much, unless it can be related to heat transfer figures or engine inlet requirements. But it can be a valuable reference number in improving or decreasing the flow as necessary, if there isn't enough cooling or if air drag is wasted in too much airflow.

Once the optimum rate of airflow is determined for a cooling duct—and it may vary somewhat with changing temperatures—it is important to let nothing interfere with that flow. Many race cars have overheated and destroyed their engines when the radiator duct picked up trash, newspapers, or even enough leaves to block the radiator core. A heavy-mesh screen placed in front of a duct opening will have little effect on airflow and yet can be angled to deflect trash away from the duct. A finer mesh screen is necessary to keep smaller particles out of the engine inlet ducts, as gravel is not only hard on the engine, but can cause the throttles to jam open.

RACING

Back in the days when movable aerodynamic devices were allowed on race cars, there was more that could be done about airflow while driving. Front and rear wings could be pivoted to increase or decrease downforce and drag at any time. The most popular technique was to design wings with the maximum downforce angle during cornering and braking, and to trim them out during acceleration. Now the driver is limited to simply driving the car.

Of course, it is possible to change wing angles during pit stops. When a stop must be made anyhow, for fuel or tires, it may be an advantage to be able to rapidly vary wing angles to adapt to changing track conditions. However, it is necessary to know exactly what wing position is desired ahead of time, for a required change in handling, since a race is no time to run experiments.

DRAFTING

There are some extremely important aerodynamic considerations which a driver must be aware of while driving, since there are other race cars on the track to cause major changes in the upstream air. If any two cars are within one or two car lengths of each other, they will have a considerable influence on each other's drag (the drafting effect) or aerodynamic lift (stability effect). Drafting has been used by racers for years but it wasn't until a study by Chrysler in 1971 (SAE Paper No. 710213) that any real data was available to show how it worked. They also demonstrated the operation of the slingshot passing technique, in which the trailing car is always at an advantage.

Two superspeedway greats, Petty and Pearson, give a good demonstration of drafting at 200 mph on the straightaway at Ontario.

The results of the Chrysler study showed that the air drag of the trailing car was reduced by about one third as it approached the rear of another car. The drag on the leading car is reduced also, but not quite as much. Therefore, two or more cars working together can increase their top speed by a considerable amount, as long as they remain in tandem. When two cars pull abreast, the air drag increases on both. The slingshot effect comes from the fact that the trailing car can accelerate into the low drag wake ahead, and use that momentum to pull out and pass. When the pass is completed, the other car is then at the advantage, and can repass at the next straightaway. In actual practice on superspeedways, two relatively equal cars may maintain their positions until the last lap, when both try to be the trailing car to slingshot around at the finish line.

But even when you know the science of drafting and slingshoting, there are some details to keep in mind. First, the trailing car may have a serious cooling problem, because not only is the frontal airflow reduced but it is filled with heat and exhaust from the leading car. Second is the question of gearing, since a pair of race cars may end up running hundreds of rpm over what seemed like the correct gear ratio in practice or qualifying.

The technique is not quite as valuable on a road racing course because of the diminishing effect at lower speeds and the difficulty in staying within a few car lengths. If two cars are perfectly equal in acceleration and they leave a 50-mile-per-hour corner bumper-to-bumper, the gap will naturally increase to two car lengths at 150 miles per hour. The reason can be seen by comparing their spacing in seconds. If the lead car is 15 feet long, then it is 0.2 seconds ahead at 50 miles per hour. But 0.2 seconds at 150 miles per hour is equal to 45 feet, or a gap of 30 feet between cars. So the trailing race car must have a slight advantage in acceleration to keep closed up until aerodynamic effects rise enough to help, or else wait to draft out of a faster corner.

STABILITY INTERFERENCES

Another serious interaction is the reduction in aerodynamic downforce on the trailing race car. The Chrysler study showed the values for large sedans, while the effect on open-wheel race cars with wings was demonstrated in a report by the Jim Clark Foundation in 1969. In both cases the results show that there are considerable changes in downforce on both cars, not only in tandem, but when they are parallel. What is worse, the changes vary greatly from front to rear, producing sudden changes in stability. For example, as the trailing car approaches, its front downforce diminishes, creating understeer, while the other car's rear downforce diminishes, creating oversteer. There have even been cases where the front of the trailing car began lifting, until the car was flipped over on its top. As long as race cars require large amounts of downforce, there is no way to eliminate this effect. But drivers should at least be aware of the problem and possible consequences, and be prepared for the change in handling.

7

HANDLING ○○○○○○○○○○○○○○○○○○○○○○○○○○○○○○○○○○○

Once the previous chapters are understood, it is possible to combine them all into one manageable whole. Tires, suspension geometry, springs, anti-roll bars, shocks, aerodynamics, and other less significant areas are all related to each other in their contribution to handling. Where some of the factors have both positive and negative aspects, sometimes undesirable results have to be accepted. But it may be possible to counteract some problems with solutions from another area.

Up to this point it was assumed that the terms "understeer" and "oversteer" were understood. In everyday language they are accepted to mean that either the front or rear wheels lose cornering power first, or that the front or rear slip angle is greater, or that the car either plows or is loose. To a vehicle dynamics engineer, however, a comprehensive explanation would take a chapter in itself. The problem is that such terms as understeer, oversteer, stability, and control are all highly *conditional*. You can't properly say a race car is understeering unless many specific conditions are defined. The stability can change drastically between high and low speeds, straight-

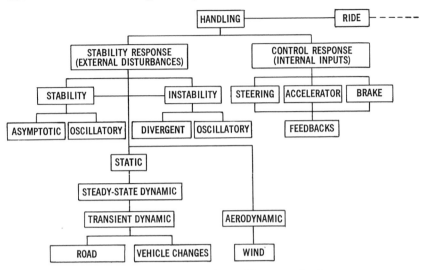

Table 2. Breakdown of handling terminology

aways or corners, steady state or transient turns, high or low loads, and can vary with inputs from steering, braking, acceleration, or the wind. Generally speaking, about all that can be said about an understeering race car at this point is that it is usually more controllable than an oversteering race car.

The first distinction to be made is between ride and handling (see Table 2). Ride, or forces and motions in the vertical direction, are relatively unimportant here. The value of proper geometry, springs, shocks, and unsprung weight in keeping the tires on the ground has been covered already. With modern knowledge and technology, it is possible to keep ride somewhat independent of handling, which concerns forces and motions only in a horizontal plane.

The previous explanations of vehicle components have only considered their effect on maximum lateral acceleration or cornering power. However, that in itself is not necessarily related to good handling. It is quite possible for handling to be so poor that another vehicle with less cornering power can be driven through a turn faster. The driver is an incredibly adaptable control system and can usually overcome some serious handling deficiencies—for a short time. But over the length of a race, it is practically impossible to avoid making a critical mistake under such circumstances.

Handling must be further broken down into stability and control, or the vehicle response to external disturbances and driver inputs. External disturbances that require a stability response include wind gusts, suddenly changing track surface conditions, bumps, and the corresponding shifts in vehicle equilibrium. The driver's control inputs that require a predictable vehicle response include steering, throttle, and brake applications.

STABILITY

Before stability can be related to the race car, it must be defined in some of its various types. (See Fig. 22.) A stable vehicle can have either asymptotic stability (returning to its original condition without any overshoot in the opposite direction) or oscillatory stability (cycling back and forth but converging to the desired condition). An unstable vehicle can have either divergent instability (a constantly increasing response in an undesirable direction) or oscillatory instability (a small disturbance creates constantly increasing oscillations until total control is lost). The condition that primarily determines whether

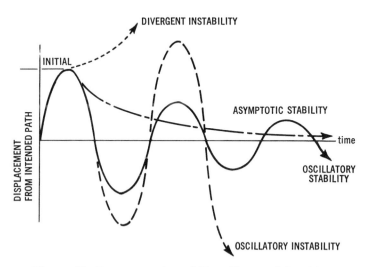

Figure 22. Representation of Four Types of Stability

stability will be oscillatory is the damping in the system. Within the limits of acceptable control response, increased damping is felt as desirable because it reduces the possibility that the driver's control could get out of phase with natural oscillations and increase instability. A good example is steering corrections in a skid on ice. As the car swerves back and forth and the driver continues to correct and then counter-correct, he may get behind in his response and end up steering the wrong way at the wrong time—which can cause the car to spin.

In addition to the various types of stability, there are four conditions under which stability must be analysed in vehicle operation: static, steady-state dynamic, transient, and aerodynamic.

Static stability is important only to something like a two-wheeled cycle, which will fall over as it approaches a static, or rest, condition.

Steady-state stability is most often considered in the analysis of vehicle dynamics since it is relatively easy to comprehend and correct. It assumes that the driver has already controlled the vehicle into a desired condition—such as a constant-radius turn, a straightaway, or constant braking force—and the vehicle is supposed to maintain that condition with minimal corrections by the driver. Any external disturbance—such as suspension deflection in the turn, road camber in the straightaway, or one-wheel lockup in braking—should be automatically corrected for within the dynamics of the vehicle itself.

Even if a race car is developed to have steady-state stability, as is usually done on the constant-radius skidpad, it is still possible for it to be unstable in a transient maneuver. Applying throttle or brakes, or turning the steering wheel, may cause vehicle response to overshoot the desired condition until it goes beyond the point at which the driver can still correct it. The most common example is the race car that appears to have perfectly neutral cornering capability on the skidpad. When driven on a race course it will probably be quite unstable (divergent, with no oscillation) upon acceleration out of a turn because it loses rear tire cornering power from forward thrust.

Finally, there is aerodynamic stability, which was briefly discussed in Chapter 6, and which can add or detract from steady-state or tran-

A badly oversteering car going out of control at the entry to a turn. Even full lock counter-steering by a skilled driver couldn't save it.

sient stability at any time depending on speed of the vehicle and velocity of any side winds or gusts. The problem of stability as a function of front and rear downforce was explained as well as possible, considering its complex interaction with load transfer. But lateral gust stability seems, oddly enough, to have inverse requirements from mechanical stability. By previous definition of asymptotic stability, it would be assumed that a side wind should have a greater force at the rear of the car, steering it back toward its previous path. However, this is felt by the driver as an unstable or oversteering condition, in which sudden, violent steering corrections are usually required. The preferred practice is to have the center of lateral pressure slightly forward of the center of gravity, so that the car must be steered *into* the gust.

CONTROL

Vehicle controllability, or response to control inputs, is the handling characteristic most associated with race cars, since that is a quality which can be sensed at low levels of performance—even though it is difficult to evaluate objectively. The most common means of measurement is the response time from a given input to a new steady-state condition—assuming a stable transient response. A sudden 90-degree turn in the steering wheel will produce a noticeably different response in a passenger car and a race car at any given speed, not only in the turn angle of the vehicle but in the time taken to settle into a constant radius turn. In imprecise language, it is the difference between a mushy feel and a nimble feel. In directional control, the most important factors are tire stiffness and suspension component rigidity. In the early days of sports cars, suspension rigidity meant stiff springs and a hard ride, but now race car suspensions are designed with soft springs and yet a great deal of rigidity in the horizontal plane. Minimum roll and pitch angles also reduce the time taken for a chassis to stabilize into its new condition. In fact, response has grown to be so rapid that sometimes shock absorbers are used to slow down the rolling of the chassis at the front or rear.

The turning response of a race car is also somewhat dependent on its polar moment of inertia, or the distribution of its greatest masses. As the major masses such as engine, driveline, fuel, and driver are pulled in tightly about the center of gravity, the rotational inertia decreases and it takes less control force to rotate the car. Unfortunately, this means that it is also easier for external disturbances to rotate the car unintentionally. With the modern mid-engine race car, it is possible that the polar moment of inertia may be less than optimum and some increase might be desirable to reduce response time demands on the driver. At any rate, it must be one of the least significant considerations in race car development once the basic layout is set. For example, a large sedan has about as high a polar moment of inertia as possible, and yet a race driver can adapt to it in such a manner that it can be driven through any set of switchbacks or esses on any race track. All it takes is some anticipation and a little pre-setup going into each turn. In fact, such cars are easier to drive with respect to the increased time they allow for steering corrections. The major disadvantage to a very high polar moment, as with a rear-engine layout, is that there is a strong tendency to overshoot when the car is rotated suddenly by a large, quick steering movement—which should never be necessary on a race track, except in a potential accident situation.

The other control mechanisms the driver has—the throttle and brakes—also affect stability but are usually less responsive in time or precision. It is seldom realized just how important it is to have a very responsive engine reaction to throttle application. But ideally it would be as precise and predictable as the steering linkage. If it were, it would make the rear wheels of a race car as steerable as the front wheels. When a car is balanced on the fine edge of stability during acceleration out of a corner, it can be disastrous for the engine to either stumble for an instant or suddenly turn on and produce a step increase in thrust—which equals a step decrease in rear cornering traction. Engine torque curves should be studied and tailored with this possibility in mind. It was just such development that Mark Donohue used to make the turbocharged Porsches so successful. Some drivers have even developed their throttle linkages to provide a slower ratio for better feel at the upper rpm, which gives better control of the axle torque.

Brakes have less effect on the control of a vehicle, primarily because the ratio is invariable between all four wheels and because they are designed for inherent braking stability. But brakes can have an important control function in critical situations. When all four tires are locked up solid and skid, the race car will tend to continue sliding in a straight line regardless of its direction, rate of spin, or the surface it is on, or its steering and suspension or failure thereof. One less important control aspect of brakes is a momentary increase in front tire traction. A sudden stab at the brake pedal may give a helpful load transfer to the front tires or drop the nose enough for better aerodynamic downforce.

To be able to control a race car at the fine edge of traction, a race driver needs many precise signals, or feedbacks, from as many sources as possible. Although none of the signals are apt to be analysed consciously, the more hours of experience a driver has, the more these signals become related unconsciously to vehicle performance. Some of the various feedbacks that seem to be of value to a race car driver are: steering wheel forces and position, vehicle heading or tire slip angle, position of the car on the track, lateral acceleration and lateral jerk, yaw rate, ride or vertical accelerations, vibrations, and sounds from the engine and tires. As yet no one has determined any relative order of importance, but it is assumed that the greater and more consistent the feedback—within the limits of comfort and tolerance—the better a driver can control his race car. Apparently the only feedbacks which can be modified independently of vehicle performance are steering force and position, but it may be possible to improve the communication between the vehicle and the driver in other ways.

OVERSTEER/UNDERSTEER

From the previous analysis of stability and control, it may be easier to comprehend oversteer/understeer in race cars at the limit of performance. The general subject is covered somewhat more completely and in greater depth by Bergman and Ellis, although they concentrate on the mathematics of passenger cars. For our purposes, we will limit the analysis conditions to cornering maneuvers—primarily transient—at speeds from 50 to 200 miles per hour, and in response to control inputs by the driver. Straightaways, disturbance inputs, and steady-state turns may be important, but not so much to the racing driver.

The mechanical setup of a race car will determine its basic oversteer/understeer characteristics in a steady-state turn at the limit of traction. But however finely the car is balanced, it still requires constant instantaneous steering motions to increase or decrease the front cornering power, which corrects for normal inconsistencies in the track surface. Braking forces may also upset the cornering balance, although the brakes may be balanced so as to simply cause the vehicle to lose lateral traction evenly between the front and rear wheels. This increases the cornering radius without necessarily requiring further steering corrections.

The balance of a race car is apt to be upset completely however, by applying large acceleration thrust forces at the rear driving wheels.

The same car with different anti-roll bars, set up to oversteer (top), or understeer (bottom) at a constant speed on a 100-foot radius skid pad. Extreme steer angle in the latter case indicates excessive understeer.

This may seem obvious, but it points out the fact that practically any high-powered race car can be made to oversteer at lower speeds by merely applying enough throttle—which has practically nothing to do with the chassis setup or basic oversteer/understeer characteristics. It is not uncommon for a race driver to get in a car with a great deal more power than he is accustomed to and claim that it oversteers sim-ply·because it is easier to break traction at the rear tires. If the car had four-wheel drive, it would appear to be relatively easy to have the application of thrust at front and rear wheels balanced—as with the brakes—to have a neutral effect.

The problem is nowhere near that simple, however, with either two- or four-wheel drive, because of so many other factors such as lateral and longitudinal load transfer, suspension deflection, tire characteristics, path requirements, and so on. The analysis is so complex, in fact, that it is beyond the comprehension of any human mind, and there is only one known computer program which can adequately predict transient cornering behavior. A joint venture between General Motors and Calspan Laboratories has produced a program which can accurately simulate a vehicle and driver. But it is so large and unwieldy, and requires so much input data, that it is virtually impractical for real-life predictions. The quickest and most reliable results still come from actual road testing.

Still, it would be useful to know what effect some individual vehicle components and characteristics have on transient behavior under acceleration. Chapter 4 (on springs and anti-roll bars) showed how the distribution of vertical loads on the tires and a knowledge of tire characteristics could be used to understand steady-state cornering. The use of springs and anti-roll bars, plus the effects of changing tire sizes and compounds, plus variations in suspension geometry make it relatively easy to produce any degree of steady-state oversteer/understeer desired. If maximum cornering speed on the skidpad were all that was necessary, it would be easy. But the car must be balanced so that it can be accelerated out of that state without becoming unstable.

To understand the transient problem, it will be necessary to return to a tire load illustration (see Fig. 23) and make a further analysis which can be varied with rear tire thrust. By careful consideration of

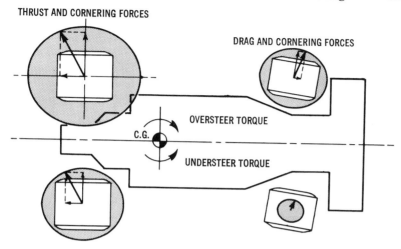

Figure 23. Tire Forces Contributing to Oversteer and Understeer

all the forces and their locations and directions, you can see that they all contribute to a torque about the center of gravity either into the turn (oversteer) or out of the turn (understeer). A breakdown of each set of forces shows that:

A. Rear tire thrust detracts from the tire's ultimate cornering capability, contributing to *oversteer*.

B. The rear tire thrust required to maintain constant velocity or to accelerate the vehicle can have either a neutral effect (with an open differential), or contribute to *oversteer* when greater thrust is available at the outside rear tire.

C. Tire load transfer to the rear increases rear tire cornering capability, contributing to *understeer*.

D. Tire load transfer off the front tires decreases cornering capability, contributing to *understeer*.

E. Front tire cornering drag forces contribute to *understeer* because of the greater load carried by the outside tire.

F. Smaller front tires have a smaller coefficient of friction than the rear tires, contributing to *understeer*.

G. Greater lateral load transfer at the front tires diminishes their combined coefficient of friction more than at the rear, contributing to *understeer*.

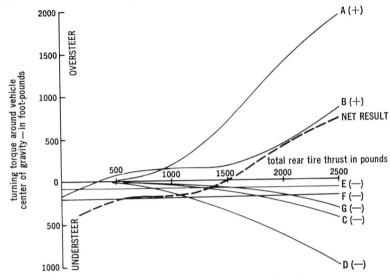

Figure 24. Dynamic Stability Graph

It would appear that the majority of factors contribute to understeer. However, the magnitude of each factor is more important to consider, as each is added for an over-all net torque about the center of gravity. It is also important to know how the magnitudes change with an increase in rear tire thrust as the car is accelerated. To find this, a given vehicle is assumed to be at maximum lateral acceleration at some given speed (which would affect only aerodynamics and perhaps tire characteristics), and calculations are made to find the actual torques generated by each factor at a number of increasing steps in tire thrusts. These points are then plotted as shown in Fig. 24 along with the net oversteer/understeer torque. The plots shown are for a typical mid-engine race car of about 1600 pounds with typical race tire characteristics. Vehicle characteristics that must be considered are wheelbase, tread, center of gravity location, roll couple distribution, and differential type (locked in this case).

It can be seen that some factors are relatively linear, if not constant, from steady-state cornering to full throttle. The effects of the front tires, whether from cornering drag forces (E), smaller coefficient of friction (F), or their greater lateral load transfer (G), are hardly changed by rear tire thrust except as diminished by the load transfer to the rear under acceleration. On the other hand, the direct consequence of rear load transfer steeply increases the understeer effect. It is greater at the front (D) because the transferred load is a larger proportion of static load than at the rear (C), and the non-linearity comes from the fact that load transfer increases with the attitude change of the chassis. But what really upsets the balance, as is familiar from practical experience, is the rear cornering loss from thrust (A) and locked axle forces (B). The locked axle oversteer effect doesn't really come into play until the thrust is so great that the inside rear tire capability is totally used up. At that point, increasing forward thrust at the outside tire rises disproportionally. Finally, by far the greatest effect comes from the actual cornering traction loss, (A) which contributes to oversteer from the very beginning.

But it is the net torque around the center of gravity that the driver perceives as oversteer or understeer. It is necessary to begin the consideration at a total rear tire thrust of about 200 pounds or (100 pounds-feet of torque at each axle for 24-inch tires), because it takes some thrust to maintain a constant speed in the corner. At this point it can be seen that there is about 300 pounds-feet of net understeer about the center of gravity. This means that the front tires must be steered into the turn until their slip angle generates the necessary balancing force. If they are 5 feet ahead of the center of gravity, they will have to produce an extra 60 pounds of cornering force. If the throttle is backed off entirely, the net understeer increases (also familiar from experience).

As tire thrust is increased, the understeer decreases gradually, until it reaches a fairly constant level at almost perfect balance, or neutral steer, where the necessary steering angle is essentially zero. This is the area of the old familiar perfect four-wheel drift. Above this point, however, or at about 1200 pounds of thrust in this example, the rear thrust effects rise so rapidly that the handling characteristics suddenly cross over into the oversteer phase. It may be possible to maintain a balance by steering out of the turn—if there is enough road to allow for the increased turn radius—but the more productive control input at this point is to back off on the throttle slightly. If not, the increasing oversteer will eventually overcome the reduced steer angle at the front until the car spins out completely.

Of course, thrust available is going to be limited by engine capability and will change with rpm, gear ratios, and vehicle speed. At high speed in a high gear, the thrust available may be less than 1200 pounds, and therefore the driver may go to full throttle in the middle of the turn without creating oversteer. It would be a good idea to add the effect of aerodynamic downforce to each tire's cornering capability as speed increases, especially if the front/rear ratio changes significantly. But this example is not intended to be absolutely accurate even for the particular race car used. All it does is illustrate trends of the different affects on transient vehicle response to control inputs. Even by using this technique it may not be possible to develop a perfectly neutral control response in a two-wheel-drive race car, but it can probably help to delay the oversteer phase as long as possible with a minimum of steady-state understeer.

FOUR-WHEEL DRIVE

Although four-wheel drive is not currently popular on high-speed racing cars, it does have some potential worth mentioning. Even if tire traction seems adequate to handle the engine output and four-wheel drive seems to be unnecessary added weight, it may add a great deal to stability—if not control. By reference to the plot of oversteer/understeer torque versus throttle application, it can be seen that there will probably be no sudden leap into the oversteer phase—at least if unlocked differentials are used at front and rear. In fact, the theory indicates that it could be difficult to keep such a race car from understeering. This brings up a great potential disadvantage: the removal of one of the driver's most familiar control functions—the ability to create throttle oversteer. All the driver is left with is steering control, which is changed a great deal by the front-wheel driving effect.

At any rate, it is possible that power-to-tire-size ratio and power-to-weight ratio may increase someday to the point where four-wheel drive becomes practical. Without going into a great deal of analysis, the previous theory predicts some basic design requirements. All four wheels should probably carry the same static weight, and roll rates and tire diameters should be the same front and rear. If some degree of steady-state understeer is desired, it probably should come from a narrower front tire. However, it is difficult to predict just what sort of conditions are required when the primary feedbacks to the driver are changed so drastically. Locked or limited-slip differentials might not be required, but there should be a drive torque bias toward the rear wheels since they still carry an increased load transfer under acceleration. The exact torque bias can even be predicted mathematically, depending on such vehicle factors as static weight, tire characteristics, wheelbase, and center of gravity location.

With current race car power, weight, and tires, some mathematical predictions indicate that four-wheel drive is negligibly faster in a steady-state turn. But it does accelerate a car out of the turn much faster in low-speed corners, with the effect diminishing at higher cornering speeds.

Above wheelspin speed in the straightaway, however, the added weight of the front-drive mechanism is a definite disadvantage. Since most passing is done toward the end of the straightaway, four-wheel drive would have to have a very strong advantage in cornering acceleration. It also adds work to be done by the brakes and complexity which affects reliability. With the unknown development requirements and unfamiliar handling characteristics, it may be some time before it becomes popular in road or track racing. But the fact that it is currently doing well under low-traction conditions in winter rallying indicates that it may be practical someday.

HARDWARE

Most of the components or systems that affect race car handling have been discussed in previous chapters. But there are some over-all vehicle design factors that don't fall in any of those categories—such as tread width, wheelbase length, and center of gravity location. Each of these is a very important consideration in basic design, although there may be little to be gained from later development and modifications. The problem is that each has a number of positive and negative contributions, which makes it hard to predict the optimum condition.

As vehicle tread width grows, lateral load transfer in cornering is reduced, which increases tire traction and minimizes suspension deflection problems. But at the same time, frontal area and air drag may increase (on full-fendered cars), the weight is increased by greater strength requirements in the suspension, and the cornering turn radius and passing ability is made worse for a given race track width. It would appear that—within reasonable limits—the net effect still balances out that wider is always better. However, the geometric relationships are such that increasing tread width has a diminishing advantage. In other words, making it wider by one inch won't help as much as making it narrower by one inch will hurt.

The same sort of relationship is also true of center of gravity height, since it is the other major factor in lateral load transfer. In this case, of course, lower is always better, except where there is too great a cost in ground clearance, weight, or driver comfort. If there is a conflict of interests here, center of gravity height may be the less significant consideration. That is not to say it should be ignored, because it also has an important effect on longitudinal load transfer, but some priorities must be kept in order.

Proper longitudinal center of gravity location, or front/rear weight distribution, is a little more difficult to analyze. Based on the consensus of most experienced race car builders and drivers, the optimum for any rear-wheel-drive race car seems to be anywhere between 60 and 70 percent rear weight bias. It should be apparent at this point that ''rear weight bias causes oversteer'' is a total myth, considering all the other factors that have an overwhelming influence on control and stability. In fact, rear weight bias *reduces* oversteer, in that it increases the acceleration traction capabilities at the rear tires. It also increases steady-state cornering capability in that it decreases the cornering drag due to load on the front tires. The upper limit to rear weight bias is the point at which load transfer to the rear under acceleration makes the steering unresponsive. As the wheelbase gets shorter, acceleration traction increases, and the center of gravity gets higher and farther rearward, there comes a point when the front wheels will be lifted clear off the ground.

The amount of dynamic load required on the front tires under the worst conditions depends on a large number of other race car factors.

But when it is difficult to steer a race car under acceleration, weight distribution is probably the last consideration. When all other vehicle dynamics factors have been tried—especially the differential type—then it may help to increase the static front weight.

When it comes to changing the weight distribution, some race car components are easier to relocate than others—but the easier ones to move are usually the less effective ones. To get an idea of the effect of a relocation, the center of gravity will move a distance which is equal to:

$$\frac{(\text{component move distance}) \times (\text{component weight})}{(\text{vehicle weight})}$$

For example, moving a 20-pound battery 100 inches from the engine room to the trunk on a 2000-pound sports car will move the center of gravity (100) (20) / (2000) or one inch to the rear. Another way to change weight distribution on a race car is to move the front wheels forward or rearward, but unless done in original design, too many other effects can be upset.

Wheelbase seems to be more closely determined by component locations than vehicle dynamics considerations. The lower limit is the necessity of fitting the engine, driveline, and driver between the axles, and the upper limit is the increasing weight of chassis material needed to resist beam and torsional loads. Within those limits there doesn't appear to be any significant control or stability effect, except as related to center of gravity height and longitudinal load transfer. Recent aerodynamic regulations, however, have created an artificial problem on open-wheeled race cars. In order to reduce the interference of rotating tires on wing aerodynamics with a limited-length car, the wings are extended well ahead and behind, while the wheelbase is shortened. When the downforce is concentrated at extreme ends, the effect of an aerodynamic imbalance on the shortened wheelbase is far more significant.

DEVELOPMENT

Optimization of total vehicle handling in control and stability is a relatively straightforward matter of following all the basic sub-steps from previous chapters and putting it all together as a package. The desired result is to have a vehicle that is asymptotically stable in both steady-state and transient cornering and one which also has quick and consistent response to driver control inputs. It would also be desirable to have this degree of stability and control remain constant with increasing speed, but that may be asking too much, considering the effects of aerodynamics. However, it is theoretically possible, as discussed previously, by having mechanical fixes for mechanical stability problems and aerodynamic fixes for aerodynamic stability problems.

Unless a racer has access to a computer simulation of total race car dynamics, such as the expensive and complex General Motors/Calspan model, a skidpad and race track will be necessary for final handling development. It will also be necessary to distinguish between two styles of driving: the step style, in which braking, cornering, and acceleration are all done in separate discrete steps; and the blend style, in which either accelerating or braking is blended into the cornering phase. Since the latter has proven to be more effective, the older step style will be disregarded.

The first stage in development is to set the car up with some degree of understeer on a relatively low-speed skidpad, or a track with a long, constant radius corner. The track and driving requirements for steady-state tests are further detailed in Chapter 13. If, at maximum speed on a constant radius, the car oversteers in either direction, then it will be practically undriveable on a race course. Of course, nearly any race car can be throttle-oversteered at low speed, but what is being tested is the stability at *constant* throttle. To eliminate steady-state oversteer, it will be necessary to increase cornering power at the rear or otherwise to change the torque about the center of gravity. Rear cornering power may be increased by larger tires, softer compound, higher pressures, or more camber. Assuming that those have already been optimized, the next step is to change the roll resistance distribution. By using a stiffer anti-roll bar or stiffer springs at the front, more load transfer is carried by the outside front tire, tending to rotate the car out of the turn. The car should begin to understeer well before the front roll resistance is so great that the inside front tire lifts at maximum lateral acceleration. If not, then it will be necessary to reduce front tire cornering power as a last resort.

Any car which is to be driven on a road course should be frequently tested in alternate directions on the skidpad. If it isn't equal in left and right turn performance, then something is out of symmetry. Original suspension alignment and balance should have taken care of obvious problems, but there is also the possibility that the effect of a live rear axle, or driver weight, or even fuel movement could affect the dynamic balance. If so, it may be necessary to pre-load slightly the anti-roll bars diagonally on the chassis until the maximum capability is equal in either direction.

It is unlikely that the car will ever have truly neutral steer characteristics on a skidpad. If it appears to, the driver should speed up slowly, with minimum throttle change, to a new constant speed—without moving the steering wheel. If the car really does have perfectly neutral response, it will move out to a larger radius with the same center and without any change in attitude.

If a race car understeers on the skidpad, it is still important to know how much. Assuming that front cornering capability is at the optimum from tire and suspension development, the rear anti-roll bar rate should be increased in steps to determine how far the handling is away from neutral steer. The steering wheel angle is also a rough indicator of understeer. If the wheel is at a large steer angle and it can be turned even more with a negligible change in vehicle attitude, then the understeer is too great. But the ideal amount of understeer can only be determined by hard transient acceleration out of this steady-state condition. If the skidpad has tangential access roads, lane markers can be set up to simulate a typical turn. Otherwise, it will be necessary to go to a race track and try the car under actual conditions.

Changing the car's oversteer/understeer characteristics on the skid-pad will give quantitative data on the effect of various changes. Subsequent changes at the race track should therefore be more predictable if based on those test figures. It prevents a driver from going out on the track with any configuration that is known to oversteer. Track testing is very expensive and relatively dangerous, so it should be limited to an evaluation of various degrees of understeer.

A combination of driver feel and accurate, repeatable laptimes will determine the optimum amount of understeer. There should be enough to allow hard acceleration out from the apex of a corner, and yet not so much that the car can't be steered into the corner or held at a high level of steady-state lateral acceleration. The ideal balance will probably even change for different road courses—from one with a number of high-speed constant-radius turns to one with a number of slow corners and long straightaways. The former would probably require a setup closer to neutral steer than the latter. Once the desired understeer is selected, it should be quantified for future vehicle setup. By going back to the skidpad and recording both lateral capability and steer angle at that speed and radius, it may be possible to avoid a lot of track testing the next time. It may be possible to reproduce the exact desired degree of understeer on the skidpad alone.

Of course, this analysis of handling only considers steady-state cornering and acceleration. Aerodynamics and braking are also important considerations, but they not only can be developed separately and independently, they *should* be. Previous chapters demonstrate how they can be balanced to have a relatively neutral influence on handling, and only as a very last resort should they be used to correct for handling deficiencies.

If everything in the past six chapters has been carefully applied, the race car should be at its optimum level of handling performance. The subject of time response to control imputs has not been explicitly covered because that is seldom a problem in race car development. It is so strongly dependent on suspension firmness and tire stiffness that if racing suspensions and race tires are used, it is hard to improve the vehicle response. If for some reason a faster response is desired, about all that can be done is to increase the steering ratio, decrease caster angle, reduce the roll angle, and stiffen the shock absorbers. Everything else has been determined for optimum vehicle capability, so only these four factors can be modified for a change in transient feedbacks to the driver without upsetting vehicle balance to a great degree.

8

ENGINE SUPPORT
SYSTEMS°°°

Although the race car engine may be one of the most important components to be engineered and developed, it will be discussed here
merely as a purchased item. The development and assembly of all-out
racing engines has reached the point of scientific art where it is impossible to do justice to the subject in less than a book. In fact, the
subject is already well covered in a number of books and countless
magazine articles from the enthusiast press. The best books are *The
High Speed Internal Combustion Engine* by Sir Harry Ricardo and
The Design and Tuning of Competition Engines by Philip Smith, both
of which are strong in engineering and theory. The best example of
practical race engine assembly, tuning, and maintenance is probably
How to Hotrod Small-Block Chevys by H. P. Books. Although written specifically about Chevrolets, it is full of information applicable
to most racing engines, particularly all American V-8's.

Because of the finesse and precision necessary to build a race
engine, not to mention the equipment required, most racers will end

up buying an assembly complete from the induction system to the oil pan. The finances available will probably determine the source and quality of the purchased engine, but one that self-destructs in the middle of a race is no bargain. However, probably 90 percent of all race engine failures are due to owner ignorance of the proper use and maintenance. Every driver and mechanic owes it to himself to know everything possible about the care of such a highly stressed component. Unless the engine is to be used once and then returned for a rebuild, the builder should supply a lot of maintenance information: ignition timing, advance curve, cam timing and lift, valve gap, spark plug heat range and gap, internal clearances, bolt torques, oil type, and oil system layout. It is also a good idea to get the dynamometer curve for that particular engine, for use in selecting gear ratios. Once all this data is at hand, it is possible to tear an engine down to check clearances and inspect components a number of times before a complete rebuild is required. One over-all tip not mentioned in most engine texts is that the pistons, rods, crank, and block all need to get "friendly" with each other before they will develop maximum horsepower. The longer a short-block assembly can be kept alive—while the heads and other external components are rebuilt—the more powerful the engine will be.

There are a number of shops that can do a fairly good job of building or race-preparing an engine, but only the most experienced and professional dynamometer shops can properly develop an engine for maximum performance. There probably aren't two dozen such race engine builders in the United States, including the people who develop components at the speed-equipment manufacturing companies. A racing engine runs on such a fine line between ultimate performance and total failure that no science is precise enough to beat trial-and-error development. It will always be possible for someone to get more power out of anyone's racing engine—but the big question is for how long. It is very difficult to compromise performance and reliability, which makes development a long, slow process of try, break, and fix. You raise the power or the peak rpm and run the engine until something fails. Then you strengthen that part and run until something else fails. When all the components are strong enough to last a race or two, then it is time to search for more power. It becomes a continual empirical struggle until every part is working at its absolute limit. It costs a lot of broken engines to get there, and it is better to do it on the dyno than on the track.

Most production engines will run forever if you keep oil and water in them—and keep the rpm low enough. Unfortunately, racing usually requires the highest rpm possible to produce the maximum power output. Component stresses rise exponentially with the increase in rpm, so an engine might last 100 hours at 6000 rpm, 10 hours at 7000 rpm, and less than one hour at 8000 rpm. That's why it pays to have an accurate tachometer and to keep the rpm as low as possible to win the race. But there are a lot of other causes for failure that aren't peculiar to racing.

It may help to list all the possible reasons for engine failure and to try and avoid it with warning devices or fail-safe systems. The most common reasons for failure probably are: overheating due to high ambient conditions or an inadequate cooling system; oil starvation due to loss of oil or a poor oil scavenge system; detonation due to improper timing or low-grade fuel; fatigue from vibration or excessive stress reversals; and electrical component overheating or breakage. There are of course an infinite number of other possibilities, but this chapter will concentrate on the optimization of five categories of engine support systems: the fuel system, the oiling system, the cooling system, the electrical system, and the exhaust system.

FUEL

The fuel system for a race car is not quite as simple as running a hose from the tank to the fuel pump. Fuel starvation can mean decreased performance or total stoppage—even destruction of the engine if it leans out and detonates badly. When restricted fuel capacity is a problem it can also be important to be able to pick up the last quart of fuel remaining in the tank.

During early development driving, the fuel pressure gauge should be frequently checked, especially during acceleration out of hard corners with a light fuel load. The gauge ought to read a minimum of

Complex plumbing in a formula car, with twin radiators, twin fuel cells, fuel reservoir, dry sump system, and automatic fire extinguisher.

4 psi, and if it fluctuates or drops to zero even for an instant, big problems are sure to follow. The most likely sources of trouble are the pickups in the fuel cell. There should be a minimum of one pickup in each rear corner of the tank, with each hose leading to a separate electric fuel pump. This way, if either runs dry under lateral acceleration and starts pumping air into the system, the other will overpower it. It is even a good idea to wire each pump to a separate switch on the dash, so that an offending pump can be cut off if necessary. Check valves ought to be added to the system to prevent pumping fuel back into the tank through a failed pump.

If, after all that, the pumps still pick up air, it will be necessary to install pickup reservoirs in the tank. A trap can be built around each pickup tube which allows fuel to flow in during lateral or longitudinal acceleration but prevents it from flowing out through flapper valves. Even a quart capacity in each corner will maintain fuel pressure until the fuel level evens out again. Race cars with multiple cells must also be equipped with surge tanks. These are designed to collect a gallon or so of fuel through one-way valves from whichever cell is upstream at the moment. In such case, a single pickup at the bottom would probably never run dry until the last ounce of fuel had passed, and one outlet pump would theoretically be adequate. But where weight is no great problem, it can't hurt to have a spare second or third pump plumbed into the system. Mounting the pumps as close to the tank outlet as possible improves their performance (it is easier to push fuel than to pull it) and helps prevent vapor lock from low pressure in the lines.

With that great length of pressurized fuel line to the engine, it is important to prevent leaks or breaks in the line. Steel tubing is satisfactory anywhere except to the pumps and to the engine, where vibration and flex could cause a rigid hose to crack. Needless to say, all connections should use threaded connectors rather than hose clamps, and all lines should be shielded and protected. If adequate pressure can be maintained all the way to the carburetor (where the pressure should be measured), then $^3/_8$-inch I.D. hose is large enough, but really long hoses may require a larger diameter.

A final word on the fuel system: find the absolute best grade of fuel available or at least the same grade that the engine was dynoed with. Due to exhaust noise, it will be difficult to detect detonation—or pinging—before the engine is badly damaged.

The Aeroquip flex hoses with braided stainless wire sheathing that are common to all professional race car plumbing are incredibly expensive if bought new. Fortunately, they are usually available through government surplus houses at prices that are reasonable for race car builders. They add such security in strength, durability, and leak tightness that even considering the cost, nothing else comes close. A catalog from Aeroquip or Earl's Supply in Lawndale, California, will give all the information necessary on types and sizes for each application, varieties of connectors, and method of assembly. While such hoses are a good idea for protection in the case of low-pressure fuel lines, they are mandatory for high-pressure oil lines and flexible teflon brake hoses.

Dry sump pump and toothed drive belt on a sedan engine. Note that the water pump belt has no idler, and rides in deep-groove pulleys.

OIL

The oiling system in a race car is seldom restricted to the inside of the engine. At the very least, it will include an external oil cooler and perhaps remote oil filters. Since oil pressures and temperatures are quite high and the consequences of loss are a ruined engine, great care is required in plumbing. Half-inch I.D. hoses are the minimum, and the more filter area provided, the less pressure lost. It may be necessary to tape up the oil cooler at times to maintain at least 200 degrees, but if things get too hot, a pair of coolers should be used in parallel—not in series. Some V-8 engines may trap oil in the rocker covers under long, hard lateral accelerations. In that case, external drainbacks will be necessary between the valve covers and the pan. Check valves will probably be required to keep the oil from flowing *up* the hoses at times.

Vent hoses and catch cans are also affected by lateral accelerations. It is very easy for the lateral forces in a 1.1- to 1.4-g corner to tilt the oil level until it starts siphoning out a vent. Or it may clog the vent until blowby pressure starts pushing oil up the line. Most sanctioning bodies require the vents to run to oil catchcans to protect the track and other cars. The best vent line routing for V-8s is to run all hoses to the top center of the engine, and then run a single large-diameter hose from there to the can or the dry sump tank. This will allow most of the oil in the lines to return to the engine by way of another vent.

The problems of tilting oil levels can only be properly solved by using a dry-sump system. But there are a number of other advantages to a dry sump. The oil pan can be made much shallower, which allows the engine to be lowered. It also permits a large remote reservoir which can de-aerate the oil and which has a more positive single pickup point. But most important, it can add as much as 20 horsepower by keeping the oil level away from the crankshaft. The oil in a wet sump is constantly whipped around by the crank, which aerates the oil and causes hydraulic power losses. Another more subtle advantage is that the stock oil pump is removed. The pump has a tendency to wear its drive gears and thereby retard ignition timing, since the distributor is also driven off of it.

The disadvantages of a dry-sump system, in addition to cost, are all the external components that can fail or be damaged. The external pump requires a toothed gearbelt which, while more reliable than a V-belt, can still be broken. And there are a number of extra hoses, fittings, and containers required, all of which have leak potential.

The design of a proper dry-sump oil pan is the responsibility of the engine builder if no pan is commercially available. The pan will have at least two scavenge pickup fittings that must be routed to separate stages in the scavenge pump. The oil is then routed to the reservoir. The reservoir should have a capacity of perhaps twice that of the previous wet pan and be as tall and narrow as possible, to improve de-aeration. If the inlet enters tangentially at the top, the swirl will centrifuge out most of the air. Oil level in the reservoir should be higher than the pump to aid in priming it, and cone-shaped to the outlet.

Oil leaving the reservoir goes back to another stage in the oil pump stack and is pressurized for the engine. Only at this point should oil coolers and filters be plumbed into the system. Again, it is easier to push a fluid through restrictions than it is to pull it. Some engine builders recommend plugging any filter bypass valves, which will require careful monitoring of the oil pressure gauge (which must measure oil pressure at the engine inlet). When the pressure starts to drop, a clogged filter should be considered first. Filter cans should also be carefully taped or safety-wired, as they have been known to vibrate loose with disastrous results. The oil cooler should be designed for minimum restriction and be able to take the kind of pressures a racing oil system can generate.

The wrong kind of oil can destroy an engine just as effectively as no oil at all. The first consideration is to use an oil with ashless additives such as designated aircraft or racing oils. Some additives in passenger car oils create deposits in the combustion chambers which can cause preignition. The distinction between aircraft and racing oils is that the latter usually have anti-foam additives to help keep the oil from aerating at high rpm. If an engine is properly clearanced and not running too hot, straight 30 weight oil ought to be adequate. As the bearing clearances wear open slightly or extreme temperatures are encountered, it may be necessary to go to 40 or 50 weight oil to maintain pressure. However, heavyweight oils require careful warmup as they may be too viscous to circulate in a cold engine. The only time that supplemental oil additives should ever be used is during breakin. New components with very high contact pressures may require a coating such as the molybdenum disulfide compounds, but the oil should subsequently be changed before racing.

WATER

The water-cooling system of a racing engine must have a capacity that is proportional to the horsepower output. If a given system is adequate for a production engine, running twice the power through it will require about twice as much effective cooling. However, since there is much greater airflow, and a lot of cooling is handled by convection and radiation around the engine itself and through oil coolers, it may not require a doubling of the water radiator size. But it's worth remembering that the cooling system is as dependent on power output as it is on ambient temperatures.

Almost any radiator a car comes equipped with ought to be sufficient if the airflow to and from the core is adequate and carefully routed, as discussed in Chapter 6. But the radiator is a very vulnerable component which should be carefully protected from puncture and vibration. A wire mesh screen (and no sharp projections) ahead of the core and rubber-insulated mounts are mandatory. All hoses should also be isolated from contact with the ground or sharp edges and insulated where they may pass the driver.

The relatively low pressures in the cooling system don't justify braided-wire hoses except where protection is worth the cost. But the effects of water loss are serious enough to require great care in all connections of any type. Only the best non-ribbed hoses are durable enough and have low enough restriction for a race car. For long, straight lengths, rigid aluminum tubing provides increased cooling surface, but it must be isolated from chafing and vibration by flex hoses at each end. Only worm-gear hose clamps are secure enough, and even then they should be tightened while hot and safety wired. All metal tube-ends should have a bead to prevent the hose and clamp from slipping off. Where long cooling water hoses are routed through a car, it will simplify filling if air bleed valves are provided at the high points, but they must also be fail-safed. A commercial leak-inhibitor solution might come in handy in the middle of a race, and a corrosion inhibitor is worthwhile for an aluminum radiator or aluminum engine components.

Since a water overflow catch can is usually required to help keep water off the track, it might as well be plumbed in as a coolant recovery system. Running the overflow tube to the bottom of the catch can and fastening the pressure cap closed provides a reservoir for water which may expand or boil out past the cap. As the system cools, the excess water will be siphoned back into the radiator.

Pressure caps and anti-freeze solutions won't improve the cooling any, but they can be a valuable aid in preventing water loss. A 21-

Engine room plumbing on a sedan includes top-centered crankcase vents, a coolant recovery can, and steel braided hoses for all high-pressure fluids.

pound pressure cap will raise the boiling point from 212 to 260 degrees, and a 50 percent solution of ethylene glycol will raise it further to 275 degrees. Of course, an engine allowed to run that hot for very long is going to have other serious problems, not to mention the power loss at such temperatures. But it is better than losing water. The best example is an unusually long pitstop where the temperature may rise into the danger zone for a few seconds and yet cool down rapidly when the car can get moving again—if all the water hasn't been dumped out. If a 21-pound pressure cap is going to be used, it is essential to pressure-test for leaks in the system before the car is taken to a track.

Water pump belts are as important to finishing a race as the tires are, and yet receive far less attention. The most efficient and durable belts are the toothed gear belts ordinarily used for external oil pumps and timing drives. They are so effective that they may be narrower and lighter than the equivalent V-belt required to handle the same horsepower. Their cost, however, has kept them from completely replacing the V-belt. At the very least, all V-belts should be the kind designated for high-rpm racing use, with reinforcement in the vee to help prevent turning over. Deep-vee pulleys should also be used to prevent the belt from walking off, and it is a good idea to fit the water pump belt tightly around only two pulleys, with no idler pulley which could loosen or get out of alignment.

IGNITION

The electrical system is often overlooked because it offers little potential for making a race car faster. But it can very easily cause the car to run poorly or not at all. The first consideration is the engine's ignition system, consisting of plugs, wires, distributor, and coil. Ordinarily the engine builder is responsible for most of that—particularly the distributor advance curve and the proper spark plug heat range. However, since the spark advance can easily deteriorate over a race weekend, it should be checked frequently against the builder's specifications.

There may be a choice in the ignition system between: ordinary breaker points and coil; a transistorized system; a magnetic pulse distributor; and/or a capacitor-discharge system. When all are working at their optimum, there is very little difference—for a short time. But only the magnetic pulse distributor can avoid rapid deterioration due to point bounce at high rpm and rubbing block wear which causes spark retardation. The magnetic pulse distributor will probably stay in adjustment for the life of the engine, while breaker points should be checked for proper dwell and advance as often as possible. On the other hand, a magnetic pulse system with capacitor discharge may be prone to sudden and total failure, and it is not easy to diagnose problems or to repair them rapidly. It is wise always to carry a complete replacement setup.

Spark plugs can tell more about the engine than the driver could possibly detect. Reading plugs is an art that must be acquired by direct observation. It is practically impossible to illustrate in photographs just exactly what the porcelain tip looks like when everything is running right, or when disaster is imminent. A spark plug engineer at professional races can probably give a good demonstration, or the following approximate description may help.

Normal: the porcelain has a light tan, or gray, or very light brown color, particularly at the base, with no specks or deposits.

Overheated (or lean mixture): the porcelain is chalky white and the electrode is apt to be noticeably eroded or melted.

Fouled (or rich mixture): the porcelain and electrodes are coated with black, sooty carbon.

Any reading will be meaningless unless the engine is first run hard with a heavy load at full throttle and then "cut clean," or immediately turned off and declutched. The reading should indicate any serious problem with fuel mixture, spark advance, fuel grade, or plug heat range. Comparison of all the plugs will also indicate any one particular cylinder with specific troubles such as oiling, wire failure, or valve problems.

Assuming that the engine electrics are well-selected and carefully tuned, they still must be protected from their hostile environment. As the saying goes, "electricity never fails—it's always a mechanical failure." The most common problems are caused by heat, vibration, and corrosion or shorting-out from moisture. Most transistorized components and magnetic devices are vulnerable to heat and should be located in a cool area or have cool air ducted to them. It is also wise to have such black-box components easily accessible and replaceable in case of failure. All electronic devices—except the distributor—should be rigidly mounted to the chassis to reduce vibrations. In many cases, all internal electronic components can be "potted" into a solid block of epoxy, which eliminates vibration fatigue and improves heat transfer.

The spark plug wires should be carefully routed through non-conductive and rigid wire mounts, but never in contact or parallel with each other for any distance as cross-firing could result. The best all-metal plug wires should be used in place of carbon resistance wires since radio reception won't be a problem. Each wire should be numbered at both ends to speed up trouble-shooting. All connections can be protected from moisture by liquid silicone sealant.

The vehicle wiring system can be as simple as an on-off switch,

An excellent example of wiring, with silicone-sealed terminals, tie-wrapped wires, looms for plug leads, and easily changed components.

fuel pump switch, and brake lights, or it can be as complex as the wiring in a production car. In an endurance racer it will be. But no matter how simple or complex, all wires should be numbered or color-coded during assembly and a complete wiring diagram sketched up for future reference. The minimum wire size should be 14 gauge, with a heavier gauge for high-load components such as fuel pumps. All wires ought to have thermo-setting insulation if they come in contact with other wires or hot surfaces, to prevent multiple melting and shorting out. For large cars with lots of wiring, or cars with lights on removable body panels, multiple-pin connectors will make it easier to disassemble the harness. To keep them from being accidentally yanked apart, they should be backed up with a solid wire cable. Every wire connection should be protected in a number of ways. Eye-type terminals are both crimped and soldered to each wire end and the exposed metal protected with vinyl shrink-tube sleeves. The terminal is held onto its stud with a lock-nut, and the whole connection coated with liquid silicone sealer. The seal not only insures that the wire doesn't vibrate loose or break off from metal fatigue. It also protects the terminal from short circuiting against other metal components.

Just in case a wire gets pinched or crimped by accident and shorts out against the chassis, it can be a great help to have circuit breakers in the system. It won't repair the wire, but it is an immediate signal of a problem and an indication of where the problem may be. It also prevents the entire wiring system from going up in smoke, so that once the short is found, no other wires have to be replaced. Fuses would do the same job, except that an instantaneous overload out on the track could blow one—say in the fuel pump system—and prevent the car from getting to the pits unless a spare fuse is at hand. Needless to say, there ought to be a healthy amperage margin, even in circuit breakers.

When all else fails, and the electrics give up in the middle of a race, it might help to have an emergency backup system. The extra wire weighs next to nothing, and even spare onboard coils, amplifiers, and voltage regulators could be worth their weight in getting the car back to the pits. The only component that can't easily be backed up is the distributor. Of course, a master shut-off switch is usually required, and it can also fail or be turned off accidentally. Therefore, the duplicate wiring system should begin at the battery, with another normally-off switch in the line. The backup system probably doesn't need to pass current to anything more than a fuel pump and the engine—assuming that it can be cut in before the engine dies and needs restarting. Still, a backup system will never substitute for adequate preparation in the first place.

EXHAUST

The exhaust system should be completely designed, built, and tested by the engine developers. Header pipe size, lengths, and layout have such critical effects on power and the torque curve that they can only

Headers designed for equal lengths, durability, and ease of installation. Note the reinforcements, safety wiring, and slip-fit into the collector.

be properly developed on an engine dynamometer. However, there are a number of areas where the race car mechanic is responsible for the installed system. The first point is that there will have to be a lot of clearance around all pipes. Engine movement due to g loadings and torque reactions can cause a half-inch of movement at the headers. Temperature clearance is also a problem if at least two inches of cool air space isn't available between the pipes and critical components such as brake lines, insulated wires, and lubricated joints. Otherwise, aluminum or asbestos heat shields will be necessary. Engine movement causes other problems because the tail pipes are supported by the chassis, so there must be some sort of loose connections in the system. If the entire header is one piece and mounted rigidly to the engine and the chassis, it will quickly crack due to the conflict in stresses. The most common solution is to have loose slip joints at the collector pipe, held together with bolted tabs. Even the bolts should be left loose (with lock nuts at their ends), and yet kept from rattling around too much with compression springs. For ease of assembly, it may be more practical to break the head pipes apart at the flange and slip them into the collector individually. This also tends to reduce stresses on the header due to uneven thermal expansion. The combination of heat and vibration is so severe that some professionals feel the only way to avoid cracking is to use stainless steel or titanium pipes. The header flange bolts must be safety-wired—nothing else will keep them tight under those conditions. At that, they should be retorqued to seal the gasket after the engine has been warmed up, before wiring them in place.

Once the engine is installed and everything is hooked up, it is a simple matter to start it up—and ruin it before it even gets warm. A race engine is a fairly reliable hunk of machinery, but it still requires a reasonable amount of care. Because of the necessary clearances, it has to be treated gently until temperatures and pressures get up to operating condition.

A fresh or cold engine should be cranked over with the ignition off until the oil pressure comes up on the gauge. If it hasn't run for some time and fresh plugs are required, it is easiest to crank up oil pressure while the plugs are out. Plug gaps, valve lash, water level, oil level, and throttle action should have already been checked. The fuel pumps should be turned on until the pressure stabilizes, and the fuel system should be checked for leaks.

Each engine induction system will have it's own peculiar starting requirements, but it is better to try and start with too little fuel pumping than too much. It isn't uncommon for a cold race engine to backfire through the inlet and start a small fire. A large, *clean* rag should snuff it out, but a CO_2 fire extinguisher may also be necessary. (The chemical types are a mess to clean up after.) And here is the most important sentence in this entire chapter: Do *not* rev up a race engine—or any engine, for that matter—until it has had a chance to warm up! The engine should be held at the minimum smooth running speed possible until the oil and water temperatures have gotten up to 140 or 160 degrees. Race cars with dry sump oil tanks can be helped along by wrapping the tank with electrical heating tape, and pre-warming the oil for an hour or so before the engine is to be started. After the engine is good and warm, it can be shut down and given last-minute checks: oil and water levels, hot valve lash, hot bolt torques, belt tensions, leaks, and the last visual inspection to insure that everything is tight and safety-wired.

Aside from that, the only race tuning that should ever be attempted at the track—assuming the engine is already developed—is fuel mixture, spark advance, and plug changes. Local atmospheric conditions may require a minor change, but running too lean, too far advanced, or too hot can be disastrous. It's better to have a slightly weak engine than none at all.

9

GEARING AND
DIFFERENTIALS∘∘∘∘∘∘∘∘∘∘∘∘∘∘∘∘∘∘∘∘∘∘∘∘∘

After a race car's handling, brakes, and aerodynamics have been
sorted out and the optimum engine is selected, it is possible to make
the final subtle changes in gearing. Gearing should be just about the
last stage in race car development. Not only does it have practically
no influence on any of the preceding considerations, but it is relatively easy to change and highly dependent on all of those other factors. Proper gearing is a direct consequence of cornering capability,
braking capability, aerodynamic drag, and engine torque curves.
Also, with the abundance of ratios available, especially with the popular 5-speed Hewland transaxle and various tire diameters, the
number of possible combinations is staggering. It is possible to find
the optimum gearing at a race track by guess and test, but the number
of choices and the scarcity of track time make it important to use
some rational method.

RATIO THEORY

By this stage the racer should know nearly all that is necessary about
a given car to make some good mathematical predictions. The neces-

192

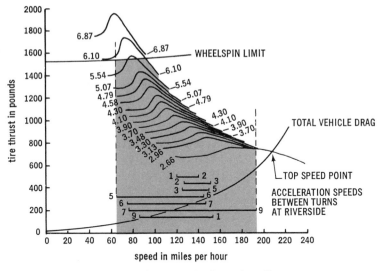

Figure 25. Gear Ratio Selection Curves

sary data includes: an engine torque curve, all numerical gear ratios available, tire rolling radius, and vehicle air drag. It is also useful to have a rough idea of the rear tire coefficient of friction, and the center of gravity height. We will arbitrarily assume the total driveline efficiency to be about 85 percent at high torques. Using this information, it is possible to plot a series of curves on a graph to show rear tire thrust at all speeds for each gear ratio. (See Fig. 25.) There are two equations that must be used for each plotted point:

$$\text{mph} = \frac{(.072)\ (\text{rpm})\ (\text{rolling radius})}{(\text{transmission ratio})\ (\text{differential ratio})}$$

$$\text{thrust} = \frac{(.85)\ (\text{torque at each rpm})\ (\text{transmission ratio})\ (\text{differential ratio})}{(\text{rolling radius})}$$

In the first equation the assumption of zero tire slippage is close enough, considering the balancing effect of tire growth at high speeds, and in both cases rolling radius is in feet. To reduce the amount of math, high gears need not be plotted at low speeds, and since all curves will have similar shapes, some can be sketched in from a few points. A pocket electronic calculator simplifies the job immensely.

The upper and lower limits of consideration are indicated by two other curves. At the top, forward thrust is limited by the traction available at the rear tires, which is a function of rear weight distribution, rear load transfer, tire coefficient, and aerodynamic downforce at high speeds. At low speeds, where it is the greatest problem, the equation is:

$$\text{thrust limit} = \frac{(Cf)\ (\text{static rear weight})}{1 - (Cf)\ (\text{center of gravity height})/(\text{wheelbase})}$$

The lower limit is the point at which total vehicle drag is greater than the thrust available in any given gear. This drag curve can be roughly approximated by data from aerodynamic development. If drag in pounds was found at 100 mph, drag figures at higher speeds are found by multiplying that force times $(\text{speed}/100)^2$. If a more precise drag curve is desired, it must include a static force component and a rolling drag force which increases in direct proportion to speed, or:

$$\text{vehicle drag} = (K_1) + (K_2)\ (\text{velocity}) + (K_3)\ (\text{velocity})^2$$

When the thrust available curve crosses the thrust required curve, that is the approximate top speed of that particular aerodynamic shape with that particular engine—regardless of gear ratio.

The use of these curves should be apparent. An arbitrary gear is selected and run up to its maximum speed in rpm (or the point at which thrust intersects the next ratio curve), and it is then shifted down to another higher ratio. Of course, the number of shifts is limited by the ratios available, so each should be carefully spaced out between minimum and maximum speeds. The optimum desired selection will maximize the enclosed area under the choice of ratios. If it were possible to have an infinite number of gears—or an infinitely variable ratio—then the rpm could remain at peak torque and the thrust available curve would be a smooth curve. In practice, each shift requires some time—say 0.1 seconds—in which *no* thrust is being generated, so there must be some balance between the magnitude and the duration of thrust.

If these curves don't provide enough range in ratio selection, it is always possible to raise or lower them by changing the over-all ratio.

A change in the differential gear ratio may be difficult (or impossible with some transaxles), but it has less effect on vehicle handling than a change in tire diameters. It may also be possible to raise the upper rpm limit, for whatever gains are available at a corresponding reduction in engine life. Unfortunately, an over-all ratio change requires a new set of calculations and curves, although the upper and lower limit curves will remain the same.

It should also be apparent from these curves that it is important to have a relatively flat engine torque curve over as broad an rpm range as possible. If engine torque falls off sharply or has noticeable dips due to intake ram tuning and exhaust tuning effects, it will be more difficult to fill the holes in the thrust curve by changing gear ratios. It makes the common practice of rating race engines by peak horsepower look relatively meaningless. Of course, the smaller the range between upper and lower speeds and the greater the number of gears available, the shorter the critical rpm span is.

TRANSMISSION HARDWARE

Even if a race car isn't equipped with a transaxle and easily changed ratios in five gears, that doesn't mean it is limited to the ratios it came with. Any manufacturer who has a competitive car probably offers a selection of ratios for the standard transmission. For example, any General Motors car that is equipped with a four-speed transmission can be fitted with any one of seven combinations of ratios in the first three gears (See Table 3.)

Gear	Muncie trans		Borg-Warner T-10 trans				
1st	2.20	2.52	2.23	2.43	2.43	2.64	3.44
2nd	1.64	1.88	1.77	1.76	1.61	1.75	2.28
3rd	1.27	1.47	1.35	1.47	1.23	1.33	1.46
4th	1.00	1.00	1.00	1.00	1.00	1.00	1.00

Table 3. Available gear ratios for a 4-speed transmission

It would be theoretically possible for a team to carry one of each set and bolt in whichever one seemed best suited to a particular track, along with a corresponding change in differential gear ratio. However, a speed chart for most road-racing tracks would show that there is no need for a low gear ratio below about 2.2 to 1. And for a reasonably flat torque curve, there won't be much difference between the remaining options in second and third gears.

Gears have some rotational inertia when freewheeling in the middle of a gear change, which means that the next two gears to be engaged will seldom be rotating at the exact proper speed. If they are forced together, there will be a destructive gnashing of the engaging teeth unless there is some sort of synchronization. Passenger car transmissions usually have friction surfaces which contact first, to match rotation speeds smoothly. In racing use, this type of synchronizer wears rapidly or is prone to more instantaneous failure. In pure racing gearboxes the gears are alternately connected to their mainshaft by lugs designed to grab the next gear very rapidly and firmly, an action too harsh for most street use. The undercut angle and corner radii of these lugs are carefully designed to catch without wearing and to lock firmly together as long as torque is being transmitted. Either type of synchronization is helped a great deal if the driver learns to match speeds between gears through modulation of the accelerator pedal—by a split-second letup during the upshift or a slight blip during the downshift. Otherwise, the synchronizers or lugs may be rapidly worn or broken, causing the driver to have to match speeds even more closely.

The strength of a transmission may become critical in the transition between a production car and a race car. But it isn't so much a factor of engine torque as it is of tire traction and driver manhandling. Torque in the driveline is limited by the traction of the rear tires, which may be doubled by an increase in tire size and rear weight bias. As the transmission is overloaded more and more, it becomes necessary for the driver to reduce shock loads as much as possible by making smoother, more precise shifts.

DEVELOPMENT

Since a transmission is a relatively fixed-design mechanism, development is limited to optimum ratio selection. To do so, a thrust/speed chart will be necessary. The one already shown is a typical example for a full-bodied race car with a 5-liter engine and Hewland transaxle over-all gear ratio selections. So far, the chart takes care of all the relevant vehicle data, but some track data is necessary also.

The ideal information would be a recording of speeds all around the specific track for a similar vehicle, from which minimum corner speeds and maximum straightaway speeds could be obtained. The second most accurate source is a driver who can note—and re-member—tachometer readings at each of these points, from which the speeds can be calculated. The last choice, for a track that has never been raced on, is an estimate from an accurate course map. Knowledge of the car's approximate cornering capability in g's and the maximum path radius in each corner, will give minimum corner-ing speed from the equation:

$$mph = (3.88) \sqrt{(g) \times (radius)}$$

The maximum speed will have to be even more roughly approxi-mated by the distance to the next assumed braking point, compared to a straight line speed/distance curve. Computer programs have been designed to do this operation with some precision, but that explana-tion would be worth a chapter in itself.

The minimum and maximum ranges of acceleration for each straightaway can then be presented as a bar chart at the bottom of the gear chart, as shown in Fig. 25. Assuming that there will be no standing starts, except perhaps for a pitstop, these are the only areas of consideration in gear selection. The highest gear must just allow the engine to peak out at the maximum speed bar. A few hundred rpm to spare at that point, however, will prevent over-revving if a "tow" is picked up, without a great loss in acceleration capability. At the bottom end, there is no reason to have a low gear ratio which provides thrust greater than the traction limit up to peak engine rpm. On the other hand, it will be necessary to accelerate the car from a standstill, so one gear should be low enough to prevent lugging the engine or slipping the clutch too much. At any rate, four ratios ought to be adequate for most tracks. The next, or second, gear will proba-bly be the lowest one used in the race, so it should have a low enough ratio not to be too far off the torque peak at minimum speed.

Still, the driver won't be able to apply full throttle until he has accelerated well out of the apex anyhow.

The first selection of the two intermediate gears might be in even numerical steps between second and fifth gears. Say second was 6.10 and fifth was 3.13, then third would be 5.07 and fourth would be 4.10. But by selecting higher ratios than that, say 4.58 and 3.70, it can be seen that more area on the graph is picked up at the higher speed than is lost at the lower speed. As it turns out, the ideal steps for maximum net acceleration will diminish in size as the transmission is shifted up.

Once the optimum ratios are selected for maximum acceleration, a check should be made for each short straightaway. The ratios should be spaced so that it isn't necessary to shift while coming out of a corner or just before getting on the brakes. Ideally, each short straight should fit the rpm range of only one ratio. This is where the compromises must be made. It is worth keeping in mind that ideal computer-simulated laps, driven by a mathematically perfect driver, may not decrease more than 0.2 percent in laptimes when ratios are changed by two or three steps. Since the driver's performance will cause more variation than that, it is probably a good idea to select ratio steps that make his job as easy as possible. Of course, even the most accurate predictions won't produce the ideal ratios for a track. Slightly increased power or cornering force may require a higher gear at any location. But the chart should improve the estimates and help avoid more than one gearbox disassembly at the track.

RACING AND MAINTENANCE

Because of the variations in gearboxes, the best advice for assembly and maintenance will be found in the factory service manual. The Hewland Maintenance and Overhaul Manuals are a must for transaxle owners, with additional valuable tips by Carroll Smith in *Sports Car Graphic,* October 1970. For adapted passenger car transmissions, all factory information should be reconsidered with the knowledge that racing will produce almost twice the stresses. The most carefully checked gear tooth alignments and patterns will change a great deal

due to deflection under stress, not only in the gears but in the case itself. Where possible, tolerances should lean in the direction to best
neutralize these deflections. Shifter forces are also likely to be especially great, so the linkage and detents must be adjusted with these
force deflections in mind.

The technique of shifting will vary somewhat with the type of
transmission, type of clutch, type of racing, and life expectancy of
the gears. A good knowledge of what happens and how it happens inside the transmission should improve the driver's performance. The
perfect driver would be able to shift quite well—up or down—
without using the clutch at all, by carefully synchronizing rpm and
shifting speed. In fact, many *im*perfect drivers can do it fairly well,
but the clutch pedal provides a margin for error. The wide-open-
throttle power shift may be a shade faster for a few drag-strip runs,
but it doesn't promote longevity in a long road race. The shock on
the driveline is far greater than ordinary racing loads, and the engine
has a tendency to over-rev by a few thousand rpm in that brief disconnected instant. As was mentioned in Chapter 5, early downshifting may reduce the load on the brakes, but it upsets the brake
balance and causes other unnecessary stresses. Stress reversal in the
driveline adds to heat input and almost doubles the total stress input.
In addition, it is easy to downshift too early, causing the engine to
over-rev with low cylinder pressures—a sure means of destruction. In
some cases it may be most practical to downshift by two gears at
once—after braking—so the linkage should have a definite reverse
lockout.

Even with the best of assembly and driving care, a gearbox and/or
differential can still self-destruct from inadequate lubrication or cooling. Ordinary gear lube isn't good enough for the extreme contact
pressures and speeds in racing. Racing lubricants have additives to
take the higher pressures and to help reduce foaming. A gearbox
which is 95 percent efficient will still have to absorb 5 percent of the
power it transmits—often more than 30 horsepower. That should
give some indication of the cooling required. If the oil temperature ever gets much over 240 degrees, an oil cooler will be necessary.
Otherwise, natural air circulation may be adequate. It also may help a

great deal to break in new gears with less than racing loads, especially hypoid differential gears. A final detail point is that high temperature does increase performance up to a point by reducing the lubricant viscosity, so it may be an advantage to start a race with pre-warmed fluids.

DIFFERENTIAL THEORY AND HARDWARE

The purpose and operation of differentials ought to be well known already, but their application to total vehicle dynamics, especially in racing, is still debatable. Considering the torque that must be transmitted while a vehicle is cornering hard, some sort of control is necessary to limit or prevent inside wheelspin. The most common methods can be broken down into the locked or locking type of differential and the friction limited-slip type. Either type will allow greater acceleration out of a turn, although both of them have a number of stability advantages and disadvantages. The open differential can't be faulted in this respect, as it always provides perfectly balanced thrust forces between left and right tires, and it limits the severity of rear cornering breakaway by reducing thrust losses on the outside tire.

Straight line stability is a relatively minor problem on a race track, but even there a locked or limited slip differential can cause instability. For example, suppose one driving wheel suddenly loses thrust traction on gravel, water, or oil—or in the worst case, due to a broken axle. The remaining forward thrust at the other tire will have such a tremendous leverage about the center of gravity that it will be practically impossible to react fast enough to keep the car from spinning. At best, it steers the car toward the more slippery surface. Then there is cornering stability, which if not reduced by a locked axle, will at least have more sudden breakaway characteristics at the rear under acceleration. In addition, some types of differentials have a relatively uneven force balancing mechanism, and can develop stick-slip or chatter in a corner, which will cause variations in the thrust at left and right wheels—an unstabilizing effect at a critical time. The limited-slips are worst in this respect, while a fully locked differential will allow a constant—if not always desirable—balance under most conditions. Still, if one wheel gets on some slippery stuff, the longitudinal forces will be unbalanced, but then the lateral consequences are far greater anyway.

One of the most popular types of locking differential in racing has overrunning clutches for each axle (Weismann and Detroit Locker),which allow either wheel to overspeed the differential. This is supposed to allow a speed or distance difference between the inside and outside tires in a turn. It works perfectly in very sharp turns at low speeds—say in the pits—but an analysis of vehicle dynamics gives some doubt whether it has any effect at all on a high-speed race track.

First, the theoretical overspeed at the outside tire is inversely proportional to the radius of a turn. For example, if the vehicle track width is 5 feet and the turn radius is 100 feet (a tight corner in racing) then the outside tire will need 5/100 or 5 percent greater speed than the inside tire. On a 500-foot-radius turn, the overspeed will only be 1 percent greater. But as was explained in Chapter 2, tires already have a slip rate when generating thrust. This slip rate, especially under hard cornering, will be over 5 percent, so it appears that the high-speed cornering overspeed required is negligible. If it were true that thrust was directly proportional to the net percentage of slip, then the inside tire would always generate more thrust, producing an understeering force which would decrease with increasing speed. However, lateral load transfer seems to have an overriding effect. It would take a computer or a great deal of experimentation to separate all the effects.

Braking stability should also be considered in the selection of a differential type. Only a locked differential will positively prevent one-wheel lockup at the rear, although other vehicle stability interactions may be more important to handling during braking. At any rate, the overrunning clutch differential appears to have the fewest of all the possible evils.

Lubrication and cooling are as important to differentials as transmissions, so the same advice applies. But a differential can have other friction effects to raise its temperature even more. The limited-slip types are especially prone to high temperatures, and if over-worked, can literally burn themselves out and revert to a relatively open differential. Even some locking differentials with friction over-running clutches can slip, which causes abnormally fast wear—especially on really low-traction surfaces.

If locking differentials seem to be the best choice, they are also rel-atively expensive and perhaps not even available for some off-brand race cars. In such a case, a solidly locked differential is a fairly good second choice in any race car with enough power to spin the inside rear wheel. If the rules don't allow a locked differential, the spider gears may be accidentally buggered until they work poorly, or a limited-slip differential can be tightened by wedging the pre-load springs almost up to a solid stack. The quickest—and most easily re-versible—method of locking a differential is to replace the spider gears with ones that have been specially machined or welded solid. On some limited-slip differentials the easiest method is to weld the friction clutch packs together on one side. But the cleanest technique is to replace the entire spider gear cage with a specially machined solid spool, which also reduces weight and rotating inertia.

DRIVELINE

As simple as they seem, driveshafts and universal joints are such im-portant links in the chain that they shouldn't be neglected. Any excess torsional strength here is well spent, as failures are usually sudden and total. Assuming that the shaft has been designed to take all the torque the tires can put to the ground—with continual stress reversals—race preparation can be concentrated on the universal joints and splines.

One last word about the drive shaft: it spins at engine rpm in high gear and any imbalance can be significant. Its trueness is fairly im-portant also, so it should be checked for runout before balancing.

There are four types of universal joints common to race cars: the cross-and-trunion, the Rzeppa caged-ball, the ball and trunion pot, and the rubber donut. The most common and inexpensive is the cross-and-trunion, which unfortunately has the least constant velocity in shafts which meet at any angle. However, if the trunions at each end of a shaft are perfectly parallel and the driving and driven shafts are perfectly parallel, then only the intermediate shaft will have rotational velocity fluctuations with each revolution. Constant-velocity universal joints eliminate this problem entirely and are mandatory for large angular deflections. The smoothness, stress, and power loss will all be optimized by laying out all joints to have the minimum angular deflection at the suspension height which corresponds to maximum acceleration. Sliding splines are usually necessary with universal joints that have no provision for changing length. These splines have tremendous torques acting on them when they most need to slide, so they should be well lubricated with the best grease available.

AUTOMATIC TRANSMISSIONS

Although automatic transmissions in road racing came and went with the Chaparrals, they still offer some potential advantages to race cars and are at least worth a mention. The advantages are all fairly obvious, with the primary one being ease of driving, so more concentration can be put into aiming the car. That assumes a fully automatic shift, however, when in fact all of the Chaparral shifting was done manually without a clutch. Depending on the system, it is also possible to have faster, more reliable, and less damaging shifts. At one time it was felt to be an advantage to have the increased torque multiplication capability of a converter at lower rpm. With the increasingly broad torque curves of larger displacement engines, however, there is less to be gained over the ratios available in a five-speed manual transmission. And finally, overrunning clutches or automatic downshifting can reduce the upsetting influences on ideal brake balance.

The greatest disadvantages are all related to weight and inefficiency. Even if fewer mechanical ratios are required, a torque converter is quite a bit heavier than an equivalent clutch. That, combined with the greater diameter necessary, means that rotational inertia will be even worse. But the most insurmountable problem is the horsepower loss in the converter, which must be added to the cooling problems and all the ordinary gear efficiency losses. In spite of the greatest care in precision design and assembly of a converter, it will still have a loss of about 3 percent even at the highest rpm where its efficiency is greatest. With the equality of competition, 3 percent loss in power can make the difference between winning and losing. So an automatic would have to have some other very significant gains elsewhere to make up the difference. At this writing, it looks as though an automatic mechanical clutch ahead of the ordinary manual transaxle may be the next stage in development.

10
FRAME AND BODY ∘∘∘∘∘∘∘∘∘∘∘∘∘∘∘

Few racers build their own chassis from the ground up. Not only is it an inefficient use of time, energy, and dollars, but it can be rather dangerous for someone without a lot of experience in either engineering stress analysis or first-hand race car chassis construction. A thorough strength analysis during the design stage is an incredibly complex task, even for an engineer with the most sophisticated computers. Even if it were economically feasible for a limited-production race car, the input loads would have to be estimated or determined by survey at all race tracks. In addition, an arbitrary safety factor would be needed for collisions or off-course excursions. Fortunately, most existing race car chassis are fairly strong, but at that they are designed and built primarily from intuition and experience. But even with a strong and rigid vehicle, there are a number of possible modifications that the racer should be aware of.

MATERIALS

Before getting into the actual hardware of frames, bodies, and components, it is necessary to consider some of the basic structural materials as they relate to racing. With all materials there is a wide range of costs per pound, ranging from reasonable for low-grade steels to astronomical for titanium and pure filament fibers. However, for one unit of anything, especially a race car, the cost of a material is usually insignificant compared to the cost of labor in design and fabrication. On the other hand, once a component or an entire race car is constructed and seems to be too heavy, the cost of labor may prevent switching to exotic lightweight materials. There has to be some consideration of the cost involved in reducing weight through a material change, up to the point where it becomes inefficient in dollars per pound of weight removed. And without an extensive test program, an engineer can't determine the precise strength requirements for a component anyway. At any rate, material costs vary so much with purchased condition or configuration, and with economic situations, that they won't be considered here.

Due to the basic nature of racing, all structural material properties must be related to density, or the material weight per volume required. And yet, for any comparison, material properties vary considerably with different compositions and hardnesses. The following table indicates general ranges for the most common race car materials:

	Alloy steel	Aluminum	Fiberglass	Magnesium	Titanium
Density (pounds/cubic inch)	0.3	0.1	0.05–0.08	0.07	0.15
Ultimate tensile strength (1000 pounds/square inch)	50–200	20–80	40–100	30–40	100–160
Strength/Density ratio ($\div 1000$)	200–700	200–800	500–2000	400–600	700–1000
Stiffness (1,000,000 pounds/ square inch)	29	10.5	3–4	6.5	16
Stiffness/Density ratio ($\div 1,000,000$)	100	105	40–80	95	105
Formability	good	good	excellent	poor	good
Machinability	excellent	excellent		excellent	fair
Weldability	excellent	good		poor	poor

Table 4. Characteristics of race car materials

Of course, with all the different compositions available in each material, the selection will be difficult without a comprehensive knowledge of component requirements and other specific material properties. Engineering assistance can save a lot of money over selecting simply light weight or a name with a nice sound. It is hard to beat the security per pound of using whatever material a component was designed around. Still, a few generalizations can be made about application to the specific area of racing.

Steel selection for race cars is usually limited to three common alloys. Common carbon steels (1010 to 1020) are inexpensive and easily fabricated but have a relatively low ultimate strength. More expensive chrome-moly steels (4130) and nickel-chrome-moly (4340) can be heat-treated to the highest tensile strength of almost any material. Heat-treating is mandatory for highly stressed components such as springs and anti-roll bars, and normalizing, or stress-relieving, is recommended for all welded parts. Each of the hundreds of race car components will have different requirements that should be matched to a particular alloy or heat treatment by an engineer or experienced fabricator. The most important considerations are usually: stiffness, ultimate strength, yield strength and failure mode, fatigue life, and formability. In addition, it may be necessary to consider high temperatures, wear, and cost. Armco Steel once sponsored a race car project to demonstrate the uses of steel alloys in racing, and some of the data was presented in SAE Paper No. 700056. The large steel companies can provide invaluable assistance through consultation and handbooks on the latest alloys.

Aluminum alloys are even more diverse in their properties and ease of fabrication. Alcoa has a series of handbooks for the engineer to use in alloy selection and component design. The same considerations for racing apply as with steel alloys except that temperatures may be more of a problem, especially in welding. The more common alloy designations and their chief attributes are: 3003—inexpensive and easily fabricated; 2024—strong and formable; 6061—more easily welded; 7075—highest strength and most easily machined. Letters and numbers following the material designation, such as T3 to T6, indicate material temper or heat treatment.

Fiberglass materials have just as wide a range in composition, especially since both the resin and the glass-fiber cloth can be varied independently. The choice of resin is usually between a polyester and an epoxy. The primary advantages of polyester are low cost and less toxicity for ease of construction. On the other hand, epoxy is so much better in strength, durability, adhesion, and temperature resistance that it is usually worth the added cost and effort in race car components. In either case, the greatest strength-to-weight ratio in the finished component comes from using the minimum percentage of resin that will hold the glass fibers together. The range can vary from 60 percent in the chopped-filament spray-ups to 40 percent in hand layups, or 30 percent in pre-impregnated cloths.

Due to all the aerospace applications of fiberglass, there is as wide a range in cloths as there is in resins. For common body components, ordinary woven boat-cloth is inexpensive, but for ultimate strength and light weight, the more sophisticated materials are worth their extra cost. If all the stresses in a structural component have been carefully anlysed, it may be best to use a non-woven, unidirectional cloth with all the fibers oriented in the optimum directions. The extreme example is pressure containers, which may be wound with a single continuous filament before the resin is applied. However, these techniques can only be applied to simple shapes and small components that can be mounted on a mandrel and/or cured in an oven. Most of the "pre-preg" cloths require external heat to cure them, and an oven provides an evenness that is lacking with heat guns or lamps.

The greatest advantage of fiberglass is the ease of forming it into large, smooth, compound body shapes. And when the surfaces are too large to support themselves, it is relatively easy to reinforce them with sandwich panels of foam or honeycomb or with integral ribs or stiffeners.

Other plastics are frequently used in race cars, although seldom for structural purposes. Urethane foams are available in either flexible form, as in bump-stops, or in rigid form, to be used as a stiffening filler or impact absorber. It is sometimes easiest to buy the foam as a two-part liquid, which foams up to fill a cavity when the two are mixed. Thermoplastic materials aren't normally used because of their

Honeycomb materials: as a sandwich with light alloy faces, and as a flexible core which can be bonded between fiberglass faces in compound curves.

sensitivity to heat and their general lack of structural strength. The exceptions are acrylics (Plexiglas), used for transparent windscreens, and polycarbonates (Lexan) for spoilers.

Magnesium is most common in racing wheels and other castings where a large given volume is required to resist deflections or buckling. In that case, its density being 70 percent of aluminum overrules disadvantages such as higher cost and casting porosity problems. Since most racers will merely buy components already produced in magnesium, it doesn't matter that it is extremely difficult to form or weld. And while it isn't easy to ignite, once temperatures get high enough it will burn intensely—especially the fine particles from machining operations.

Titanium is the strongest metal available in absolute strength per pound. In addition, it has about the best fatigue resistance of all racing materials and maintains its strength at very high temperatures. This makes it ideal for reciprocating engine parts and exhaust headers. Unfortunately, it is practically impossible to cast and very difficult to machine, weld, or lubricate, which limits its usefulness primarily to forged connecting rods. It has been used for race car chassis and suspensions, but most often only when cost was absolutely no object.

Spin-offs from the aerospace industry are making other forms and combinations of materials available to racing people. Where large flat areas are required to support a lot of weight without buckling, as in fuel cell containers or aerodynamic surfaces, metal or plastic sandwich materials are being used. These can be in any combination of materials that can be welded or bonded together. The most familiar combinations are probably fiberglass skins over a core of urethane foam or aluminum skins over a core of aluminum honeycomb. The chief drawbacks are that they are difficult to join at their edges and practically impossible to form into compound curves.

The last material to be mentioned is almost beyond consideration at this point. The failure point of any material is usually determined by inescapable impurities in the composition. But if the material is literally *grown,* molecule by molecule, in an inert atmosphere, then absolutely pure fibers or whiskers can be created. These pure filaments have proven to have strength-to-weight ratios far greater than even titanium. Of course, their cost is also comparatively great. But when formed into components, such as a replacement for glass fibers in an epoxy binder, their strength and stiffness is incredible. As material production increases and race car construction costs rise, they could become practical.

TYPES OF FRAMES

The simple ladder frame is so poor in torsional stiffness per pound that only tubular space frames and monocoque construction can be considered for race cars. While popular choice has fluctuated between the two for years, it is probable that the best solution is a combination of the two. Monocoque, or stressed skin construction, is most efficient where large areas carry a distributed load, such as aerodynamic surfaces and fuel containers, or where the skin serves a double purpose as structure and body. On the other hand, a tubular space frame is most efficient where there are a few specific highly-loaded points to be connected, such as engine mounts and suspension brackets. Other important considerations include space limitations, access, ease of construction and repair, and cost. So the choice between monocoque and space frames is not an "either-or" based on stiffness versus weight. The selection should be based on particular require-

A monocoque chassis with large cross-sections provides a good rigidity/weight ratio, but doesn't easily accept "point" suspension loads.

ments in each particular area. The choice is further confused or assisted by the popular use of the engine and transaxle as a structural member.

The primary requirements for a race car frame are ultimate strength, or resistance to structural failures, and torsional rigidity. Other problems common to production cars, such as beaming rigidity and vibration frequencies, are seldom a problem. By far the most important principle in structural design is that stiffness increases exponentially with increased cross-sectional area. So for given strength requirements and minimum weight, the taller and wider the frame, the better. But since few racers build their own frames anyway, this section will concentrate on improvements and other modifications.

The first step is in knowing how to form and join metals, particularly riveting in the case of monocoque and welding in the case of tubular frames. Durability and safety are so important that only a fabricator familiar with aircraft construction techniques, or perhaps a certified welder, should be allowed to build or modify any critical components. In the search for absolute weight efficiency, the chassis is only as strong as its weakest link—which could be one bad weld. For those fabricators with some experience who *must* work on their own race cars, Carroll Smith gives many important construction tips on riveting and welding in *Sports Car Graphic,* July 1970. Otherwise, the best bet is a quick course in aircraft fabrication or at least a handbook on the subject.

STRENGTH

Before a chassis can be modified, there must be some means of determining how strong it is already. Early in the original construction stage or at any time thereafter, the bare chassis and suspension components can be loaded and twisted while deflections are measured. The maximum twist load that a race car is likely to be subjected to will be the entire front weight carried by one front wheel, which may then be accelerated upward at 2 to 3 g's due to bump loads. That is multiplied times the chassis tread width to get the torque in pounds-feet. With a torsional test setup as described in Chapter 13, the chassis can be stressed and measured, and if the angular deflection is excessive, the frame or suspension should be reinforced. For light road-racing cars, 3000 pounds-feet per degree of twist is a nice ballpark figure. However, if there is an easily-met minimum weight, more is better. If the front wheels seem to "patter" excessively over rough sections of track, regardless of shock absorber settings, then the chassis may need more stiffness to resist torsional vibrations.

When the chassis is bolted to the floor or a bedplate, and weights or other large, measurable forces are available (such as hydraulic or pneumatic cylinders), it is also quite educational to stress the suspension. Rough calculations can be used to estimate the input forces due to tire traction in acceleration, cornering, and braking, and the loads can be simulated by forces acting on torque arms bolted to the hubs. With enough hardware, an accurate simulation can be made of combinations such as increased vertical load, and braking and cornering forces on the outside front suspension. The corresponding deflections or deformations are likely to be frightening enough to motivate

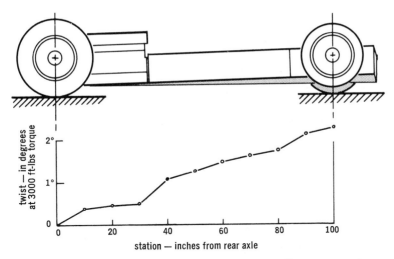

Figure 26. Chassis Torque Deflection Curve

stronger reinforcements. It isn't unusual to see the suspension and/or frame deflect by some degrees under realistic loads.

A great advantage to such static testing is that the weakest locations can be pinpointed (see Fig. 26) rather than having to make intuitive or massive corrections. By using a rigid base surface and a number of dial indicators, it is possible to localize the major sources of deflection and to evaluate the corresponding reinforcements.

Once this setup and development is completed, it isn't hard to go to the next step—durability testing. If there is some means of continuously varying the loads, a representative frame and suspension can have racing loads cycled into it until the weakest link breaks. Then it can be repaired and cycled again until something else breaks—and on and on until its strength and durability are well known quantities. Then an all-new chassis can rise from the ashes. The cost of such a test program may seem to be out of the question, but it will inevitably save weight and avoid failures, and perhaps even help avoid a serious track accident.

In addition to major structural changes, it will frequently be necessary to add or alter brackets and other miscellaneous attachments. A

Chevrolet Engineering test facilities which can rapidly stress-cycle a bare chassis and driveline for durability—in this case, a lightweight Stingray. (*GM Photograph*)

failure here may not affect the safety of the vehicle as a whole, but it can still cause the loss of a race in many cases. It is important to remember that all supports must not only carry some static component weight, but that there will be frequent high g loadings from bumps, and there will be continual high frequency vibrations caused by the engine. Exhaust systems and supports are particularily prone to failure from high temperatures and vibration fatigue. The best insurance is to make all brackets as stiff as possible with adequate triangulation, and to feed their loads into major chassis components.

The best race car chassis may be designed very close to its ultimate limit of failure. As a chassis gets older and gets handed down and raced over a number of years, many changes take place. Metal fatigue may begin to affect chassis components that are not easily removed and inspected, and a suspension bracket is as important as the suspension itself. Then too, racers tend to update older cars with larger tires and engines. So as the chassis gets older and weaker, it is also subjected to greater forces from increased weight and cornering loads. A car's weight should never increase merely by the added weight of a heavier component; there should be a proportional increase in the strength (and weight) of supporting structure.

Large production cars modified for racing usually don't have critical strength problems. Still, they aren't designed for the kind of loads that can be generated by increased tire capabilities, and they are apt to have an undesirable amount of flex. The most common problem is how to remove unnecessary structural weight and yet add back the minimum amount needed to increase torsional rigidity.

So much can be done to a passenger car body and frame that it may be fastest to start with a new unleaded and unpainted shell. The first step, when allowed by the rules, is to acid-dip all non-structural components—and even all structural components that will later be reinforced by a mandatory roll cage. There are a couple of aerospace companies in the Los Angeles area that have the capacity to dip complete full-size automobile bodies, and they have a lot of experience at it. The operation takes some care in planning for the amount of metal that can be safely removed without weakening large panels too much, and it may require extensive masking for those areas where no metal removal is desired. It is also somewhat expensive, but it is a very rapid way to cut the weight by many hundreds of pounds. Even when the minimum race weight is specified by the rules and is easy to meet, acid-dipping is still a worthwhile process. By removing the maximum amount from the front and top of the body, it becomes possible to replace the weight in ballast where it is more useful. It may be possible to move the center of gravity down and rearward by inches by the careful placement of hundreds of pounds of ballast.

A lot of other components can be weight-reduced also, including subframes, substructure, suspension hardware, and even the engine block and heads. Critical components should be acid-dipped with care. The only time it can be done at all is when they are later reinforced by a more efficient use of material.

Whether dipped or not, all spot-welded body seams, and all intermittent welding on frame rails, should be completely seam-welded into one rigid unit. The factory doesn't do it for cost reasons, but racing demands it for the added strength and durability. In the case of previously used components, sandblasting is not only necessary to clean the metal for welding, but is an alternate means of weight reduction for non-visible panels.

Cast-iron engine blocks and heads have been acid-dipped with some success, but the lost weight is hardly worth the effort involved. Usually a finished block must have all its machined surfaces masked off before dipping, including bores, bearing surfaces, and all flat mounting faces and threaded holes. An alternate procedure is to start with an unmachined raw casting and have it completely machined after dipping. In either case, there is always the unknown question of durability from reduced wall thicknesses.

The first and major reinforcement to a production chassis is the roll cage. Most race sanctioning bodies specify minimum requirements in terms of tubing size and locations and amount of triangulation. NASCAR probably has the safest and most elaborate roll cage specifications, which are good to follow in any instance where the weight is no great penalty. But for lighter cars on slower tracks, the SCCA specifications are relatively safe.

As long as the roll cage has to be there for safety's sake, it might as well serve some structural purpose. As far as the rules go, all it has to be is a protective box around the driver. But by fully triangulating the box for stiffness, and connecting it to the front and rear spring mounts, it can become a fully adequate space frame in itself. Some racing sedans would probably be just as strong with none of the production body components or frame members at all. The body tends to be no more than an easily replaced external skin.

Where some attempt is made to maintain the original body and frame—because the rules demand it or cost is a problem—then the cage will have to fit whatever exists. The major points to be connected by the roll cage tubing are: front spring and shock mounts, engine mounts, front subframe mounts, and all rear leaf spring and shock mounts. In the case of unit-construction bodies, it will be nec-

A good sedan roll cage may have enough tubes, cross-bracing, and triangulation to be an adequate space-frame in itself.

essary to have reinforcement plates to spread the load on the sheet metal wherever a tube is to be welded in. Otherwise, in the case of separate frames, the cage must be welded to the frame itself. If the body normally rests on rubber insulators, it will add to chassis stiffness if they are removed and the body is welded or bolted rigidly to the frame. If the engine is not used as a structural component, it is probably better to keep it on rubber mounts to absorb some of the vibration.

The best time to open up the wheel wells and fenders for greater tire clearance is during construction. Tire sizes will often become larger than anticipated and it can be very difficult to relocate roll cage tubes which may be in the way. Also, cutting and rewelding all that sheet metal can have a disastrous effect on body stiffness, which can be corrected with properly located roll cage tubes. The same is true

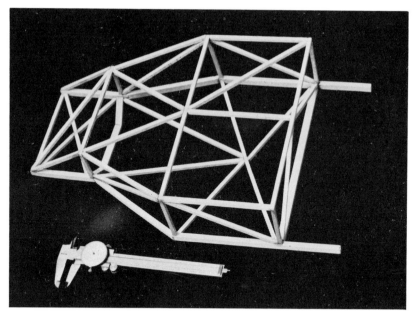

This balsa wood model of a sedan subframe can be qualitatively evaluated for rigidity per pound with various combinations of bracing.

for suspension travel clearances, where lowering the chassis creates some interference with the existing frame. There can never be too much suspension clearance—until the frame or body hits the ground.

Finally, all that roll cage material can protect a lot of other valuable things in a collision besides the driver. For safety, the fuel cell should be well surrounded, and for insurance it helps to have the engine room somewhat enclosed also. Any serious accident will probably tear off the wheels and suspension and a lot of sheet metal, but everything else should be salvageable.

If it isn't obvious, any rectangular arrangement of reinforcing structure is very inefficient in terms of stiffness per pound. There are very few places in a race car where full triangulation of all members is impossible. It is not too practical to have a diagonal tube crossing the windshield, and it will be necessary to leave a space up front for engine removal—although bolt-in diagonals are sometimes used. If there is any question about optimum tube locations, it is fairly easy to make small test models out of balsa wood. These models can be loaded or twisted by hand and measured for deflection with a dial gauge. Making a number of configurations and comparing their stiffness per pound will at least give a relative value for different tube arrangements.

On the subject of models, it is possible to get far more accurate data from small models, which can be scaled up to the final chassis. Properties of metal components in full scale can be duplicated by the properties of certain plastics in smaller-scale thicknesses. Steel, for example, can be simulated by the use of clear, rigid polyvinyl-chloride-acetate (PVC-A), which can be easily fabricated by thermo-forming and welding. It is possible to fabricate a perfect scale model of a proposed chassis, perform small-scale tests for strength, deflections, and vibration frequencies, and then accurately scale the data up to the actual chassis. The automobile industry commonly does this with complex unit-body designs, and it is a simple operation for much more straightforward race car chassis. It takes some complex

Stress, deflection, and vibration data on a chassis can be accurately scaled up from models in PVC plastic, such as this 1/4 scale 1967 Camaro. (*GM Photograph*)

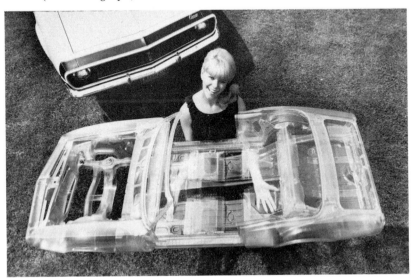

mathematics to make accurate scale factors, but the process is still valuable even for qualitative evaluations. Elliott, in SAE Paper No. 710262, goes into more detail. The effort spent in building models of a proposed chassis could save a lot of expensive rebuilding or reinforcing in the final product.

Race car bodies are primarily an aerodynamic consideration, and better covered in that chapter. But they tend to make up such a large part of a race car that they should also be considered structurally. As long as a body has to exist for aerodynamic reasons or rule requirements, it might as well serve another purpose as a structural member whenever possible. Assuming that the final external shape is resolved in original design and won't have to be experimented with or changed, the only restrictions are due to access. Unfortunately, practically every enclosed space on a race car will require access at some time or other, so it has to be a matter of compromises. At any rate, locations requiring only occasional access, such as over fuel tank bladders or the pedal areas, can be taken care of by using structural cover plates.

At the very least, bodies should use their skins efficiently enough so a minimum of frame structure is necessary to support them. Downward air loads are hopefully great enough to require a lot of strength also, and the lifting forces due to negative air pressures shouldn't be ignored either. With some forethought, a fiberglass body skin can be designed with integral stiffeners and a continuous shape that is totally self-supporting. And finally, even if the body is strong enough in itself, it had better be attached with some care. It is nice to be able to get a panel or body off in a hurry to make repairs, but not if an aerodynamic surface can come loose at high speed. The loss of bodywork has had fatal consequences in racing—not to mention all the lost races it has caused. With the magnitude of downforces that are being generated, the strength of body panels can be every bit as critical as suspension components.

11

SAFETY ∘∘∘∘∘∘∘∘∘∘∘∘∘∘∘∘∘∘∘∘∘∘∘∘∘∘∘∘∘∘∘∘∘∘∘∘∘∘

Race car safety is a responsibility that tends to be left up to the sanctioning bodies. Every racer's first consideration is simply to win, and the thought of something going wrong, or of an accident, is usually so remote that few are prepared for it. Even when it is considered, not many racers are anxious to sacrifice weight—much less money—for safety equipment that gives no improvement in performance and will only be put to use one time. But safety involves more than protection in case of an accident. An equally important aspect is avoidance of the accident in the first place. Accident avoidance is something that means money in the bank, by protecting the car investment and insuring a finish. Racing is an inherently risky business, but the risks can be greatly reduced by taking certain precautions and *knowing* things that are easy to check.

ACCIDENT AVOIDANCE

FASTENERS
The first and most obvious means of accident avoidance is to make sure nothing becomes disconnected or falls off. This requires a good

221

knowledge of fasteners and how to fasten them. Most auto mechanics are familiar with the SAE standards for bolts, which are coded on the bolt head. There is no reason to ever use anything less than a Grade 8 bolt on anything that could cause the loss of a race or loss of the car if it failed. But in addition, better bolt standards are set up by the government: AN specifications for aircraft; and NAS specifications for aerospace. Such bolts are not only of a much higher quality in strength and dimensions but far more expensive and difficult to purchase. However, due to government inefficiency, they are often available at surplus stores at prices usually lower than new SAE bolts. All a mechanic has to do is search through bins with a ruler and a list of the sizes needed. It helps to know the code of designations, but the important considerations of diameter and length are obvious—keeping in mind that AN/NAS bolts have a shorter thread length so that the threads never carry shear loads. Bolts designed primarily for shear have thinner heads, and in many cases the heads come pre-drilled for safety wiring. NAS 12-point bolt heads indicate extremely high-strength bolts that will outlast just about anything they could be attached to. Then there are also titanium bolts, which are just as strong and yet will save some weight, but which are seldom worth it for their tendency to gall and corrode—and their expense.

Racers who know (accurately) what loads are to be carried by specific bolts can also save weight by not using unnecessarily large diameters. Ultimate tensile strengths vary from 125,000 psi for AN bolts to 160,000 psi for NAS bolts. It is a simple matter to divide the load by the strength to get optimum bolt cross-section area, even if it isn't easy to anticipate exactly what the real loads are going to be, due to accelerations, shocks, and vibrations. It takes a complicated analysis with a lot of other considerations, so a large margin of safety should be allowed.

The strongest bolt is worthless if the nut can't be kept on. Racing vibrations and fluctuations in stress will inevitably loosen any nut that isn't locked on in some way. Lock washers are relatively undependable and have a tendency to tear up the light alloy materials in race cars. The most familiar lock nuts are the type with integral plastic rings which are usually available at surplus stores. They come in fine and coarse threads and even half-heights for shear-only applications. Most can be reused many times before the nut can be freely turned by hand. For temperatures over 250 degrees it will be necessary to use all-metal lock nuts, which may not be reusable, or castellated nuts with cotter pins. For absolute security, and a constant visual indication that everything is tight, it is hard to beat safety-wiring. It may even be the only answer in the case of bolts in tapped holes. After the wire is threaded and twisted, it should be wound slightly clockwise around the bolthead or nut before anchoring.

Tension bolts must be carefully pre-stressed with a torque wrench. For really critical applications, such as connecting rod bolts, it is far more accurate to gauge the tension by measuring bolt elongation with a micrometer, but the torque wrench is otherwise more convenient. The problem is that bolt torque is strongly affected by friction at the threads and bearing surfaces. This can be minimized by using washers under each bolt head and nut and by lubricating the surfaces with an anti-seize compound or moly grease. Proper bolt torques for each type and size and proper torquing techniques are usually provided with torque wrenches.

When all else fails, there is always Loctite, an essential but expensive series of liquid resins used to lock any two tightly-fitting fasteners together. It requires careful pre-cleaning and application but is self-hardening and stronger than most lock nuts. In addition, it prevents fluid leakage and corrosion. There are many grades and types for applications from locking to sealing to bonding, and for other cases of excess clearance such as bearing fits. However, since it is expensive and takes some time to apply correctly, other locking methods are more convenient.

Other fasteners may have to be released during a race, for access or to replace a damaged body component. A number of quick-release pins or fasteners are available, but the most common are the familiar hood tension pins with a wire locking clip. Where removable shear pins are required, as in hinges or on highly-stressed components, ball-lock pins, or pip-pins, are the best answer. These are hollow pins with button-operated detent balls to hold them in place. Because they

A good example of safety fasteners, including the Dzuz fastener (top right), ball-lock pin (bottom right), lock nut, and safety wire.

are hollow, shear strength is a little less than a bolt, although they are usually made from high-grade steels. Flush quick-release fasteners such as the Dzuz fastener are inconspicuous and neat but have less holding strength and can be difficult to operate in a real emergency. They should be used only for non-critical, non-aerodynamic body surfaces. For the same reasons, all body panels should have edges protected so that the airstream can't get under them and rip them off. If overlapping edges can't be arranged correctly, it may be necessary to seal the gaps with racer's tape.

INSPECTION

Since the nature of race cars is to have all components as light-weight and structurally efficient as possible, frequent inspection for potential failure is mandatory. Given a high-power microscope and enough time, a mechanic could go over every component inch by inch to find beginning stress cracks. Due to similar aircraft requirements, however, fast and sensitive crack-detecting systems are available at reasonable prices. But first, the surfaces of all critical components should be carefully prepared and cared for. In initial fabrication, large radii and careful polishing (in the direction of stresses) reduces the concentration of stress. In addition, shot-peening increases the ultimate strength by pre-stressing the surface material. From then on, the components should be carefully protected from corrosion, since stress and corrosion contribute to each other.

If there are no obvious surface flaws, there are still three methods of finding any microscopic or invisible imperfections: X-ray, magnetic particle, and dye penetrant inspection. X-ray is relatively expensive and necessary only once, to show up any subsurface flaws, voids, or casting porosity. If it is going to be done, it is best to do it before the raw forging or casting is machined, to save that much expense. But if there is a history of component failures, and the manufacturer doesn't X-ray, it may still be worthwhile to do it after purchase.

Magnetic particle inspection, or Magnaflux, is the most popular technique for finding external flaws, but of course it is only possible with ferrous parts. The component must be removed and cleaned, magnetized in a solution of metal particles and fluorescent dye, and inspected under black light. Any surface cracks or flaws will show up as obvious red lines. All non-ferrous materials such as aluminum and magnesium must be inspected by a dye-penetrant technique such as Zyglo, which is similar except for the magnetization. Portable and inexpensive kits are available which can be used at home. However, professional service is available at any airport large enough to have a good engine rebuilding shop, and some race sanctioning bodies require official inspection certificates for critical components.

The big question is in trying to determine which parts are critical and how often they should be inspected. There are a few life-or-death components on every car, such as axles, hubs, spindles, hub carriers, and steering arms, which could cause a serious accident. But there are other highly-stressed parts, especially in the engine, transmission, and driveline, which would merely cost a lost race and some internal damage. The cost of inspection is insignificant compared to normal teardown time and the potential loss from failure. Where possible, of course, the best practice is to anticipate the potential for failure, and minimize the damage by providing a fail-safe design. The best example of this is dual isolated braking systems. The more a driver knows about the condition of his car, and the care the mechanics are putting into it, the more he can concentrate on the other risks of racing.

DRIVER PROTECTION

When the most careful efforts toward accident avoidance fail and the inevitable accident occurs, the driver is going to be praying for every protection device available. There are so many possible types and combinations of accidents that it is impossible to be prepared for everything. But the driver, engineer, and mechanics should be aware of some of the more likely ones, so they aren't left to the random standards set by sanctioning bodies. Their safety rules are the *minimums* they will allow, and more is always better. In the long run, more protection will even be worth what it may cost in lost performance due to increased weight. In fact, one of the biggest problems in providing accident protection is minimum weight regulations that are too hard to meet. If minimum weights are high enough, everyone can add more protective (and stiffening) structure and better fire prevention equipment with no one at a disadvantage for it.

To understand a total safety system, it is necessary to break an accident down into four common ways a driver can be injured: excessive decelerations, impact with the interior of the car, collapse of the car, and post-crash hazards such as fire or suffocation. Any one of them alone can be fatal, so each one must be anticipated and protective measures taken.

DECELERATION

Healthy humans can survive decelerations of over 40 g's for brief instants under ideal conditions. Using the equation for deceleration versus distance and speed from Chapter 5:

$$g = \frac{(.0334)\ (mph)^2}{(distance)}$$

will show that it is theoretically possible to stay within the 40-g limit at 70 miles per hour if the driver is evenly decelerated in about 4 feet.

This racing seat provides lateral support for left turns. Note the six-point safety harness, and padded head rest with pit radio behind it.

In other words, the driver could walk away from a collision with a concrete abutment at 70 mph if the front of the car could be designed to collapse evenly for those 4 feet. Of course, it isn't easy to provide such ideal collapse, but then it isn't common for drivers to ram walls head-on either. The point is that more available crush distance is a tremendous advantage to survival, especially in glancing blows.

Even at 200 miles per hour, 33 feet of constant deceleration is theoretically survivable, but that is obviously beyond any potential in chassis collapse. Race track owners and race drivers debate the relative value of rigid versus absorbent barriers, and whether the errant race car should carom off or be swallowed by the barrier. Chain link fences have proved to be able to stop light race cars at about the correct rate—with minimal damage to the *car,* much less the driver. But, given the illogic of rigid walls around some race tracks, the chassis designers must provide as much carefully thought-out crush space as is reasonably possible.

A survivable limit of 40 g's assumes that the driver doesn't contact any rigid part of the vehicle interior, which could cause bone breakage or tissue damage. This is the purpose of the seat, seatbelts, helmet, and other padded surfaces. The ideal seat might be something like an astronaut's couch, designed to distribute high g forces evenly over the maximum body area and to enclose the driver as much as possible to prevent undesired motion in any direction. No padding is necessary if the seat contacts only soft fleshy areas, so a perfectly rigid shell could be adequate. Of course, the mounting brackets must be able to handle the forces from a 40-g impact in any direction. It is especially important to have a headrest designed for such impact forces from the rear, and perhaps even from the sides, except for the visibility problems.

RETENTION

Seatbelts are fairly well defined by most racing groups. In any kind of accident in any kind of car, they have proved to increase survivability by at least a factor of ten. The desirability of being thrown free is a total myth from the standpoint of tolerable g's and required deceleration space. The absolute minimum belt standard is a four-point system, and one or two extra crotch belts to prevent submarining may also be necessary. There are even experimental systems that include a helmet-restricting strap. Belt anchorages are critical, in both ultimate strength and the angle of pull on the driver's body. A final precaution is to protect the buckle from accidental snagging, which could release it at the most unfortunate time.

Crash helmets are also closely regulated, but there is some choice as to style. The full-coverage type is superior in every safety consideration, although it is slightly hotter and heavier. That little extra area of fiberglass and padding can save a lot of face from impact or flame. If it seems like a lot of weight to carry in constant high-g corners, then stronger neck muscles or a lateral restraint strap will be necessary. The most valuable and irreplaceable component in any race car is the driver's head. Protection is a bargain at any cost.

The impact-absorbing rigid foam in helmets is a good example for protection in other locations. Soft, flexible foam rubber is totally useless in a race car, since it will bottom from the slightest impact. Foam helmet liners are designed to crush at the optimum rate at high decelerations, and to have *no* rebound, since any rebound would produce further undesirable forces. Therefore, these foams can only be used once. In fact, they may even deteriorate with time and should be replaced or updated every few years. Ideally, the same sort of rigid foam would be used to line every inch of a race car interior. But these potential driver impacts are less understood, so other rigid urethane or styrene foams may be adequate. It may even be worthwhile to surround the entire seat with foamed-in-place polyurethane.

At the very least all rigid metal components should be as far from the driver as possible. Under extreme conditions, seatbelts stretch many inches, allowing the driver to contact ordinarily unreachable surfaces. Similarly, the steering column should be collapsible, or very short, or fitted with universal joints, and it is a good idea to have a rigid foam pad in the center of the wheel.

COLLAPSE

If the driver is not to strike any interior surface of the car, his compartment has to be rigid enough that it doesn't collapse around him. He should also be protected from striking any external surface such as the ground, walls, trees, or other immovable objects. And after the car has stopped completely, it should be possible to remove the driver without special tools or large forces. This is no great problem in large sedans, where roll cages can be designed to withstand incredible impacts and repeated pounding from rollovers and flips. Both NASCAR and SCCA have elaborate specifications for materials that can be used, size of tubing with respect to car weight, fabrication methods, and layout. In addition, restraining nets are required or recommended for the driver's window, to prevent his head and arms from flailing out against something. It has to be an extremely violent or freak impact to critically injure a driver in such a cage.

Open sports cars have traditionally been required to have only a rollover bar or hoop behind the driver. This is relatively inexpensive and simple to construct, but it ignores the possibility of frontal impacts. Recently, wiser drivers have been equipping open sports cars with full roll cages forward over the windscreen. Any disadvantage in weight can be more than made up for in reduced chassis structure required, if the cage is also used for structural stiffness.

For some obscure or commercial reasons, race sanctioning groups don't seem to care as much for the lives of drivers in lightweight race cars. They still have good standards for rollover hoops to protect the driver's head, but they ignore the mass damage possible from any other sort of impact. A frontal or diagonal collision, or an end-over flip at any speed, almost guarantees severe injury or death. There have been instances of drivers taking it upon themselves to install cages or at least long diagonal braces forward of the cockpit—as is common in dirt-track sprint cars. But they haven't become popular yet, perhaps because of the stigma of overcaution or the imagined disadvantages in weight or a higher center of gravity. Without such equipment it is not unusual for the entire front chassis of a race car to be ripped off in a collision, exposing most of the lower half of a driver's body. The only alternative to better protective structures being required is for someone to win a few races with a roll cage in his formula car—or to walk away from a violent accident in one. The best that can be said for the safety of sophisticated monocoque formula car chassis is that they may distribute the load well as they collapse about a driver's body, and they are relatively easy to tear apart to remove the remains.

FIRE

When an accident occurs, there is still avoidance and protection to consider in the case of fire. With the severity of impacts, the amount of fuel carried, and the lightness of race car structures, a post-crash fire is almost inevitable. But aerospace technology and lots of experience have produced some very effective avoidance and protection systems.

The fuel cell has probably saved more lives than any other safety device in a race car except for seat belts. Only its cost prevents it from being a valuable item in passenger cars. The flexible bladders themselves are so well specified and standardized by sanctioning groups that all a racer has to do is select one to fit his capacity, filling, and fuel requirements. If a standard volume or shape won't work, they can easily be custom-fitted to any application—at a much higher price. Most bladders are filled with blocks of a porous foam,

A destruction test of a 22-gallon fuel container, which left the bladder intact. The inner foam shows where the filler plate was removed.

which reduce the interior volume by about 5 percent and should be considered when capacity is marginal. The foam has practically no effect on fuel movement (as demonstrated by the fact that a 22-gallon bladder can be filled in 4 seconds), so it will have little effect on slosh or leakage if the tank is torn open. The primary purpose of the foam is to prevent explosion in the bladder by slowing down the flame front, but it also helps hold the bladder in shape even when it is empty.

Although all bladders are practically crushproof, leakproof, and explosion proof, they can still be cut or punctured by a sharp object, so they need to be enclosed by a metal container. Most regulations require a minimum of 20-gauge steel or .060-inch aluminum for the container, with some sort of double-wall honeycomb or sandwich metal being even more efficient. As long as that material is required, it ought to be possible to use it as stiffening structure, although it isn't wise to use it as an external skin which is highly vulnerable to impact.

Even with the best fuel bladder and container, it is still possible to lose the fuel through other broken lines or openings. For all race cars

The typical dry-break fueling system for sedans and sports cars includes the spring-loaded receptacle on the car (top), and matching nozzles on the 11-gallon filler cans with vented handles (below).

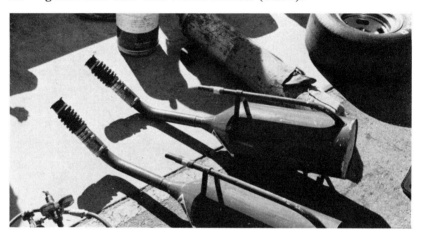

that don't ordinarily make a pitstop for fuel, a flush positive-locking or screw-type filler cap is best. Where long filler necks are required for fast fuel stops, a one-way check valve or flapper valve is mandatory, in case the neck gets ripped off. Some racing rules even require dry-break connections which prevent spillage from either the filler neck or the fueling cans. Fuel tank vents can be a bigger problem. They have to: allow air to enter as fuel is consumed, let air out in a hurry as the tank is being filled, not dump any overflow fuel in a dangerous location, and have a check valve to prevent drainage if the car is upside down. The best and most expensive solution is a portable, transparent overflow catch can to match another dry-break connection on the vent.

The fuel pumps and lines are just as important to safety. The lines should be routed in the most protected locations and perhaps even be shielded by heavy metal tubing. In the most violent crashes, a line will inevitably be pulled apart, so it is a good idea to have the pumps as close to the tanks as possible, to block the flow when the electricity goes off. NASCAR requires mechanical fuel pumps, however, perhaps with the reasoning that when the engine blows or dies, the pump stops automatically. It may be possible to use fail-safe line fittings which "break-shut," but they aren't currently available for race cars.

When something does break and fuel starts escaping, a master circuit breaker may help prevent a grand flame-up. This switch cuts *all* electricity from the battery and is marked and located for easy access by course workers. It might even be handy to have a second switch in the line within reach of the driver, in case help is late in arriving or the driver can anticipate the impact. To further prevent sparks—and acid spillage—the battery should be enclosed in an all-plastic marine battery box, and the battery cables should be well protected or shielded.

When every avoidance measure fails and the car does go up in flames, it is too late to wish for more protection equipment. Sometimes a race track fire truck can't get to an accident for over a minute, and a hand-held fire extinguisher doesn't stand a chance against 20 to 50 gallons of burning fuel. If the on-board fire extinguisher and the driver's protective gear aren't adequate—it's too late. Large sedans and sports cars with some distance between the tank and the driver have the advantage of a steel firewall—as long as it holds up and is fuel-tight. But the driver of an open race car can measure his survival time in seconds.

Although chemical fire extinguishers (a minimum of 2 to 5 pounds) are required in all race cars, that's just barely adequate to put out an engine-room fire. There are many automatic, integrated systems available, however, with remote routing lines and various types of sensors. These are somewhat better—but hardly foolproof, as each has its own particular drawbacks. The first question is where to route the distribution lines. They can be in the tank location or engine room to put out the fire before it grows, or in the driver's compartment for protection in case fuel is splashed in, or a combination of both which spreads the effect too thin. Then there is the problem of what to use for a sensor or trigger. Whether it is flame actuated, heat actuated, impact actuated, or manual, there is always the possibility that it will go off at the wrong time or that the signal won't be strong enough to set it off at all. If the extinguisher is triggered while the car is still traveling at some great speed, the chemicals will be totally used up or blown away by the time the car comes to a stop. There seems to be no one right answer, unless it is a combination of all of the above, with some provision to keep the chemicals from escaping the cockpit. In any event, the main extinguisher system should be located close enough to the driver so it won't disappear if parts of the chassis are torn away in the accident.

Fireproof clothing is a tremendous survival advantage, but it can only go so far. Three critical problems are involved. First, the material must resist burning through under the direct flame from burning fuel, which can be from 1800 to 2500 degrees Fahrenheit. Second, there must be some thermal insulation to prevent tissue damage from contact with the material. And finally, it must be impermeable so that fuel will not penetrate it and start burning on the inside. From simulated tests, the best that can be expected of a firesuit is that it protect a driver for at least 60 seconds. After that much time the driver should be free from the flames or he is likely to be fatally injured by breathing superheated air or flames. If some way can be found to enclose his head at such times, suffocation is far more survivable.

It wouldn't be quite so difficult to meet all these problems if it weren't for some comfort requirements. Clothing must be light enough not to unnecessarily restrict the driver's movements, and it must be porous enough to allow some airflow for cooling under normally hot conditions. There are a number of fabric combinations that will satisfy all the requirements to some degree, but any selection will naturally have to be a compromise between protection and comfort.

A crash helmet is adequately fire resistant, but since it doesn't cover the neck and face, a fireproof hood should be worn under it. In addition, goggles or a Lexan face shield—even in a closed car—will protect the driver's eyes from flame for a short time. The driving suit itself is only as strong as its weakest link. All seams must be sewn with fireproof thread and preferably internally stitched. A one-piece suit will prevent a gap from opening at the belt line. Leather gloves and shoes are allowed because they are not flammable, but they shrink so badly in a flame and transmit heat so easily that they are only slightly better than nothing. The best fireproof suit, face shields, gloves, and shoes are the cheapest insurance a driver can buy.

All sanctioning bodies have lists of other safety items, modifications, and procedures that everyone must follow. And again, they are *minimums*. Anyone with any sense will use them merely as guidelines to better accident avoidance and protection. But there is one last point worth considering in the interest of finishing races. After the most extreme off-course excursion, it may still be possible to continue in the race if the car has been prepared for such rough treatment. Protection should include the vital components of the car, such as the radiator and hoses, brake and oil lines, and electrics, so they aren't damaged by small impacts or by sliding over rough surfaces. Tires will inevitably go flat, so it should be possible to get to the pits on whatever is left. If the car isn't damaged so badly that the officials take it out, there is always a chance to salvage something from the race.

12

THE DRIVER ∘∘∘∘∘∘∘∘∘∘∘∘∘∘∘∘∘∘∘∘∘∘∘∘∘∘∘∘∘∘

Race car drivers have to perform such complex and strenuous tasks that it is important to make their job as comfortable as possible. Every means of simplifying the driver's job should be explored: fitting, convenience, comfort, sensory feedbacks, and mental programming. This chapter may seem to be somewhat dehumanizing in considering the driver as simply a part of the guidance and control system to be optimized. But in fact, the ideal driver is one who acts very much like a machine or a computer. His function is to determine the ultimate limit of the car's performance at every point on the track, and to guide the car to that point repeatedly and precisely. A sophisticated electronic guidance system might be built to do the job even better, except for the necessity of constant sensing and adaptation to other cars and drivers. Unfortunately, race driving is no place for any human characteristics such as emotions, errors, or imagination. For the fastest and most consistent laps, the driver must be able to concentrate *totally* on keeping the car at its critical limit.

236

FITTING AND COMFORT

The driver has such intimate contact with the seat that a proper fit can improve his performance considerably. With the kind of accelerations possible today, lateral support is even more important than vertical support. To prevent the driver from having to hold himself upright by the steering wheel, well-fitted lateral support is required at the thighs, hips, rib cage, and especially the shoulders. If these contact points distribute the load over large, fleshy areas of the body, there is no need for padding. In fact, padding adds practically nothing to impact safety, and is likely to obstruct cooling air flow to the driver's backside. A series of holes drilled in a rigid seat shell will improve circulation, allow perspiration to escape, and reduce weight. Mounting an unpadded seat shell rigidly to the chassis also improves the driver's ability to sense every minute force and motion in the car. The commercially available Racemark seat (designed by the author

This form-fitting racing seat shell provides full lateral support for the legs, chest, and shoulders, plus an integral head rest.

for Mark Donohue) is a good example, although it only fits drivers in the 140- to 180-pound range. Any seat should be fully adjustable in travel, height, and tilt, until the driver is satisfied that he has exactly what he wants. Possible considerations are: arm extension, visibility, leg travel, and leg interference with the steering wheel.

All the controls should be individually fitted to each driver. It isn't necessary to have the steering wheel at arm's length, because the ideally set-up car should never need more than a quarter-turn of travel at the wheel. But it is a good idea to have it far enough away so the driver doesn't elbow himself in the abdomen when an emergency correction is necessary. The brake and clutch pedals should be far enough away so the driver's leg is almost straight at full travel since that is where it develops the maximum force. It is also a good idea to have adjustable pedal stops to prevent a strong and overenthusiastic driver from bending the linkage. The brake and accelerator pedals must be positioned perfectly to the driver's satisfaction so that he can heel-and-toe (or toe-and-heel) to his preference during braking and downshifting. The optimum position is probably to toe the brake pedal and heel the accelerator, since the brakes require more sensitive control at that point. At any rate, the steering wheel, pedals, and shift lever should all be fully and independently adjustable, until the driver is satisfied and has a written record of all the necessary locations carefully measured.

Enough drivers have blamed a stuck throttle for loss of control, for the entire accelerator linkage to be carefully designed and installed to eliminate it as a possible cause. Since the engine is apt to move around due to accelerations and torque reactions, any rigid linkage of rods and ball ends will probably be out of alignment at some time. The best solution is a tension cable in a flexible steel housing. Motorcycle control cables are adequate, but heavier industrial control cables and housings are available which can also take some compression forces. The reason for compression action is in case the throttles stick or the return springs fail. A toe-hook on the pedal can be used to push the throttles closed. Not less than two of the highest quality throttle springs should be used. And, needless to say, all throttle butterflys and shafts should be absolutely free from misalignment or

All instruments in this sedan are arranged for the needles to be vertical at peak operating conditions. Note the pit signal reminder list.

binding. The accelerator linkage, as well as the brake and clutch linkage, should be designed with its inherently variable force and movement ratio in mind. Ideally, the ratios should vary so that there is quick action at the start of travel to take up slack in a hurry, and slow action at the end to allow precise modulation.

All that is required of gauges is that they be accurate, easy to read, and reliable. The necessary gauges, in approximate order of importance, are: tachometer, oil pressure gauge, water temperature gauge, oil temperature gauge, and fuel pressure gauge. If any other component in the car is marginal in performance or durability, a gauge may help to keep an eye on it, whether it is the charging system, differential temperature, brake vacuum level, or whatever. But the driver is usually so busy that more than four gauges are almost beyond comprehension. At that, it can be a good idea to back up the really critical gauges with big, bright warning lights. Not only will they alert the driver when he can't easily check the gauges—say in a series of turns—but they provide a quick double-check if an instrument seems to have failed. Failure in an oil or fuel pressure gauge can be disastrous, so it is a good idea to provide shutoff valves in their lines to prevent loss of fluids during a race.

Every gauge should be assumed to be inaccurate until it is tested and calibrated. A new tachometer should be taken to a reliable test shop, and the person doing the testing should be impressed with the importance of even a 100-rpm error at 8000 rpm. The zero or idle calibration can be off, as long as the needle is accurate at the top end. Temperature and pressure gauges and switches can be tested at home using boiling water and welding gas regulators for reference. In addition to a tachometer, it might be good insurance to have an electronic rpm limiter. The best choice is one that doesn't suddenly kill the engine but gradually breaks up the sparks instead, and one which is nearly failure-proof. Still, the driver should be provided with a bypass switch in case of failure, or in case he absolutely *has* to have an extra few hundred rpm to draft past a relatively equal car.

To minimize a driver's visual transition from the road to the instruments, they should be as close to the driver's line of sight and as far away as reasonable. They may be arranged in any grouping the driver is most familiar with, but rapid comprehension is the primary consideration. Each gauge should be well identified with large labels, and the danger zone should be marked in red. It helps to rotate each dial face until the optimum needle position is perfectly vertical, so an undesirable condition is immediately apparent. In addition, all switches must be well labeled and within arm's length—and yet not close enough to be hit accidentally.

The value of vehicle feedbacks to the driver was mentioned in Chapter 7. The better a driver can perceive these signals, the more precisely he will be able to control the vehicle. The feedbacks can be categorized by the driver's senses: vision, for the perception of the location of the car (and other cars) on the track; feel, for the perception of forces, accelerations, jerks, and vibrations—both linear and rotational; sound, for the perception of road speed, and component failures; and perhaps even smell, for the perception of overheated components. So far, it hasn't been possible to measure the relative value of these sensory inputs in optimizing control. It would make an interesting research project to try and study them by establishing a simulated driving task, while totally eliminating each input in sequence and measuring the dropoff in performance. It is interesting that Formula car drivers have been moved into a more vertical sitting position recently—which can't help but improve visibility and the perception of horizontal forces and accelerations. Anything that can be done to improve the driver's intimate contact with the vehicle and its motions will help—at least until the contact reaches the point of discomfort.

Aside from all the factors involved in the driver's control system, there is still the very important and often neglected consideration of comfort. There are many areas where small changes can noticeably improve the driver's maximum effort and endurance—although they may be so subtle that the driver is not consciously aware of them. In the midst of a race the driver probably won't notice that vibrations are affecting his vision or that engine noise has deafened him to the sound of grinding brake pads. Vibrations and noise should be reduced as much as possible within the limits of performance, and the driver should be protected from excessive heat, fumes, buffeting, and vision interruptions.

Sealing the firewalls ahead of or behind the driver is not only an obvious safety precaution but keeps heat and fumes from leaking into the cockpit. Gasoline and exhaust fumes can have serious effects on a driver before he is even aware of a problem. For the same reason, most regulations require tailpipes to be rearward of any cockpit openings. Even when weight is a problem, a little bit of fiberglass or asbestos insulation and sealant may be worth its weight in driver endurance. In front-engine cars, a tremendous amount of heat is radiated from the firewall, transmission tunnel, and the floorboards above the exhaust pipes. A driver will probably know quite well when more cool air ducting is required, and he deserves all he wants. The effect of cooling ducts on external air drag is hardly worth considering. But it won't help much if the radiator is ahead of the driver and is pouring hot air either into the cockpit or into the driver's cool air ducts.

For longer races the driver will probably require a drinking water supply. Water might be provided during pitstops, except for the obstruction of full-coverage helmets and interference with other more necessary pit chores. The water container will have to be insulated and mounted near the driver. Location of the container and drinking tube can be a problem, to avoid natural siphoning action under hard horizontal accelerations. If the driver should stop sucking and take a breath at such times, a drastically tilted water level could maintain the flow enough to choke him. The container should be more than a 45-degree angle below the driver's mouth.

The windscreen on an open car is usually a compromise between visibility and wind forces or buffeting. The optical problem is that any transparent material becomes very difficult to see through at a large angle, and pits, dirt or oil will make vision practically impossible. The proper angle, however, with perhaps an added curved lip, can deflect the airflow high enough so the driver can be positioned to see completely *over* the windscreen. But this still allows the driver's goggles or face shield to collect some trash, so spare lenses or stripable covers should be provided. Flat black paint on all visible surfaces will cut down on glare that might temporarily blind the driver.

The final, if not most important consideration, is for the driver's mental comfort. If the driver can be sure that the owner, engineer, and mechanics all know their business and that they care a lot for the driver's health—and for finishing races—then he can be confident that they have done everything possible to keep the car together. A driver who has faith in his car and the team can afford to concentrate on the business at hand and will probably feel more free to take other risks that only he is responsible for.

LEARNING

There is still the matter of programming the computer/driver/machine to take full advantage of the race car's potential. This doesn't sound quite so cold and calculating if it is called ''learning'' and the driver is an actively willing participant. Of course, everyone knows how to drive and the racing driver knows his business better than anyone standing in the pits. But he doesn't necessarily know the peculiar characteristics of that particular car or setup, and he can't out-sense electronic instrumentation.

For the driver who is just starting out in road racing—and for some drivers with a lot of unsuccessful experience—the first step is to learn the friction circle concept. This was explained more logically and completely in Chapter 2, but in a sentence, it means that the fastest way around a track is to keep the tires at their maximum friction capability in any direction—laterally or longitudinally, and especially during the transitions. This means that braking, cornering, and accelerating will usually overlap each other. As easy as it is to say, it takes a lot of practice and sometimes a lot of relearning.

If a driver is stepping into a race car for the first time, or into a radically different kind of race car, the experience probably ought to be taken in small steps. One of the best places to start is at a combination drag strip and skid pad. The long straightaway gives the driver a chance to practice up- and downshifting and braking at the limit of lockup, and gives him a feel for high-speed straight line stability. The skidpad will give him a chance to get used to the maximum lateral capabilities without the risk of sliding off a dangerous turn. And it is not a coward's way out. Some of the best race drivers in the world insist on driving a new car on the skidpad before taking it to a race track.

Another practical suggestion is to get as many driving miles on a particular race car setup as possible. There are few drivers who can step from a passenger car into a race car and make the instantaneous transition required in responses and control movements. The more familiarity a driver has with *his* car, the better he can control it and the less chance there is for him to make a mistake. If the race car is a converted production sports car or sedan, it might even be possible to add a few street items such as mufflers and lights, and get a lot of ordinary highway miles on it.

Of course, it is insane to try to practice race driving on public streets and highways in any kind of car. The conditions are so far removed from actual racing that it is a total waste of time, energy, the car, and the tires. The only way to practice realistic race driving is at the absolute limit of traction and at both edges of the road. If it were possible to do that on public streets, it would be homicidal. The only time a real racer drives fast off the track is when he's in a hurry—not because he's practicing. However, there is *one* kind of practice that is safe in public—smoothness. When a race car is balanced precariously at the limit of traction, any sudden movement of the controls can send it off the track or lose some seconds. Every driver, race or otherwise, would find it productive to practice smooth driving at all times.

A real race track can't be beat for realistic racing practice. Unfortunately, the rental cost for exclusive practice time is usually out of the question, and race weekends are so crowded that very little practice time is available to any individual driver. Amateur races provide inexpensive practice or development time for professional drivers, but by the time a driver has reached that stage, he can usually adapt to a track relatively rapidly.

The best investment in cost per hour of learning time is probably an electronic performance recording system. If a race car is wired to record both speed and lateral acceleration constantly (or the *net* acceleration in any horizontal direction) as described in Chapter 13, the driver can learn more in minutes than by hours of practice driving. If a faster, more experienced driver is available, he can set a performance baseline to be matched. Or two fairly good drivers can compare their recordings and learn from each other, since each will be better than the other in some distinct areas. But even a single driver can learn by studying the output charts and seeing where his performance is not at the limit. In any case, it is more convenient to use a distance-base in the recorder instead of a time-base so that all laps come out exactly the same length on the chart paper and can be directly overlaid for comparisons. For example, two drivers may have about the same laptimes in the same car but learn from comparing recordings that one is faster in the corners, while the other brakes later and harder. Both may be able to learn to drive faster by knowing exactly where someone else has already done it. The recordings will also graphically illustrate just how smooth a driver is, and where and how he can improve in this respect.

Such training instrumentation isn't just for beginners. For the experienced professional driver, it may be the only way to find areas for improvement when there are no observers or instructors as skilled as he is. It isn't easy to sense the point at which the car is at its absolute limit without taking the chance of going over that limit. It is much more precise—and safer—to find the limits by electronic instrumentation. In addition, the speed and acceleration curves are invaluable records for setting the car up for that track the next time. An article by the author in *Sports Car Graphic*, January 1971, gives examples of such comparisons for Mark Donohue and Milt Minter in a Javelin at Riverside.

For actual beginning race-driving training and experience, it is hard to beat the professional race driver schools, where they teach such things as the proper position and control motions, paths to take on the track, and how to deal with other cars. Second best, but far less expensive, are the SCCA driver's schools, where they teach about the same thing with perhaps less experienced instructors. And finally, it helps to read and think about the right way to do it. One of the best books on driving technique is Alan Johnson's *Driving in Competition*.

EMOTIONAL PROGRAMING

Great racing drivers are *made,* not born, and no one can make a driver great but himself. The difference between a very good driver and one who becomes a successful professional is all in their heads— not their physical makeups. There seems to be no correlation between any physical characteristics such as reflexes, eyesight, or build and a driver's accomplishments. Of course, most drivers are physically strong and quite healthy, but that is probably an effect, not a cause.

While there aren't any distinguishing physical characteristics, there do seem to be a number of personality characteristics that frequently set the great driver apart from most other people—even those who are successful in other competitive activities. A psychologist, Dr. Keith Johnsgard, has made studies of over five hundred race drivers, from beginners to World Champions, and found definite distinctions between them and the average population. The discussion of these characteristics might seem out of place in a technical book, except for the fact that they might help a car owner or team manager to select the optimum driver component for his car or help him to program that component for better performance. Although that may sound coldly exploitive, the fact is that the driver is usually getting *paid* for the ultimate performance, and he ordinarily wants to improve himself.

Probably the most significant trait in successful drivers is their overwhelming motivation to win at any cost—the killer instinct.

Many times this isn't apparent in a driver's outward appearance, but it can show up in different forms. Some drivers demonstrate it on the track by driving like maniacs when they get behind—although those types don't usually last very long. The opposite extreme is the driver who spends every waking hour building and developing his car, and honing his own skills to perfection. But in either case, there is an unusually high need to be best, to be successful, to accomplish tasks requiring skill and effort, to be a recognized authority. Their average need for achievement is higher than 90 percent of all college students. And they are likewise defined as tough-minded, self-reliant, and no-nonsense when it comes to the job of winning. The motivation for this drive doesn't seem to be important. It can be either to attain recognition in front of large audiences or simply a personal obsession to beat the other guy.

Similarly, the most successful driver is usually highly assertive and has a high need for dominance. His assertiveness shows up as independence, aggressiveness, and stubbornness. He is a self-motivated, self-directed person. He will be quite willing to argue for his own point of view, to be a leader of whatever groups he *must* be associated with, and to be able to persuade and influence others. However, since the need for this trait is often strongest *off* the race track, some relatively quiet and humble drivers have done very well with the assistance of team managers who always handled those particular conflicts.

To balance these strong drives and traits, racing drivers must also have good control over their emotions and behavior. They are perhaps compulsively self-disciplined. But at the same time, they are not neurotic nor unusually sensitive to emotional problems in themselves or others. In most situations, especially during a race, they are more casual, relaxed, and composed than the average population. They are relatively decisive and imperturbable, and don't waste a lot of effort in self-criticism. They are emotionally mature in their personal responsibility. Another balancing factor is that most of them are able to listen to criticism from others objectively, and they welcome constructive suggestions from qualified persons.

There are a number of other characteristics which fall outside the range for the average population. Racers generally are more intelligent and more capable of abstract thinking. They have a good perception of reality. The brighter a driver is, the more successful he tends to be. He also has a high capacity for endurance in the face of frustration and physical hardships, and he is willing to adventure, to take chances in pursuit of his goals.

But what do all these studies and analyses mean to the race driver himself? If a driver is relatively unaware of his own attitudes and feelings, it is possible for him to take some psychological tests and discover his strong and weak areas. He might learn how he compares with other more successful drivers and try to learn to compensate or develop his personality to compensate for his weaknesses. It is important to keep in mind, however, that these statistical studies are all averages of a large number of drivers. Some World Champions are low in some desirable characteristics, and some losers are high in all of them.

There is another personality characteristic which is not recognized by standard psychological tests, and that is an empathy for machines. There are two diverse approaches to the matching of the man and the machine. At one extreme is the highly logical and systematic driver who learns everything there is to know about the machine and who adapts that machine to fit his own precise personal preferences. At the opposite extreme is the driver with strong instincts for the right responses, who can take any vehicle and adapt to its particular characteristics. The former method seems to be more reliable and consistent, while the latter usually takes many thousands of miles of experience. But in either case, there is a strong feel, or empathy, for the car.

Race driving is unlike most other competitive sports in that an extremely complex machine is involved. A ballplayer or a track and field man is born with most of the hardware he needs to compete, but a driver must learn to use complex extensions to his body. And the characteristics of those extensions can change totally from car to car, and even from moment to moment in a race, requiring tremendous adaptation skills. It usually takes years of practice for the racing driver to learn accurate perceptions of all his feedbacks and the proper control responses required. It must be as though the steered wheels were the driver's hands and the driven wheels were his feet. He doesn't really feel the steering wheel and pedals as much as he feels the track at the tire contact patches. There must be a direct, instantaneous connection between the ground and his mind—without conscious comprehension of all the hardware in between. When a tire locks up in braking, there has to be an immediate automatic response to ease up on the brake pedal—as though that tire were simply another part of the driver's body.

It is theoretically possible to build an ultimately perfect electronic driver. Enough is known about the psychology of driving, race strategy, cybernetics, computers, servo systems, and inertial guidance to do the job—given enough time and money. It is even possible right now to select mathematically the perfect line for a car to take in the corners, although it takes a precise map of the course and a lot of computer time. Such an electronic driving machine would be able to drive any race car at the absolute limit at all times, always select the optimum path, never fatigue, and never make a mistake. But then, which is more interesting, competition between machines or competition between men in equal machines? It is an important consideration in racing even today.

13

TESTING ∘∘∘∘∘∘∘∘∘∘∘∘∘∘∘∘∘∘∘∘∘∘∘∘∘∘∘∘∘∘∘∘∘∘∘∘∘∘∘

Automobile testing is an incredibly broad and complex subject worth a book in itself, but the more limited discussion of race car testing can be covered in a chapter. All too often race car mechanics, drivers, and even engineers assume that all you have to do is put the right pieces in the right places and you can go out and win races. But in fact, testing and development are far more important than basic design. It is almost a truism that a well tested and developed old design will be more successful than the most advanced new design. Most of the other chapters in this book mention specific tests in their areas, but this chapter will go into more detail about the necessary test hardware and equipment and the proper test procedures.

PHILOSOPHY

Before getting into the specifics, there are a number of basic points to be made concerning testing of any kind. First, it is important to realize that there will always be a large number of uncontrollable variables that can have great or small influences on the area to be studied.

In some cases it may be possible to compensate for them, but even if not, they should be known and considered before any results are accepted as fact. At the very least, all vehicle and environmental conditions should be recorded so it is possible to analyse inconsistencies later. A partial check list of factors is given in Table 5.

Location, date	Suspension	Tire size	Spoiler heights
Driver	Spring rates	Compound	Wing angles
Mechanic	Ride height	Rim width	Temperatures
Engine	Shock settings	Pressures	Barometer
Transmission ratios	Caster, camber, toe	Rolling radius	Wind
Weight	Anti-roll bars	Condition	Track condition

Table 5. Check list factors for engineering development

Plus, of course, notes concerning the purpose of the test and any driver comments. As memorable as all those may seem at the time, it won't be that easy to recall the details, and there is always the possibility that the person who remembers won't be around forever.

The second point is that *all* tests should be baselined. There is no way to know whether a change is positive or negative unless there is some well-known, fixed basis of reference. If a change in suspension geometry seems to make the car faster, it must be possible to go back to the original setting, to make sure the change wasn't simply due to driver improvement. Sometimes it is even more important to be able to go back to the original condition when a change had negative effects.

Third, never make more than *one* change at a time. If two things are changed at once and the car becomes slower, there is no way of knowing which change had what effect. It is quite possible that one of them actually added to the performance. On the other hand, the car may be made faster through mass changes but no one will ever know exactly how or why.

It may be a good idea to make changes large enough so the results will be obvious. This makes it possible to bracket the optimum result, avoiding the need for eternal and indeterminate small improvements.

The exception is any place where a great change may make the car dangerously uncontrollable or liable to critical failure. Track testing can be far more dangerous than race driving, even if there are no other cars on the track. Many components are usually being altered and vehicle characteristics change a great deal between runs. In addition, few teams can afford the corner workers and safety personnel that are always present during a race. At the very minimum, an ambulance and para-medic should always be present.

The most valuable test instrument is the driver. He is the one who operates the test, and he is the first one to recognize—or suffer—the results. Therefore, there are certain characteristics that are essential to a test or development driver—above and beyond the skills of a mere race driver. Of course, whether racing or testing, consistency is of primary importance. One superfast lap out of ten scattered laptimes is meaningless in either case.

Since the driver is the most variable input, nothing can be determined until he can continually repeat good laptimes within a few tenths of a second. This requires the driver to be familiar with the car and the track and to have a lot of practice before vehicle testing begins. It also helps if the driver has had some experience with a wide variety of handling characteristics, so he will *know* what feels good or bad—and how to cope with the bad. Still, consistency is far more valuable than ultimately low laptimes or years of experience.

There are other personal traits that mean a lot to the mechanics and engineers and speed up development immensely. The driver must know the language—as expressed in this book, for example—so he can communicate what is happening to his crew. He also has to be physically sensitive to all the various feedbacks he gets, such as steering wheel forces and movements, vibrations, noises, smells, and so on, and to be able to distinguish the most subtle changes. In addition, he has to have the patience to wait through interminable delays and interruptions and to watch for the most minor improvements. Finally, the test or development driver has to be absolutely honest with himself and the crew, to avoid the search for problems that were actually the result of driver error.

HARDWARE—THE INSTRUMENTS

Before getting into the description of test instruments, three measurement terms must be understood: precision, accuracy, and repeatability. "Precision" is determined by the smallest increment on the measuring device. On a yardstick, precision may be ¼ inch; on a micrometer caliper, probably .001 inch. "Accuracy" is the relationship to *absolute* standards as established by the National Bureau of Standards and depends on the accumulation of errors in successive measuring devices. For example, when a tachometer is calibrated, what is used as the reference? "Repeatability" is a function of the human element. How close can a person "eyeball" the readout, and was there any change in the object between measurements?

Test gear can range anywhere from a stopwatch to hundred-thousand-dollar rolling laboratories of telemetry and recording instruments. The major auto and tire manufacturers can afford to be the most advanced in this area, with lightweight systems that can record *anything* they could possibly want to know about a car or driver at any time or in any place. It is possible to record simultaneously and continuously dozens of channels of information on speed, acceleration, displacements, locations, temperatures, forces, pressures, strains, and events. But since the racer should never change more than one thing at a time, he shouldn't need to record more than a couple of variables at once. The following discussion will concentrate on more reasonable and available hardware.

FACILITIES

The first thing necessary is a reliable, repeatable, and safe surface on which to test. A great deal of the basic vehicle test work can be done on simple drag strips, most of which are longer and wider than typical race track straightaways. Drag strips are usually inexpensive to rent during the week, are smooth and level, and are far safer than a racetrack or deserted country road. If they can be rented exclusively, two-way runs can be made, which improves accuracy and cuts down on test time. This may be a good first exposure for any new car and/or driver, as it allows familiarization of the shifting, braking, and high-speed stability without the complication of cornering problems.

The interior of a Chevrolet R & D instrumentation van, with (from left) automatic-wind light table, 10-channel strip chart recorder, telemetry receiver, and portable calibration reference box. (*GM Photograph*)

Ideally, the dragstrip should have an adjoining skidpad on which to test steady-state cornering. There are few criteria for a skidpad, other than it be level, as smooth as possible, and have a consistent and high-coefficient surface. It is also necessary to have a guide circle painted on the surface. The accepted minimum radius seems to be about 100 feet, while the maximum desirable size is limited only by the available surface area. In small or isolated cities it may be possible to rent or borrow a large, unobstructed parking lot, although it takes a strong underbase to resist the pounding and cornering forces from large race cars. In the case of NASCAR sedans or Indianapolis cars, a skidpad isn't apt to have a high enough speed capability to raise tire temperatures to a simulation of high-banked turns. However, the smaller asphalt oval tracks themselves serve roughly the same purpose. In a pinch, any long (180 degrees or so) constant-radius turn is better than nothing, if a precise path can be marked on it and followed by the driver.

Going to a race track is the last stage—or as a last resort can serve as the first stage. At any rate, consistency and safety will be the greatest problems. A road-race course is *designed* to be a challenge to the driver and the total capabilities of a vehicle, not to isolate test factors. It could help to put down very distinct markers (braking and cornering) to follow, so as to reduce driver inconsistencies. There usually isn't much choice among available road-racing test tracks, but if a track has some particularly unsafe areas, the car can be timed through limited sections, since overall laptimes probably aren't that important. A final consideration on any surface is its cleanliness. Obvious dust, dirt, or gravel that can blow or wash across a track surface can be a real problem in any minimum-traction sections. But in addition, oil from broken engines or oil heat-seeping out of the track can hurt. On the other hand, a lot of tire rubber can help, unless rains have washed the surface clean.

A stopwatch is an absolute necessity. The older dial watches are adequate, though they can't match the capabilities of modern electronic, digital-readout watches with memories. Any watch is good enough for test work as long as it has a precision of hundredths of a second and has split action for sequential timing. The electronic variety, however, offers the option of remote control and can be triggered by external switches or photocell timing traps. If automatic timing traps are not used, the greatest inaccuracy with any watch will be the operator. At best the operator will find it difficult to get his own two thumbs to agree within a few hundredths of a second, much less his perception of when a car passed a certain point. Automatic timing traps have become inexpensive enough for the amateur, but the time and difficulty in setup seldom justify the increase in timing accuracy. In any case, some common sense is necessary in the analysis of elapsed times with any watch on any course. It is not simply a matter of taking the best time (which may be timer error), or the average of many times (which may include a driver error). The most reasonable figure is probably an average of the three best times after any unusually low time has been thrown out.

ELECTRONIC INSTRUMENTS

So many race car factors require continuous data recording that an automatic recorder is highly desirable for serious development work. The proper type of recorder and its satellite gear should be fitted to the purpose by a test engineer, but some of the criteria and choices

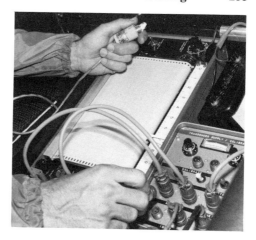

A two-channel variable-speed strip-chart recorder, with an unmounted accelerometer (top) being wired into the calibration box (below).

can be mentioned in a few words. Purely mechanical recorders are occasionally used, with the recording paper driven by the speedometer cable and displacements recorded with cable-operated pens. However, electronic recorders offer so many advantages and are available at such low prices that they're hard to beat. Prices range from thousands of dollars down to $250 for a simple build-your-own kit.

The first decision is the number of channels required. One channel is barely adequate and won't save very much money considering the time and cost of multiple test runs. Two channels will handle most race car tests. The second decision may be the paper span, with 10 inches about the best. Five inches is the minimum, since precision in such measurements as speed and acceleration is minimal below that point. Frequency response and paper speed are minor considerations, since the test data will be relatively slow compared to the capabilities of most recorders. Size and weight are worth some thought when a really light race car is being tested, but most recorders weigh less than 5 gallons of fuel and can be fitted in the space required by a fuel bladder. Some recorders may be sensitive to g loadings or vibrations, so it may be necessary to mount them in certain positions or in shock-absorbent materials. They may also be sensitive to unshielded electronic ignition interference. There are at least three choices in writing method: ink, thermal, and light-sensitive. The first two are the most common—with thermal being less messy and more reliable. The light-beam oscillograph is very expensive and is used primarily for high-frequency response and many channels of information. Finally, it may be desirable to record data as a plot on a single sheet of paper, in which case an X-Y recorder is necessary. Otherwise, the continuous-strip chart recorder is more versatile. Of course, any electronic recorder will require a power source. Most of them are designed for house current, so an inverter will be required, capable of producing the appropriate voltage, frequency, and wattage. More sophisticated recording systems can be built using tape recorders and/or radio telemetry, but the cost and complexity are hardly worth any advantages they may have in weight or space.

The transducers, or measurement sensors, are where the real engineering comes in. It is always necessary to convert whatever quantity is to be measured into electrical signals that are compatible with the recorder. The most common measurements desired in race car development are usually speeds, accelerations, displacements, forces, and temperatures, and occasionally pressures and stresses.

Speed in miles per hour or rpm can be sensed by two methods, depending on the use of the data. Most common is the tachometer-generator, which when mounted to a wheel or the engine, generates a precise DC voltage signal proportional to rpm. When it is also necessary to know the total distance or number of revolutions, it is more practical to use a digital sensor. A large number of magnetic slugs are glued evenly around a rotating circumference, and a magnetic pickup is mounted near enough to produce digital pulses. Speed is then proportional to the pulse frequency, and distance is proportional to the sum of the pulses. In addition, electronic circuits can be designed to differentiate the velocity change to give a signal proportional to acceleration.

For recording straight-line or slow cornering speeds, a fifth wheel is ordinarily used, since it has minimal diameter change effects. But for race car use, it is more practical to use a road wheel to avoid swingout due to lateral accelerations. A front wheel is best, preferably the outside wheel, as it has the least effects from lifting or slipping.

Accelerations can be measured in many ways. Forward or coasting

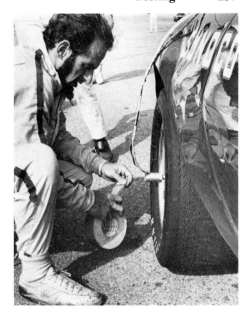

A tachometer-generator (center) has been mounted to the hub of a front wheel, and its wires are being taped to the fender lip.

accelerations are usually so small that taking the slope of the speed curve (differentiation) is most accurate. For transient lateral acceleration (non-skidpad) or braking, however, the most direct method is the electronic potentiometer accelerometer. These can occasionally be found through aerospace surplus stores in the desired 2.0-g range and are easily wired in with an accurate fixed reference voltage. A bubble level is also necessary to insure a perfect zero free from gravity effects.

There are also some relatively inexpensive non-electronic accelerometers, which have certain other drawbacks. The commercial pendulum-type and fluid manometer-type are incapable of permanent recording, which means that continuous recording is practically impossible. There is one type with a pendulum which scribes lines in a film on the inside of a hemisphere that can be analysed for changes and magnitudes of horizontal accelerations. But after a few corners on a road course the scribed lines get rather confusing.

Displacement sensors are most commonly used to record suspension, steering, or throttle movements. In some cases a linear potentiometer may be available with enough travel to fit the total displace-

A displacement transducer being used to measure suspension deflection. The rotary potentiometer and its cable reel are strapped to the fender, with the cable leading to a swivel at the center of the hubcap.

ment. But a more flexible device, in both mounting and total travel, is a rotary potentiometer attached to a spring-loaded cable reel. This can easily be attached to any fixed surface, with the wire cable connected to the moving component. With a 10-inch paper span, inches of travel can be equal to inches of stylus movement.

Forces are difficult to measure if no movement can be tolerated, in which case strain gauges are necessary. Otherwise, the easiest technique is to allow movement against a known-rate spring and again record the displacement. Wheel loads or vertical aerodynamic forces are most often measured in this way, by recording the average suspension deflection at a specific speed. Strain gauges have the capability of measuring forces very precisely with no displacement, but they are inconvenient for all but the most precise stress work. They require professional attachment and careful calibration, and they tend to record every little unimportant force or vibration. Forces in fluid pressures can also be measured through the use of aerospace pressure transducers, to record fuel, oil, brake, or air pressures.

It may also be desirable to record temperatures in the moving race car, especially other than by the fluid temperature gauges available to the driver. Thermocouples can be mounted on the brakes, exhaust, or air inlets, and wired into the recorder for a continuous record. However, in most cases the *peak* temperature is all that is wanted. If so, it is far easier, faster, and cheaper to use a simple heat-sensitive positive indicator. The most familiar device is called Temp-Plate, which consists of a row of colored dots on an adhesive strip. The dots blacken successively with precise increases in temperature and are available in increments of 10 to 50 degrees, anywhere from 100 to 1100 degrees Fahrenheit.

When anything is measured indirectly, as with transducers and a recorder, accurate calibration is critical. Forces can be calibrated by loading with known weights, and displacements calibrated by measuring with an accurate tape measure. With accelerometers, 1.0 g can be checked by using the earth's gravitation, while anything greater

This strip of Temp-Plate being attached to a transmission case will blacken its indicator dots up to the maximum temperature encountered.

will require a centrifugal acceleration wheel. Time can be checked with an electronic stopwatch, or a constant accurate time reference can be provided with a standard frequency oscillator wired to the recorder. It can also be useful to have an accurate digital voltmeter when setting up a recorder and potentiometers. Finally, it helps to have all calibration gear easily accessible and to have the recorder controls within easy reach of the driver. It is often necessary to record just one small segment in a series of laps or for the driver to stop and check the calibration out on the track.

PRESSURE INSTRUMENTS

For any aerodynamic work beyond random experimental changes in shape and the measurement of lift and drag, some pressure instrumentation is desirable. Very little is available off-the-shelf to suit

Pressure measurement equipment being fitted to a duct includes: multi-tube manometer, Strip-a-tube, pitot-static tube, and pressure rake.

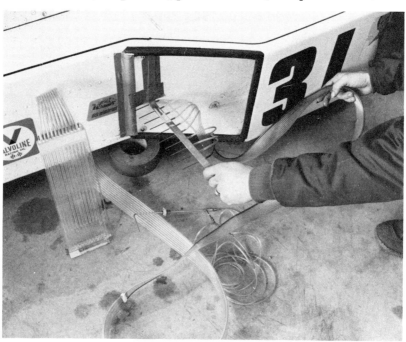

The manometer is connected by tubing to a pressure pickup strip taped to the body, with pressure holes numbered from 1 to 10 from the nose.

race development work, but it is relatively easy to build. A commercially available pitot-static tube is useful to measure both free-stream dynamic pressure and free-stream static pressure to use as a reference. Other necessary commercial products are fluids and hoses. Water is perfectly adequate, but a colored manometer fluid will have the same density and be easier to read. For the measurement of multiple pressures at one time, a flexible plastic hose called Strip-a-Tube is available with up to 10 separate tubes formed in one flat strip. Otherwise, a hundred feet of individual model airplane hose will work as well, though somewhat messily. A manometer, pressure rake, and surface pressure strip will probably have to be built from scratch.

A multi-tube manometer will require at least 12 tubes; 10 for measurements and one on each end for reference static pressure. A capacity of 12 inches of water will handle most pressures at reasonably fast air speeds. The easiest material to use is acrylic plate and tubing, which can be sawed, drilled, and glued to shape.

A pressure rake is simply a row of short lengths of brass tubing soldered to a flexible metal strip. The strip can be taped above a body surface or in a duct, and connected by flex hose to the manometer.

The surface pressure strip is designed to be taped flush to a body of any compound shape, to read the air pressures acting perpendicular to the surface with a minimum of intereference to the airflow. The best material is probably flexible vinyl sheet, which can easily be cut and glued into a ten-channel strip and yet will be flexible enough to follow all but the sharpest body contours. To reduce airflow disturbance, the pressure pickup holes should be in the center and smoothly drilled, the strip should be of minimum thickness, and it should be taped to the body as smoothly as possible.

It is very important to make every hose and tube *air* tight, or observed pressures will be meaningless. It is even necessary to test for pressure leakage between tubes or channels, especially in the surface pressure strip. This can be done by applying pressure to one channel at a time and watching for pressure readings in neighboring tubes. Leaks can be found by watching for bubbles when the entire setup is immersed in water.

OTHER EQUIPMENT

Tire or suspension development will inevitably require the use of a tire pyrometer, or electronic thermometer. Tire company engineers are usually available to take temperatures at professional races, but for personal use, a reasonably quick, reliable, and accurate pyrometer can be bought for a few hundred dollars. Tire temperatures change so fast that convenience and speed are essential. For truly accurate measurement, some companies have developed infrared sensors which can read and record surface temperatures on a tire at high speed. They are so expensive, however, that stopping and contacting the tire is usually fast enough for most engineers.

Engine development has reached such a level of sophistication that it is beyond all but the largest professional teams. Even then, the

Tire engineers using an electronic pyrometer to measure the temperature—and its variation across the tread—of a race tire.

engine is usually considered a simple "lump" which is purchased and installed as is. Still, the cost of dynamometers has come down to the point where one can be bought for the price of a V-8 engine rebuild. A chassis dyno is out of the question for all but the smallest race cars because horsepower measurements are limited by tire slippage on the rollers, and such dynamometers are inaccurate for anything more than A-B tests.

The most practical dynos are the portable water-brakes, which can be bolted to the engine bell housing on an engine stand or to the output shaft on a transaxle. Of course, all engine development work should be done by the builder in a dyno cell before the engine is even installed. But the racer with a few less dollars or an off-brand engine he has to develop on his own can learn a lot faster on a dyno than by cutting and trying and measuring laptimes. Although straightaway acceleration runs are simple, a dyno can save time and improve precision.

A wind tunnel is a piece of development hardware so expensive it must be rented by even the largest teams. For a race car that is already built and running, it is far more practical to do aerodynamic development by measuring changes on the existing bodywork. For a

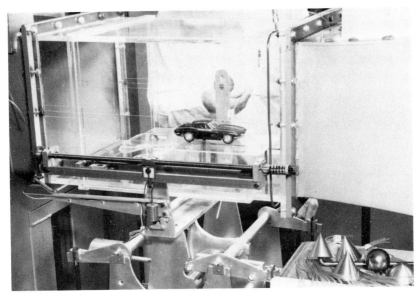

The Chevrolet R & D wind tunnel, with a 1/25 scale model Corvette mounted to a force balance in the test section. (*GM Photograph*)

radical new design or elaborate changes, however, a wind tunnel can save time and money even at rental rates of hundreds of dollars per running hour. But it is such a complex operation that an experienced test engineer has to set up and run the tests and analyse the output data. For those engineers who would like to prepare themselves better for such development work, two of the best references are by Pankhurst and Holder, and Pope and Harper.

TEST PROCEDURES

Even with the best equipment, a test may be meaningless if some small step is overlooked. An accurate test requires careful preparation, precise execution, and often a lot of practice. After the driver has become familiar with the car and track, sometimes it takes still more practice to become familiar with a particular test procedure or the instruments involved. If there is room for a passenger, and if he doesn't suffer from motion sickness while reading instruments, some of the responsibility and concentration can be taken off the driver. But for single-seaters, there isn't much choice—the driver will have to be a test engineer also.

ACCELERATION

Acceleration tests are probably the most common. Although an engine may be perfectly developed and tuned to the last horsepower, there are other factors that must be resolved on the track. The dynamometer can't quite simulate the response requirements of a driver accelerating out of a turn, or the inertia, air drag, and air pressure effects on the system. When gear ratios are changeable, they too must often be selected by trial and error.

For most racing situations—except drag racing—acceleration from a standstill is irrelevant, and acceleration with wheelspin is more of a tire test than anything else. Therefore, a good acceleration test will be from the end of wheelspin capability up to the maximum possible speed. If the gear ratios are already determined, the engine output can be analyzed in just one gear—from some reasonable rpm to the upper rpm limit. Before the test, certain conditions must be standardized, such as tire pressure and temperature, engine and gear lube temperature, exact total vehicle weight, and precise shift rpm. If there is any possibility of a road grade or wind, all runs must be made in both directions. Assuming that acceleration is measured by the time interval between velocities rather than with an accelerometer, the velocity signal must be accurately calibrated, and there must be a precise "event" mark at each given speed. If the time is measured with a stopwatch against the tachometer, a greater time span will improve accuracy. If the time interval between speeds is taken from a continuous speed recording, it is much easier to identify precise speed points but still necessary to have an accurate time base on the recorder paper.

For a simple A-B test between two configurations, is is a simple matter to compare elapsed time between two speed or rpm points. However, it is possible to convert the figures into acceleration in g's, or thrust force in pounds, or horsepower at any given point. In addition to the change in miles per hour (V-v) and elapsed time (t), it is also necessary to include the exact test weight (W), times a factor to include rotational inertia. The equivalent weight due to rotational inertia may vary from 3 percent for a large sedan, to 6 percent for a light race car. Therefore, the equations are approximately:

$$\text{force} = \frac{(.045)\ (1.06\ W)\ (V\text{-}v)}{(t)}$$

$$\text{horsepower} = (.0027)\ (\text{force})\ (\text{average mph})$$

Both force and horsepower figures are applicable only at the specific average mph point, or (V + v) / 2. By taking data at a number of points, it is possible to plot a curve of the net acceleration force or horsepower above that required to overcome friction and aerodynamic drag. An article by Ronald Brown in *Road & Track,* November 1970, goes into a more detailed explanation, with examples and illustrations.

Of course, simple knowledge of the horsepower curve doesn't make a race car any faster. It is possible to plot the thrust, or power, or g curve in each gear, however, to locate the optimum shift rpm for each gear ratio. When many ratio selections are available, this can be used to help select the optimum gears—in addition to the technique described in Chapter 9. Finally, acceleration tests will give an elapsed time evaluation and subjective feel for engine response to sudden throttle applications, especially at low rpm or during a fast shift.

BRAKING

Brake tests are all too often left until the end of the straightaway on a road racing course, where any error can mean disaster. No wonder few drivers are willing to use their brakes to the limit—even if they are aware of what the brakes are capable of. The ideal test location is at the center of a long straightaway such as a drag strip, so that two-way runs can be made and so that there is plenty of safe escape road. A race car should be tested with a full fuel load for maximum stress, but since the tanks are unlikely to be exactly at the center of gravity and fuel slosh can have a considerable effect, the car should also be tested for balance while half-full and empty. It is also necessary to

Getting out of shape in a brake balance test. Note wires leading to tachometer-generators mounted on the right front and rear wheels.

warm racing brakes up to some typical operating temperature and break in any new pads before testing begins. This is a good time to evaluate the modulation, or the ability of the driver to hold the brakes right at the verge of lockup without flat-spotting a tire. It should be just barely possible to get short, instantaneous bits of sliding without full lockup, with the performance smooth and consistent throughout each and every application. A good test of consistency is to make repeated complete stops from a specific speed while measuring each distance. Declutching at the same time will prevent engine interference or stalling. The driver should be able to begin the braking within a few feet of a given fixed marker and keep each stopping distance within a 5 to 10 percent variation. This is also a good test for maximum average capability in g's, knowing the initial speed in miles per hour (V) and the stopping distance in feet (d).

$$\text{stopping g} = \frac{(.0334)\,(V)^2}{d}$$

The actual instantaneous deceleration will be greatest at higher speeds, where aerodynamic drag and downforce contribute to stopping power. To measure the actual rate of deceleration, it is necessary to have an electronic accelerometer wired into a strip-chart recorder. But aside from pure research, about all that will show is whether the driver is using all available brake capability at all speeds.

Braking stability tests are probably more meaningful with respect to vehicle development. The question of whether and when the front or rear brakes lock first was discussed in detail in Chapter 5. If the braking g's are much lower than the tire capabilities seem to be, or if the rears lock first, some front/rear ratio change will be required. In addition to the previously explained procedure of an outside observer determining which locks first, an onboard recorder can be used. Having a velocity sensor on both a front and rear wheel can even measure the relative slip rates in braking. If a two-channel recorder is used, both wheel speeds can be measured, but even a single channel recorder can be used if a circuit is designed to compare the two speed signals constantly and read out the result. Finally, even if the brakes could be perfectly balanced for continual variations in weight distribution, aerodynamic downforce changes, and engine drag at the rear wheels, there would still be another change from straightaway tests to a road course. Since the ideal situation is to brake deeply into a turn and there is more lateral load transfer at the front, it will probably be necessary to reduce the front bias even more to avoid inside front wheel lockup at the limit.

Brake durability tests are fairly difficult to perform, and there is the basic problem of accurately simulating real requirements. Tests can be made by driving back and forth and braking on a long straightaway if all the necessary maximum and minimum speeds are known, but a race track is an unquestionable real situation. The most valuable information is the temperatures at the disc, the pad material, and the fluid in the caliper. Even without a recorder and thermocouples, positive-indicating Temp-Plate will give the peak figures if the brakes are truly forced to their limits. The most severe conditions are; full fuel load, high ambient temperatures, maximum traction coefficient, and a comparatively low average-speed course to minimize high-speed cooling. During these temperature tests it is a good idea to keep a record of pad thickness versus miles to get an indication of durability, if that isn't known from previous racing experience. Enough testing may even show the variation in wear rate at different peak temperatures, which may be very important if pad life is marginal in a race.

AERODYNAMICS

Aerodynamic drag and downforce tests are most easily performed on a long straightaway, preferably one that is perfectly flat and free from any winds. The only way to *know* that grade or wind has a minimal effect is to run all tests at the highest possible speed and to repeat each test in the opposite direction immediately. The most convenient test for air drag is the coast-down run, which can be recorded in a number of ways. If the car has a very precise and accurate speedometer, a stopwatch can be used between any two speeds. Otherwise it will be necessary to use an electronic speed signal and record it with a precise time or distance base. Another alternative that is sometimes used is electronic speed traps in the road. However, at least three triggers are required, and precision, accuracy, and reliability tend to be worse than with continual speed recording.

The test procedure is practically foolproof. To minimize friction drag, the tires are overinflated and all lubricants and bearings warmed up. The driver accelerates to the highest speed that will allow some coasting distance, shifts into neutral, and coasts with a minimum of steering fluctuations.

The air drag in pounds at each speed is calculated the same as acceleration force was, where the difference in two speeds is $(V-v)$, the elapsed time is (t), and the test weight of the vehicle includes some rotational inertia factor $(1.06 \ W)$. Therefore:

$$\text{force} = \frac{(.045) \ (1.06W) \ (V-v)}{(t)}$$

That will be the drag force at the average speed $(V + v) / 2$. It is generally assumed that air drag increases with the square of velocity, but plotting a number of points at widely varying speeds will indicate the actual force curve with mechanical friction drag included. Alternately, it is possible to design an electronic circuit to differentiate the speed curve continuously and produce a signal proportional to g's.

Aerodynamic downforces are best measured in pounds at the front and rear axle centerlines and at a given fixed speed. As explained in Chapter 6, the forces should be measured at a constant speed, to include rearward load transfer due to air drag. The test setup includes some sort of suspension deflection sensors mounted at the front and rear, and either observation or a continuous recording of the deflections. For a solid rear axle, the mounting point should be the center of the housing to eliminate any asymmetry or roll effects. Most independent suspensions have an anti-roll bar between the two sides, so the best mounting location is a lever arm fastened to the center of the bar. The best calibration, or scale factor, is probably to have 1 inch of chassis deflection equal to 1 inch on the chart recorder.

After the instrumentation is set up, the actual suspension ride rate in pounds per inch must be determined. Assuming that downforce is going to be recorded—rather than lift—the best method is to load the chassis with known weights and note the corresponding deflections in inches. For close approximations and relatively linear suspension spring rates, it can be simplest to have a known-weight person climb on the chassis, and then note that single weight/deflection point. Otherwise, for greater precision, or non-linear springs or anticipated high loads, it will be necessary to use a number of large test weights. It is also important to load the chassis *directly* at each axle centerline, and carefully to bounce out any friction or hysteresis in the suspension before each reading. Knowing the pounds-per-inch rate and the deflection in inches due to downforce, it is a simple matter to calculate pounds of force.

The test itself takes some care to get any accuracy or repeatability. Headwinds or crosswinds can have such odd effects that averaging two-way runs under such conditions is only slightly better than nothing. It is also necessary to have the test speed be as constant as possible during a run, and also from run-to-run. Suspension friction can be great enough to hold the chassis as much as an inch away from the true force-balanced height, so it should be carefully shaken free at the test speed. If road roughness isn't enough to keep it free, it will be necessary to blip the throttle and rock the steering wheel slightly to get it balanced out from previous acceleration or cornering deflections. While the suspension deflection instrumentation is set up, it can be worthwhile to record maximum pitch angle during braking and acceleration. The figures may come in handy when working on suspension travel, anti-dive or anti-squat effects, or in correcting accelerometer readings.

Air pressure measurements or air velocity profiles on a body are fast and easy to record with a multi-channel recorder, hundreds of pickup points, pressure transducers, and multiple-scanning valves. However, with the less elaborate and less expensive equipment described previously, taking pressure measurements over an area of any size is a long and laborious process. Ten points or readings are about all that can be conveniently taken at one time, so it takes a lot of equipment-relocating and test reruns to cover a large surface.

The most difficult part of a test setup is to find an accurate and constant source of reference static pressure. A race car will have varying pressures everywhere in and around it as the speed changes. Therefore it will be best to use the static pickup holes in a pitot-static tube, and the tube will have to be mounted some distance away from the body to avoid interference. Four to 5 feet above a body, or 8 to 10 feet ahead, should be good enough, but a check can be made by using a very sensitive absolute pressure gauge at rest and at high speed. Commercial mechanical absolute pressure gauges may also be used for body pressure readings, except that their cost and bulk doesn't justify any added precision.

The pressure pickup strip and total pressure rake are taped to the body or in a duct and connected by flex tubing to the multi-tube manometer. The two outside manometer tubes are connected to the static pressure reference, and the manometer is filled about half full with colored water. It is practically impossible for a driver to read or mark the fluid levels at speed, so a passenger will be necessary or perhaps a camera to record the water levels.

The test procedure is to drive at a specific constant air speed—repeated carefully run-to-run—while the pressures are recorded. It is a good idea to approach the speed slowly, because extreme pressures can run the fluid out the top or bottom of some manometer tubes and it can be difficult to work air bubbles out again. It is probably fastest to mark the plastic face of the manometer with a wax crayon and transfer the various inches of water to paper during a pickup relocation stop. For accurate figures in inches of water, it is also important to keep the manometer tubes perfectly vertical while recording. Later, the figures can be converted to average air pressure perpendicular to the surface, or velocity of the airstream at a given speed, by the relationships:

$$1 \text{ inch of water} = (5.2) \text{ pounds per square foot, or}$$
$$1 \text{ inch of water} = (.00023) \text{ (mph)}^2$$

Of course, it is also possible to measure true air speed for the vehicle by comparing the static pressure reference to total frontal pressure from the pitot tube.

HANDLING

Skidpad tests can be the most productive and exciting tests for a road racing car, but they are also highly demanding on driver precision and consistency. It may take a lot of practice laps before the driver can maintain a nearly constant throttle and steer angle and get lap times to repeat within a few hundredths of a second. But a lot of valuable data can be obtained at low cost and low risk on a skidpad, so it is well worth the effort. The test setup will vary depending on the data needed, but driving technique is simply to keep the car on a precise circular path at the highest possible constant speed. To a driver who is used to clipping corner apexes with the inside front tire, it is probably easiest to try to keep the inside front tire on the painted circular stripe. That tire will also be least affected by a change in friction coefficient due to the painted stripe.

Maximum lateral capability can be measured by one of three methods, or all three together, if accuracy demands it. The first is to use an electronic speedometer and record the speed constantly. The disadvantage is that it is hard to take the average speed, and the recorded speed is affected by lateral tire slippage. A more direct method is to use an electronic accelerometer mounted laterally in the

Measuring cornering power and handling on a skidpad. The car is held at maximum speed on a precise circle—indicated by the white line.

car. But again, it is hard to take an average of all the fluctuations, and the reading has to be corrected for roll angle. The easiest, fastest, and probably most accurate method is to take the laptime for each complete revolution on the circle. This merely requires a split-action stopwatch and someone with a very precise eye and thumb, or an automatic trap switch to start and stop the watch. A timer's accuracy can be improved by having a distinct mark on the circle and noting the instant the car's front tire hits it. It is also a good idea for the timer or someone else to watch the car and make a note whenever it moves noticeably off the marked path. As with any other data-taking, any particularly low figure will have to be backed-up before it is credible. Of course, tires should always be scrubbed in and warmed up until laptimes reach a consistent and low level, and the turn direction should be reversed frequently. The relationship between lateral acceleration, radius, speed, and elapsed time is given by:

$$g = \frac{(.067)\,(\text{mph})^2}{(r)} \qquad g = \frac{(1.22)\,(r)}{(t)^2}$$

where the radius (r) is to the center of gravity of the race car, or the inside tire path plus one-half the tread width, plus some slip angle displacement.

Steady-state stability can be evaluated at the same time as maximum lateral acceleration. This is the tendency of the race car to maintain a stable non-oversteering condition at top speed on the skid-pad, as discussed in Chapter 7. As various factors, such as springs, anti-roll bars, or tires are being changed, the steering angle necessary to balance the car will change. It should be possible to see the increase in laptimes as the car becomes unstable and uncontrollable with oversteer. But it is also possible to measure the oversteer or understeer by recording the steer angle. At a very low speed—say 5 miles per hour, or the minimum possible—a given steer angle (Ackermann steering) is necessary to keep the car on the circle. As the speed is increased, the necessary steer angle will either increase (understeer), remain constant (neutral steer), or decrease and require quick and violent corrections (oversteer). For a smooth understeer condition at the limit, it may be possible to simply hold the wheel at a constant angle and mark its position with a piece of tape. Otherwise, it will probably be necessary to connect the steering wheel to a rotary potentiometer and make a continuous recording of the angles, from Ackermann to the limit of control. The data plotted in Fig. 27 is for a car that oversteers in one direction and understeers in the other. By considering the total steering ratio between steering wheel and road wheel, it is even possible to approximate the difference in tire slip angle between the front and rear tires. (If the steer angle averaged out to zero, front and rear slip angles would be equal.)

Transient tests can only be positively made on a skidpad that allows entry and exit from the steady-state circle, or on a race track, of course. However, if there is even a little extra room on the skidpad, it is possible to get a feel for transient response. There should be enough understeer so the car can be accelerated relatively rapidly without losing traction at the rear. In other words, there shouldn't be any drastic throttle oversteer. Conversely, there shouldn't be a sudden change in stability due to a complete throttle-off at the limit. It can also be an educational experience to brake hard from maximum lat-

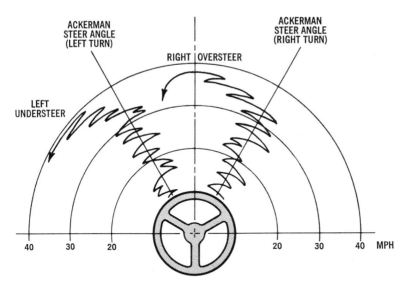

Figure 27. Steady-State Stability Measured at Steering Wheel

eral acceleration while trying to maintain the path radius.

When it comes to checking fuel and oil pressures, the skidpad is far safer than a race track, if not quite a perfect simulation. Naturally the driver should always be aware of oil pressure at high lateral accelerations, but the skidpad allows him to watch it more closely over a longer period. If the oil level is ever going to settle to one side of the pan and starve the pickup, it is better for it to happen on a skidpad where there is a greater opportunity to shut the engine down immediately. The same is true of fuel pickup systems, especially in trying to determine how completely they can drain the tank without picking up air and leaning-out the engine. The greatest problem with the test is that in many cases the worst possible situation is compounded by the addition of braking or acceleration forces.

Suspension deflections can be important to know, especially in development of geometry and ride rates. Deflection measurements on the skidpad will merely show the maximum roll angle, how close the components are to bottoming, and how great the jacking effect is. The test setup is about the same as for aerodynamic downforce, except that the deflection sensors are mounted as close to the wheels as possible, instead of in the center of the car. Ideally, there would be a continual recording at each wheel, but if only one channel is available rather than four, the test must be carefully repeated four times. The best location to record suspension deflection is probably at the centerline of the spring, although it may also be useful to know the *wheel* deflection. In that case, a swivel anchor can be mounted to the exact center of the wheel, and the sensor can be mounted outside and above the wheel—as on a fender lip or extended bracket. For real-life conditions such as bumps, dips, and combinations including acceleration and braking, only a test on an actual race track will suffice.

TIRE TESTS

Tire tests are one of the most valuable uses for a skidpad, once the chassis has been fairly well developed. There is no other way to determine accurately the optimum tire compounds, temperatures, camber angles, or pressures. Results obtained from race track testing would have to be far more significant to eliminate driver inconsistencies. The test setup simply requires a race car and driver that can run all day long at low speeds and high lateral acceleration, with no fatigue, overheating, or variation in performance. It is also important to remember that only a pair of front or rear tires can be tested at once, since the car will be limited by either front or rear cornering capability. The best practice is probably to develop front tire cornering performance first (since the car should be understeering), and as it becomes better, to keep increasing the front anti-roll bar rate as necessary to avoid oversteer. When no more front cornering power is available or the front roll rate is so great that it lifts the inside front tire off the ground, then it is time to work on increasing the rear tires' capabilities. The rear anti-roll bar rate may then be increased to create oversteer, as a rear tire limiting condition to overcome.

Tire test procedure is simply to record average laptime or lateral acceleration for each configuration change. However, it will be necessary to monitor tire temperature constantly, since its effect is great enough to cancel out other test conditions. The first test with any tire should be a comparison of g's versus temperature, to determine the optimum and the dropoff on either side of the optimum. Since it is difficult and expensive to record temperatures continuously, it will be necessary to stop the test at intervals and check the temperatures as rapidly as possible with a tire pyrometer. The best technique is to run in two or three lap increments, with one person timing, and another taking temperatures as fast as the car can be stopped from its high lateral condition. It shouldn't be necessary to take over half a lap to stop, and the tire technician should be right *there* at the stopping point. Within 10 or 20 laps the tire should be at its maximum temperature, or past its peak cornering capability. It can also be valuable to know just how fast the tire cools off, to get an idea of what the true temperature is while the tire is working. This can be estimated by watching the temperature fall in a given location over a matter of seconds and projecting the result. Since the test accuracy is poor, it is a good idea to repeat it after, or as, the tires cool off, and in both directions around the pad. Of course, the *outside* front or rear tire temperature is of greatest importance.

From then on, all tests with that particular tire should be run at the optimum temperature or at least corrected for any dropoff. This data will also come in handy at the race track, to determine whether a tire compound is too hard or too soft for the work input under a given ambient temperature.

When tire compound and temperature can be held constant, then optimum tire pressure and camber angles can be determined. Proper camber angle will show up in skidpad lap times, tire wear profiles, or temperature differences across the tread, but the last method is quickest for tire development work. The pyrometer must be used rapidly to get three readings (inside edge, center, outside edge) before the natural heat conduction in the tread evens out the temperatures. It isn't reasonable to expect them to be exactly equal, however, since the car will be at maximum lateral acceleration camber angle only for very short periods.

When everything else has been developed to the optimum on a skidpad, it can be a good place to teach the driver what extreme variations in handling feel like. If the car is ever going to lose a shock absorber, or break a front anti-roll bar and oversteer, or have a tire go soft, or otherwise become unmanageable, the skidpad is the safest place to learn the feel and the corrections required. Just knowing the feel of ordinary changes from oversteer to neutral steer to understeer is an invaluable aid in later analysis of a race car on a race track.

TRACK TESTING

An actual race course is the last place where any serious or accurate development work can be done. Only after the car has been otherwise ideally set up will race track laps be meaningful, and then primarily with respect to the driver's performance. For vehicle evaluations, it will still be necessary to break the track down into braking, cornering, and acceleration segments, as opposed to over-all laptimes. The timing isn't as difficult (with an electronic split-action watch) as it is to find a spot where the car can be seen at many locations around the track. At Riverside, for example, it is possible to see a car most of the way around the track from the roof of the timing tower. A sample of segment times is shown in Fig. 28.

This is also the best way to find out how a competitor's car really compares—as opposed to average laptimes. If the other driver is sandbagging, it will probably show up in a particular segment. But if the other car is quicker, it is helpful to know exactly where, to know where there are some capabilities to be gained. In the example shown, car B is apparently better in acceleration, which means that car A is probably adequate in handling and braking but should have more power or lower air drag. Some people have also developed electronic gunsight tracking devices to record comparative speeds around an arc. There are other more sophisticated spying devices to analyze competitor's cars, which are more accurate and more complete. But, needless to say, they are much more expensive and complex—and confidential.

Probably the best race driver teaching device known to man is a continual recording of speed and horizontal accelerations around a race course. It won't say much about the car unless there are other recordings of the same car in another configuration, or other recordings of other cars, to compare with. But such recordings will tell a

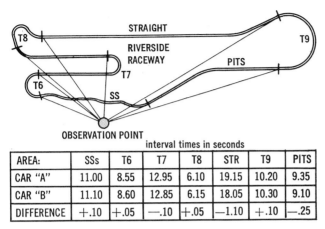

interval times in seconds

AREA:	SSs	T6	T7	T8	STR	T9	PITS
CAR "A"	11.00	8.55	12.95	6.10	19.15	10.20	9.35
CAR "B"	11.10	8.60	12.85	6.15	18.05	10.30	9.10
DIFFERENCE	+.10	+.05	—.10	+.05	—1.10	+.10	—.25

Figure 28. Comparative Interval Times for Two Cars at Riverside

great deal about the driver's ability to take advantage of the car's capabilities. The best test setup is to have a two-channel recorder with speed and acceleration inputs. The speed can come from a front wheel pickup, preferably the outside wheel, to avoid lift or lockup problems in cornering and braking. The g sensor can be either a single lateral accelerometer or a combination of two arranged at right angles. An electronic circuit can be designed to calculate the net horizontal acceleration in any direction and produce a signal proportional to the percentage of traction used versus traction available. A more thorough explanation is given in Chapter 12.

Other tests that can be performed on a race track were previously explained under straightaway or skidpad testing. However, in general they tend to be tests of the track configuration rather than of the vehicle. Unusual suspension deflections are mostly dependent on surface condition or grade changes or bankings. Different tire or brake temperatures are a function of track coefficient and distribution of time spent on cornering, acceleration, and braking. Vehicle transient response characteristics will change with respect to the types of corners on a given race track. If there is enough time, a race car can be set up to the optimum for each particular track's predominant characteristics, but it is likely to take at least a few days of track rental and exclusive running. It helps a great deal to have a lot of experience at a particular track and at a wide variety of tracks. But for those with no experience or for a new track, a careful analysis of speed and g recordings can work almost as well.

Of course, in the absence of any recording instrumentation at all, stopwatch times in various track segments will probably indicate the worth of any vehicle changes. Handling or tire improvements should show up in the low-speed cornering segment times, aerodynamic downforce should show up in high-speed cornering segments, engine power should show up in the straightaways and so on. The overall improvement will probably show up in total laptimes, but less significantly.

This leads to the question of the relative value of various vehicle improvements. Racers tend to concentrate on making improvements in the areas they understand or enjoy the most rather than those where the potential gains may be greatest. It isn't that hard to determine just what these relative values are, however. A computer can be—and has been—used to put a numerical value on various race car improvements, but any racer can find the numbers for his own car on any particular track by the handicap method. If it isn't easy to *improve* a car's performance, it is all too easy to *diminish* it. All that's necessary is to know the amount by which the effect is reduced and the increase in laptime which results. The effect will be linear enough over a reasonable range to project from a decrease in performance to an increase in performance due to a positive change.

The most obvious example is in determining the effect of reduced weight on laptimes. All that is necessary is to plot laptimes versus fuel consumption in pounds. Say that a 2000-pound race car consumes 200 pounds of fuel during a race, while its average laptime decreases from 90.0 seconds to 88.2 seconds. Then, assuming that all other factors remained equal during the race, a person could project that a 10 percent reduction in vehicle weight would produce a 2 percent reduction in laptimes—at that track. Other factors may be as easy to degrade as weight: power reduction with throttle-stops, air drag increase with a flat plate, tire traction reduction with lower pressures, and braking capability reduction with lower temperatures.

However, it may be somewhat difficult to quantify the exact value of the change in the factor. But once the relative positive effect of various changes can be estimated, the proper concentration of efforts can be allocated. Of course, even the most scientific approach must be adapted to fit the capriciousness of racing regulations and the availability of time and dollars.

Most racers feel that durability tests are also beyond their limits in available resources, so they tend to use experience, intuition, and luck instead. The only way really to know whether a car can be raced hard for 24 hours or 500 miles is to *race* it hard for that time or distance. If it is done in a test session and nothing breaks, then the car can be totally rebuilt as new for the real race—and still fail due to some random faulty new component. Even if experience is the best judge of durability, that sort of experience can be bought. A brand-new design may be faster but it definitely doesn't have a history of reliability. The best insurance is in knowing that a particular design or component has been around for a long time without unusual failures. At the very least, it is a good idea to know a car or component's history, and its average life expectancy before inspection, rebuilding, or replacing is necessary. On the other hand, if durability testing is feasible, the biggest mistake is to try and make the car survive under those conditions. Instead, the idea is to *try* and break the car under reasonably severe simulated usage, rather than pussyfooting it around. However, it is wise to test on a track where a failure doesn't have consequences as critical as they could be in a race.

STATIC TESTING

There are also a number of static tests or measurements that may be necessary or desirable for further development work. In the first place, it will frequently be necessary to know the exact rolling tire diameter. Since there is some static deflection due to weight, the most accurate means is to measure the rolling *distance* and divide by 3.14. In fact, it is more accurate to roll the loaded tire for 10 full, exact revolutions and divide by 31.4.

Center of gravity height is of more than just academic interest,

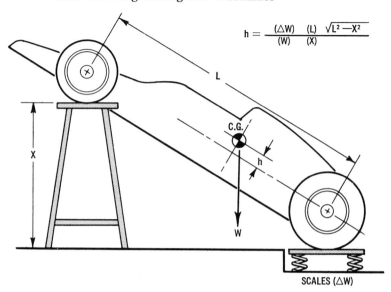

$$h = \frac{(\Delta W)}{(W)} \frac{(L)}{(X)} \sqrt{L^2 - X^2}$$

Figure 29. Locating Center of Gravity

since it is required for many performance calculations. There are many ways to locate it by suspending the car from a single point or by mounting it on a teeter-board, but the following is easiest for most racers' limited facilities. (See Fig. 29.) First, it is necessary to realize that *any* fluid movement during a test can falsify the results. It will be necessary to drain all fluids, including oil in the pan and water in the cooling system. At least two precise platform scales will be necessary, plus a hoist to raise the front of the car and tall stands to set the front wheels on. With the rear wheels resting on the scales, the front is raised and the tires set on stands, while the increase in rear wheel load is noted. Obviously, when the center of gravity is directly over the rear axle centerline, the weight on the rear will be total vehicle weight. Well before that point is reached, the center of gravity height can be calculated by:

$$h = \frac{(\Delta W)(L) \sqrt{L^2 - x^2}}{(W)(x)}$$

Where: (h) is height of the center of gravity above the rear axle centerline in feet, (W) is total vehicle weight, ($\triangle$W) is the increase in rear scale weight, (L) is the wheelbase length in feet, and (x) is the raised height of the front tires in feet. The higher the front tires can be blocked up, the greater the increase in rear scale weight and the more accurate the calculations. The rear wheels may be blocked on the scales, but the front wheels must be free-rolling on perfectly horizontal stands to avoid any weight effects at the scales.

Chassis deflection tests can also be important for a race car, especially lightweight, open cockpit chassis. Beam strength is seldom a problem if the torsional stiffness is adequate, since nothing is as critical in the longitudinal plane as front/rear resistance and suspension alignment are with respect to twisting. There are no accepted minimum standards, but 3000 pounds-feet per degree of twist is acceptable for most lightweight road-racing cars, with a figure many times that being common for a sedan with an integral roll cage.

The test procedure requires some heavy equipment, including anchors in a concrete floor; hundreds of pounds of weights; a long, stiff beam arm to hang them from; and solid links to replace all four suspension springs. It is most convenient to measure the deflection with dial gauges in a number of locations. The race car chassis is mounted with the rear hubs anchored firmly to the floor, the front center of the chassis resting on a knife edge, and the weight beam connecting the two front hubs. As the weights are loaded on one end of the arm, torsional deflection can be measured with dial gauges at two points on the arm. The deflection in degrees for each torsional load is equal to the difference in readings, divided by the distance between the gauges, times 57.3. If the stiffness falls much below 3000 pounds-feet per degree, then it may help to take deflection readings at various locations along the chassis length to find any particularly weak sections. Then it may be possible to reinforce the chassis with panel stiffeners or tubes and recheck the over-all rigidity.

14

THE PITS ○○○○○○○○○○○○○○○○○○○○○○○○○○○○○○○○○○○○

Even if a race car is perfectly set up and the driver is fast enough to put it on the pole, the race can still be lost in the pits. In fact, a great many races are won by slower cars because their pit crews were quicker or they used better strategy, or simply because they prepared and maintained the car better. There are a number of important considerations beyond the engineering and development of the machine. Ideally, the entire team, including car, driver, mechanics, pit crew, timer/scorer, signalman, and equipment will all function perfectly as one well-oiled machine.

The attitudes of the individuals who make up the team and the way they relate to each other is a primary factor. The team members seldom get the recognition that a driver, owner, or sponsor will, so they have to be rewarded in other ways, whether by money, association, travel, or simply love of the action. In any case, it takes a tremendously wise team manager to hold them all together. Supervision and management skills may even be more important than ultimate technical knowledge, and it couldn't hurt to study ordinary business management techniques. Personal factors such as commitment, responsibility, teamwork, and personal pride are as valuable as knowledge or experience. When all those qualities are found in a mechanic or manager, he ought to be recognized and rewarded, because such people are hard to come by at any price.

The team manager is also responsible for a great deal of planning and paperwork—the dull, but critical clerical work. This includes records, entry forms, do-lists, check lists, schedules, reservations, purchasing, and bird-dogging late or lost items. There are no end of projects to make a race car faster or more reliable, but some sort of priority must be established. At short intervals—from weeks to days—the do-list should be revised to suit the remaining time schedule. It may even be necessary to break all jobs down into three categories: Must do, Important, and Also. The first category would include work on safety and durability, plus any necessary repairs. Second would be any changes that might make the car faster or more comfortable. And last would be cosmetic jobs such as paint and polish. Polish will never make the car faster but is a great psychological advantage over competitors when they realize that *everything else*

Crew prepared for a tire change pit stop, with tires, jack, and pneumatic wrench ready. Two fuelers are out of the picture on the right.

has already been done to your car—at least as long as your car is fast and doesn't break.

RECORDS

Check lists are highly underrated and underused, considering the complexity of a race car. And they shouldn't be regarded as an insult to the intelligence of a mechanic, because *no* one can remember every little critical detail. When more than one person is involved, each will assume the other has done everything. There are even many different types of check lists. There can be a detailed assembly check list for separate areas on the car such as engine installation, suspension assembly, or brake rebuilding. Then there is the pre-race check list, to make sure every last-minute preparation detail has been checked, such as all fluid levels, tire pressures, fasteners, and adjustments. And finally there is the logistics check list, to make sure everything and everyone is always in the right place at the right time. This includes everything from a packing list, to schedules and reservations, to equipment in the pits. The assembly and pre-race check lists can be started by using a commercial Race Car Inspection Form available from Auto World, and additions can be made by going through this book and including more details. The logistics list is a combination of all necessary procedures and all necessary pieces of hardware that might be needed. The best way to reach a compromise between taking everything and leaving out that last important item is with careful hindsight and a reasonable amount of forethought. Experience will indicate what parts are most likely to fail or wear out and the tools necessary to do the job. The time will come when an experienced mechanic will tire of the check list and graduate from it. And the time will invariably follow when some tiny detail will be ignored or forgotten and it will cost the race.

There are other necessary records besides those kept on the engineering, testing, and development of a race car. Once the car is at the track, it is essential to know just what kind of mileages can be expected from all consumables. Total fuel and oil mileage should be obvious. But it is also necessary to know at what exact point the car's

A timing and scoring team with pit board (right) and blackboard to communicate position and intervals to a signaler at the pit rail.

performance suffers from fuel or oil starvation, because it is quite possible that a poor fuel pickup will cause the engine to lean out with a few gallons left in the tanks. It helps to carry the absolute minimum weight in fluids, but it may be more valuable to have a safe margin to allow for changing conditions. In long-distance races, tire wear and brake pad wear must also be known with some accuracy so that pit stops can be precisely scheduled. Careful pre-planning in scheduling replacements can save a lot of time. Tires should be changed at the same time as brake pads—and the car should be fueled also if there are enough crew members. But since it is only practical to have two wheels off the ground at once and the outside tires and brakes wear faster, it is quicker to change only one side per pit stop. Careful record-keeping will make it possible to keep the number of pitstops and the time lost to a minimum.

TIMING AND SCORING

Timing and scoring are the most difficult kinds of records to keep during a race. Simple lap timing can be done by almost anyone, but the added complications of counting laps, taking intervals, and scoring all cars on a lap chart makes it a challenge for two or three experienced people. The subject is too involved for the space allowed here, so a potential timer/scorer should enroll in one of the training schools held regularly by sanctioning groups, and get some practice with them at amateur races. But for those with a little experience already, a few tips may help.

First, a timer/scorer must have a very strong and stable personality, to face the inherent pressures and to maintain the necessary concentration. There will be 20 to 40 cars going by—multiplied by perhaps hundreds of laps—and all a scorer has to do is miss *one* car to disorganize a lap chart completely for the rest of the race. Distractions such as spectators' questions, rain, pit stops, calls of nature, and cars blowing up must be completely ignored. It will probably also be necessary to be in place and working whenever the cars are on the track—even during practice—to make checks on competitors' cars, and to become familiar with all the car numbers and colors. The pit position of such people is particularly important. They should have a clear view of a reference point on the track (and some space ahead to anticipate in) that will not be obstructed by spectators or other cars. If a timer can see far enough ahead, it may be possible to present the driver with information on his *current* lap—not on the previous lap. Timers should be easily accessible to the team manager—and no one else. The primary purpose of a timer/scorer is not to check the accuracy of the officials but to provide continual running information for the manager and the driver.

The relative value of the different types of information to be gathered varies completely with the nature of each race. For the average short amateur race, all the driver really needs is his time interval from the next car ahead or behind, and perhaps the laps remaining. It may not be necessary to keep a lap chart to identify which cars are immediately competitive and which ones are some laps down. Over-all

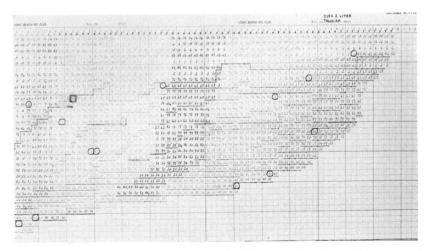

A professionally prepared lap chart. Different colored pencils are used every ten laps to help keep order, and circles indicate car retirements.

consecutive lap times are insignificant unless the driver is trying to improve his consistency or finds it necessary to maintain a certain predetermined average speed. In a long-distance race, perfect strategy would determine the ideal average speed to have the car just slightly in the lead at the finish without overstressing it to the point of failure. Total number of laps completed may be extremely important—particularly when fuel mileage is marginal—but that is simple enough so every member of the crew should keep a running tally. When races are run on total length (versus overall time), it is important to distinguish *race* laps remaining to the driver so he can plan his strategy accordingly.

For longer races, and all races with scheduled fuel stops, it will be necessary to keep a lap chart. Otherwise, no one will be quite sure just who is immediately ahead or behind, much less what position the car is in. A driver may find it possible to pick up a position or two with a little extra effort, if he knows where he stands. Conversely, he could risk destroying the car trying to pass another car that was actually a lap down. Keeping accurate lap charts, however, requires careful training and a lot of experience. This is especially true where mixed classes and pit stops are involved, and on short, high-speed tracks where thirty-three cars may be coming around once every minute. These, and endurance races which run from 4 to 24 hours, are a real challenge even for professionals. It may be possible to get car positions from the officials during a race, but at best the information will probably be a few laps old, even if electronic computer-scored systems are used. If there are enough stopwatches to go around, it may be best for each member of the team to have a specific timing assignment and perhaps even keep track of laps on a couple of the nearest competitors. Before the race, the driver and manager should come to an agreement as to what information is going to be most valuable to the driver. The driver may also arrange certain signals to the pits, to request particular data such as intervals or remaining laps to a pit stop.

Some sort of communication system with the driver is always needed. Two-way radios have recently become popular, but they are expensive and just one more complication. Also, the driver may be unnecessarily distracted by an incoming voice while he is involved in a critical maneuver. But in signaling from the car to the pits, a one-way radio avoids the problems of hand signals and allows much more information to be transmitted. Otherwise a driver is limited to a small number of prearranged signals for anticipated situations. He may have signals to request certain information or to warn the crew that he needs fuel, oil, water, a tire, brake pads, or even a driver change. But if it is something else, such as a V-belt or a spark plug, or he needs a door taped shut or a plug wire replaced, it will take some explaining. If the crew isn't prepared when the car comes in, it may save time for the driver to go back out for another lap while they get the parts and tools set up.

Signaling the driver from the pits is easier and more common. The methods can range from a simple blackboard, to commercial number flip-boards, to metal boards with magnetic letters and numbers. Regardless of the board, there are certain sign conventions that are ordinarily used: P-3 indicates third position; L-29 indicates either 29 laps down or 29 to go (the driver ought to know the difference) with a final IN sign for the last lap before a pit stop; and +3.5 or −3.5 indicates that the driver is either 3.5 seconds ahead of or behind the

Signalers at the pit rail, with various types of pit boards. Some of them are also doing their own lap and interval timing.

next nearest competitor. Laptimes can usually be given in two-digit numbers, such as 6.5 to indicate a lap of one minute and 56.5 seconds, since the numbers shouldn't vary by more than a few seconds. An additional blackboard offers the chance to make other odd comments to the driver, such as "faster" or "conserve fuel." But they had better be simple and obvious to avoid confusing or worrying the driver. Finally, the signal board will have to be well located and easily identifiable, since the driver is very busy out there and it can be hard to distinguish individuals at the pit wall. The board should be well marked and its visibility checked at changing sun angles. The one person who is allowed out to the pit wall for signaling will be in the best position to watch for any obvious problems on the outside of the car—a low tire, body damage, leaks, or whatever. It might be a good idea to have another person on the other side of the track to watch the other side of the car. After a little shoving out on the track, a driver may be very interested in knowing whether a bent fender seems to be rubbing on a tire.

A NASCAR fuel stop. Man at left is removing an empty can, man in center will insert a second can, and a third man catches the overflow.

PIT STOPS

There are two kinds of pit stops to be prepared for—the ordinary scheduled pit stop and the unexpected occurrence. The first kind of stop requires a great deal of planning, special hardware, and practice. The hardware ordinarily consists of every conceivable device that will speed the addition of fluids or the changing of components. Quick-fill fueling systems are an art in themselves, but since overhead tanks have been generally outlawed in favor of eleven-gallon cans with dry-break couplings, fueling has become much more standardized—and safer. But the internal design of cans, tanks, and spouts can often be revised to pick up a few seconds. The air vent or overflow tube may also be reworked to get the air out faster and insure complete filling. Oil and water, when necessary, can be added by using dry-break connectors in the engine compartment. Because there is less danger of fire, a predetermined amount can be injected very rapidly from pressurized containers.

With the method of tire changing being generally open under the rules, there have been a lot of clever developments to speed up the process. Knock-off hubs are not allowed in most cases, so it is a matter of getting the lug nuts off and on again in the absolute minimum time. Ordinary pneumatic impact wrenches are used, but they are souped-up, or modified by drilling out the air passages, and the pressure regulators are boosted way up. Even the sockets are custom-ground to slip on more easily. All of the wheel studs and lug nuts are modified to guarantee that they will go on *right* and *fast* with no chance of cross-threading. The threads are usually machined off the first ¾-inch of the stud to guide the nut on straight. And all nuts are carefully lubricated before the race.

Special lightweight hydraulic jacks are available, and some crews even add more exotic materials to lighten them further. Jack wheels are seldom necessary, and they have a tendency to sink into hot asphalt, so a skid plate is usually substituted. The jacking point on the car is well marked, as is the proper insertion distance on the jack. The jack is pre-set to about the right clearance, and the jacker should know just how many pumps are necessary. It is also a good idea to try getting the jack under the car with one or both tires flat on that side.

The wheel can be mounted much faster if there is a tapered centering cone on the hub and the stud holes in the wheel are chamfered slightly. There are a number of ingenious methods for getting all five nuts started rapidly. The simplest technique is to have five new—and cooler—nuts ready by hanging them on a string from the tire changer's mouth. The old hot huts simply lie where they fall. New nuts may even be pre-attached to their proper bearing surface on the wheel, by gluing them in place with trim cement. They slip on the studs as the wheel slips on the hub, and the impact wrench will still turn them up tight. But the most sophisticated technique is to have the nuts permanently retained on the wheel by the use of a spring-loaded plate that allows them to back off but not fall off.

Brake pad changes are least frequent and most difficult. It is best to schedule them at the same time as a tire change when the car is up and the wheels are off already. Then the removal and replacement of pads shouldn't take more than another minute at the worst. The greatest obstacle is that the pads and disc will probably be literally red hot, so the old ones will have to be removed with pliers or asbestos gloves, and the new ones must be installed with great care. Retainer pins must be fail-safe and yet easily removed and reinstalled. The problem of squeezing the caliper pistons back to make room for thicker linings is best handled with a vacuum retractor system, as described in Chapter 5. The next best method, which is cheaper, but much slower, is to build a screw-operated spreader device to push the pistons back in. It is worth another mention here that all new pads should be pre-burnished, or broken-in before race time.

That fairly well covers the scheduled pit stop, but there must also be some anticipation of and preparation for the emergency stop. Experience and pessimism are the best helps here. If what was going to fail were known, it should be improved or made fail-safe instead of making it rapidly repairable. The only exception is collision damage that prevents the car from continuing or slows it down for a greater net time loss than a pit stop would cost. Ordinarily, about all that can be repaired fast enough to keep the car competitive is bodywork. Racing cars usually have lightweight fiberglass body components that can be replaced rapidly with quick-release fasteners—providing there are spare panels immediately accessible. Otherwise, a lot of silver racer's tape, bungee cords, and wire may be used to hold the remaining fiberglass together. Some thought should be put to the changed aerodynamic characteristics also, as the loss of certain surfaces may make the car dangerously unstable.

For metal-bodied cars, the most common problems are fenders collapsed onto the tire and broken windshields. Heavy sledges and long, forked pry bars are common in NASCAR pits to bend the metal away from the tire. A pneumatic chisel might even be used to snip the wheel well open. (Acetylene torches are suicide in a fueling pit.) The problem of windshield replacement is eased by merely resting the glass in a rubber-lined frame, and holding it in with the required safety clips. It ought to be possible to get the old windshield out and a new one in, in a few minutes. If the old glass is merely cracked and not shattered, it might even be left under the new windshield. Other

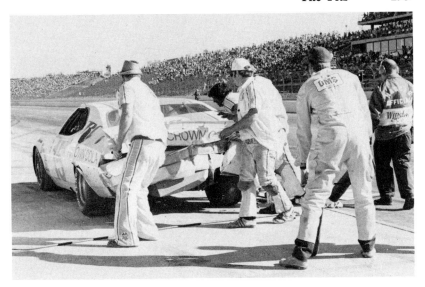

A good example of the mass damage that a well-prepared race car can survive. This car went on to finish fifth in a 500-mile race.

than external problems, about all a crew can do is to have as many tools and spare parts as possible—at least suspension, brake, and engine components—in the back of the pit. Still, there comes a point where the time required to get the car going again will put it too far back to be worth the panic and effort.

Since the pit crew is what makes or breaks a fast pit stop, their attitude and skill is more important than the hardware involved. First, it is critical that everyone know the rules of the game. If too many people are involved, if they move too soon, or if they do something they shouldn't, the car could be disqualified. Second, they must know what is happening at all times and be prepared for immediate action. They may get no more than about 10 seconds' notice before the car comes to a stop in the pits, or they may have to go out and find or fix it somewhere on the track—if that is legal. But most important, the crew must have a lot of practice at doing the jobs they know they will have to do: fueling and tire changes. There is no such thing as too much practice—just as a driver can't practice his job too much. But as a crew member does his assignment, he ought to have his priorities

The beginning of a fast fuel and tire stop. Two men fuel, two remove and replace the tires, one jacks the car, and one carries the spares.

in order. First and foremost, the job has to be done *right*. There usually isn't any second chance—a wheel may fall off, or the pits may go up in flames. Doing it *quickly* is only the second priority. The possibilities for lost time due to a mistake are far greater than any possible gains in split seconds. And yet, it *can* make a difference when races are won or lost by a car length. About all that can be expected of the crew during an emergency stop is that they be fast thinkers and even faster workers. It is worth a note here that any time the car comes in unexpectedly, time should be taken to fuel it up unless it has enough to finish the race. That precaution could save another fuel stop later.

The actual steps and movements in fueling or tire changing ought to be planned and choreographed as well as any ballet. The crew members themselves can probably come up with the optimum arrangement after a few rehearsals. One man might remove the filler cap for the fueler and then return for the second fuel can. The jacker might clean the windshield while the tires are being changed, or pass a new tire at the precise moment the old one comes off. The instant the jack drops might be the signal for the driver to drop the clutch. There are a thousand possible arrangements and tricks available to the crew that keeps watching, plotting, and practicing.

Safety is still a problem in the pits, even with safer fueling rigs. It is wise for fuelers to wear flameproof coveralls or old driver's suits, even if it looks kind of peculiar. Goggles and fireproof hoods ought to be required protection. And the crew has to recognize the fact that another driver in the pits may care more about a fast pit stop than their personal safety. The pits are just about the easiest place there is to get hit by a speeding car. The faster a pit stop is, the less exposure time there is for the crew.

Assuming the driver has first choice of pits, there are some very rational selection criteria. Usually, it is best to have the pit closest to the slower end of the track. If there is a slow turn just before the entrance to the pits, that end is the best location, because the car is already going slowly and that gives the length of the pit straight in which to accelerate again. Other less significant considerations are: to be close to facilities, to be close to the official timers, or to have the high ground if it rains. In practice, the driver should also practice full-blast pit stops to learn just where the last possible shutoff or braking point is. If he overshoots his pit, he will probably have to go around the track again—whether he has enough fuel or not.

If all goes according to the script, the actual racing pit stop itself will be anticlimactic. The car will be in and out in a matter of seconds with little apparent concern or drama. If things *don't* go so well, the longer a car sits, the sicker it gets. The engine will start to overheat if it has to idle much longer than an ordinary tire change, and if it is shut off, there is the possibility it will heat lock and not restart. It may be possible to spray the radiator with water, but it makes the pit a mess for fast starts. Also, the brakes will be blazing hot from the last stop, and they can boil the fluid or warp and crack the discs if the wheels aren't kept ratating. And finally, when the pit stop is over, one assigned crew member must act as a traffic cop and keep the driver from pulling out in front of another pitting car. Otherwise, the race may end right there in the pits.

BIBLIOGRAPHY ◦◦◦◦◦◦◦◦◦◦◦◦◦◦◦◦◦◦◦◦◦◦◦◦◦

TIRES AND WHEELS

Harvey, W. L. & Ressler, D. B. *Competition Setup—A Chassis Adjustment Analysis.* Rochelle Park, N.J.: ADI Press, 1973.

Kummer, H. W. & Meyer, W. E. *Unified Theory of Tire and Rubber Friction.* University Park, Pa.: Pennsylvania State University, 1966.

SUSPENSION GEOMETRY AND ALIGNMENT

Harvey, W. L. & Ressler, D. B. *Competition Setup—A Chassis Adjustment Analysis.* Rochelle Park, N.J.: ADI Press, 1973.

Wakefield, Ron, *Suspension and Handling Supplement. Road & Track* Magazine, June 1970.

Winkelmann, O. J. *Handling Requirements,* SAE Paper No. S220, New York: Society of Automotive Engineers, 1959.

SPRINGS, ANTI-ROLL BARS, SHOCK ABSORBERS

Dinkel, John, *Shock Absorbers for Your Car. Road & Track* Magazine, October November 1974.

Kruse, D. F. & Edwards, R. C. *Automotive Suspension Bumpers.* SAE Paper No. 680471. New York: Society of Automotive Engineers, 1968.

Speckhart, F. H. & Harrison, E. *The Design of a Shock Absorber to Improve Ride Comfort.* SAE Paper No. 680472. New York: Society of Automotive Engineers, 1968.

BRAKES

Douglas, J. W. & Schafer, T. C. *The Chrysler "Sure Brake"—The First Production Four-wheel Anti-skid System.* SAE Paper No. 710248. New York: Society of Automotive Engineers, 1971.

Ihnack, J. J. & Meek, J. F. *Mark II GT Sports Car Disc Brake System*. SAE Paper No. 670070. New York: Society of Automotive Engineers, 1967.
Newcomb, T. P. & Spurr, R. T. *Braking of Road Vehicles*. Cambridge, Mass.: Robert Bentley Inc. 1969.
Rusnak, R. M. & Schwartz, H. W. & Coleman, W. P. *A Comparison by Thermal Analysis of Rotor Alloys*. SAE Paper No. 700137. New York: Society of Automotive Engineers, 1970.
Schafer, T. C. & Howard, D. W. *Design and Performance Considerations for a Passenger Car Anti-skid System*. SAE Paper No. 680458. New York: Society of Automotive Engineers, 1968.
Smith, Carroll, *Stop That Car*. *Sports Car Graphic* Magazine, February 1971.

AERODYNAMICS

Abbott, I. H. & von Doenhoff, A. E. *Theory of Wing Sections*. New York: Dover Publications, 1960.
Aerofoil Report. London: The Jim Clark Foundation, 1969.
Cornish, J. J. *Some Considerations of Automobile Lift and Drag*. SAE Paper No. 948B. New York: Society of Automotive Engineers, 1965.
—— *Trapped Vortex Flow Control for Automobiles*. The Aerodynamics of Sports and Competition Automobiles. Los Angeles: American Institute of Aeronautics and Astronautics, 1974.
Fackrell, J. E. & Harvey, J. K. *The Aerodynamics of an Isolated Road Wheel*. Los Angeles: American Institute of Aerodynamics and Astronautics, 1974.
Fink, M. P. & Lastinger, J. L. *Aerodynamic Characteristics of Low-Aspect-Ratio Wings in Close Proximity to the Ground*. Technical Note D-926. Washington: National Aeronautics and Space Administration, nd.
Hoerner, S. F. *Fluid Dynamic Drag*. Midland Park, N.J.: Published by the author, 1958.
Reilly, D. N. *Aerodynamics of the Airfoil*. Road & Track Magazine, June 1969.
—— *NACA Ducts—What They Are and How They Work*. Road & Track Magazine, March 1970.
Romberg, G. F. & Chianese, F. & Lajoie, R. G. *Aerodynamics of Race Cars in Drafting and Passing Situations*. SAE Paper No. 710213. New York: Society Of Automotive Engineers, 1971.

HANDLING

Bergman, Walter, *The Basic Nature of Vehicle Understeer-Oversteer*. SAE Paper No. 957B. New York: Society of Automotive Engineers, 1965.
Ellis, J. R. *Vehicle Dynamics*. London: London Business Books Limited, 1969.
Milliken, William F. *Research in Automobile Stability and Control*. London: The Institution of Mechanical Engineers, 1957.

ENGINE SUPPORT SYSTEMS

Fisher, Bill & Waar, Bob, *How to Hotrod Small-Block Chevrolets*. Tucson, Arizona: H. P. Books, 1973.
Ricardo, Sir Harry, *The High-Speed Internal Combustion Engine*. 4th ed. London: Blackie & Sons Ltd., 1967.
Smith, Phillip H., *The Design and Tuning of Competition Engines*. 5th ed. Cambridge, Mass.: Robert Bentley Inc., 1971.

GEARING AND DIFFERENTIALS

Gregorich, H. L. & Jones, C. D. *Mark II G. T. Transaxles*. SAE Paper No. 670069. New York: Society of Automotive Engineers, 1967.
Smith, Carroll, *Prepare to Win—Part 5—Engines and Transmissions*. *Sports Car Graphic* Magazine, October 1970.

FRAME AND BODY

Elliott, W. A. *Plastic Models for Dynamic Structural Analysis.* SAE Paper No. 710262. New York: Society of Automotive Engineers, 1971.

Looby, L. F. & McKee, R. S. *Taking the Materials Approach to a Can-Am Chassis.* SAE Paper No. 700056. New York: Society of Automotive Engineers, 1970.

Smith, Carroll, *Prepare to Win—Part 2—Rivets, Riveting, Welding, and Basic Metal Work. Sports Car Graphic* Magazine, July 1970.

SAFETY

Henderson, Michael, *Motor Racing Safety.* London: Patrick Stephens Ltd., 1968.

DRIVER

Johnson, Alan, *Driving in Competition.* Newport Beach, Calif.: Bond, Parkhurst Publications, 1971.

Van Valkenburgh, Paul, *The World's Most Advanced Race-Driver's School. Sports Car Graphic* Magazine, January 1971.

TESTING

Brown, Ronald F. *Your Car's Horsepower. Road & Track* Magazine, November 1970.

Pankhurst, R. C. & Holder, D. W. *Wind Tunnel Technique.* London: Sir Isaac Pitman & Sons Ltd., 1965.

Pope, Alan & Harper, John J. *Low Speed Wind Tunnel Testing.* New York: John Wiley & Sons, 1966.

THE PITS

Stropus, Judy, *Stropus Guide to Auto Timing and Scoring.* Norwalk, Conn: Sports Car Press, 1975.

Thompson, Jerry. *Do Your Homework Well. Corvette News,* April/ May 1974.

Wyer, John, *Motor Racing Management.* London: St. Anne's Press, 1956.

GENERAL

Campbell, Colin, *Design of Racing Sports Cars.* Cambridge, Mass.: Robert Bentley Inc., 1973.

Mezger, Hans, *Engineering the Performance Car.* SAE Paper No. 700678. New York: Society of Automotive Engineers, 1970.

Smith, Carroll, *Prepare to Win.* Fallbrook, Calif.: Aero Publishers, Inc., 1975.

Steeds, W. *Mechanics of Road Vehicles.* London: Iliffe & Sons Ltd., 1960.

Terry, Len, *Race Car Design and Development.* Cambridge, Mass.: Robert Bentley Inc., 1973.

INDEX ○○○

ABOUT THE AUTHOR

Practically every phase of Paul Van Valkenburgh's professional career helped prepare him to write this authoritative book. After studying Mechanical and Aeronautical Engineering at the University of Kansas, he obtained his most valuable education as a Research Engineer with Chevrolet, working on the highly confidential "racing team." His last project was a computer simulation of race car performance that led to construction of the famous Chaparral "sucker" car. He then became Test Editor for *Sports Car Graphic* magazine, where he developed the first electronic road test system for consumer publications, and in two years analyzed over eighty of the world's most exotic sports and race cars. A close association with Mark Donohue led to his co-authorship of Donohue's autobiography, *The Unfair Advantage,* which revealed Donohue's winning secrets. Mr. Van Valkenburgh is also the author of *Chevrolet—Racing?,* the story of Chevrolet's secret racing programs.